ATTACHMENT, PLAY,
AND AUTHENTICITY

ATTACHMENT, PLAY, AND AUTHENTICITY

A *Winnicott Primer*

Steven Tuber

JASON ARONSON

Lanham • Boulder • New York • Toronto • Plymouth, UK

Published in the United States of America
by Jason Aronson
An imprint of Rowman & Littlefield Publishers, Inc.

A wholly owned subsidary of
The Rowman & Littlefield Publishing Group, Inc.
4501 Forbes Boulevard, Suite 200, Lanham, Maryland 20706
www.rowmanlittlefield.com

Estover Road
Plymouth PL6 7PY
United Kingdom

British Library Cataloguing in Publication Information Available

Library of Congress Cataloging-in-Publication Data

Tuber, Steven, 1954-
  Attachment, play and authenticity : a Winnicott primer / Steven Tuber.
    p. ; cm.
  Includes bibliographical references and index.
  ISBN-13: 978-0-7657-0541-9 (cloth : alk. paper)
  ISBN-10: 0-7657-0541-9 (cloth : alk. paper)
  ISBN-13: 978-0-7657-0542-6 (pbk. : alk. paper)
  ISBN-10: 0-7657-0542-7 (pbk. : alk. paper)
  1. Winnicott, D. W. (Donald Woods), 1896-1971. 2. Child analysis. 3. Infant
psychology. 4. Play--Psychological aspects. 5. Mother and infant. I. Title.
  [DNLM: 1. Winnicott, D. W. (Donald Woods), 1896-1971. 2. Child
Psychology. 3. Play and Playthings. 4. Mother-Child Relations. 5.
Psychoanalytic Theory. 6. Psychoanalytic Therapy. WS 105.5.P5 T885a 2008]
  RJ504.2.T83 2008
  618.92'8914--dc22   2007037410

Printed in the United States of America

⊗™ The paper used in this publication meets the minimum requirements of
American National Standard for Information Sciences—Permanence of Paper for
Printed Library Materials, ANSI/NISO Z39.48-1992.

This book is lovingly dedicated to the three people who would appreciate it most:

Max Tuber
Bella Tuber
And
Dr. Goldye Meyer

And to the three people I cherish the most:

Jacob Tuber
Savi Tuber
And
Dr. Jodie Meyer

You have all been far more than a "good enough" holding environment for me.

Contents

Preface

IN MY THIRTY YEARS OF BEING ENGROSSED in the intertwining fields of child diagnosis and child therapy, the clinical acumen and humanity of D. W. Winnicott have always been something to aspire to, something to cherish, and something almost limitless in their usefulness. I write this book, therefore, in large part to pay homage to the man and his work. In some small but real way, I believe that in teaching his work to my students, I help expand them the way he has expanded me. This book will not be a biography, nor a comprehensive review of his work, nor a complete distillation of his ideas by theme. I think that a respectful way to approach his work is to think dynamically, in the literal sense of that word. I will attempt to see and play with his ideas as a presentation of paradoxes, never fully resolvable by words alone, yet capable of stirring us to find greater and deeper meanings to even the simplest of gestures, squiggles, and words, both in the consulting room and beyond. Therefore I'd like you, the reader, to approach this book with paradox and dilemma solving/making as your frame of reference. The book is derived from a series of lectures I have given to my graduate students in the doctoral program in clinical psychology of the City University of New York at City College. Most chapters will begin with a dilemma or paradox that Winnicott has posed for us and will focus on a close reading of one or two of his articles that speak most directly to this conundrum within the human experience. Often I will set the stage for the chapter with a song or reading from outside our field to convey the way in which Winnicott's musings have large, at times universal, application. As you will see, the capacity for play has been understood by Winnicott to be the gold standard for determining the capacity to be fully alive and human. Given that lectures have served as the segue to this book, many of the chapters will also be filled with references to my own clinical work and occasionally to personal experiences as a parent that have served to convince me of the heuristic value of Winnicott's thinking and writing. I trust and hope that these references will augment your understanding of Winnicott and not get in the way. It is my attempt at play; I'd like to think that Winnicott himself would have approved.

Acknowledgments

I HAVE BEEN HELPED BY MANY PEOPLE during the process of writing and producing this book and their genuine care and, in many cases, love and devotion, has been so very important. I'd like to first thank my dear colleague and friend, Professor Arietta Slade, who kindly and beautifully helped edit the manuscript. Another colleague at City College, Professor Lissa Weinstein, was the true catalyst for this book in the first place. Several people were especially generous in helping me negotiate the publication process: Michael Moskowitz, David Scharf, A. J. Franklin, Paul Wachtel, and especially Art Pomponio, editor at Jason Aronson, who has been a staunch advocate and supporter of the work from the moment he read it.

The book was spawned by a class I teach on Winnicott as part of the curriculum of the doctoral program in clinical psychology at CUNY. The curiosity and receptiveness of the students in the class in the spring of 2006 were instrumental to the writing of this book—Alex Crumbley, Wendy Cummings, Ben Harris, Melissa Jacobs, Maia Miller, Aoife West, and Rachel Wolitzky, I owe many thanks to you all. My wife, Dr. Jodie Meyer, sat in on the class and it was her ample yet subtle notes that provided the bedrock to bank on in the writing process.

As this book has almost as much to do with teaching Winnicott as it does with "playing" with him, it has made me think deeply about, and with great appreciation for, the many teachers I've been blessed with over the years. This seems like a most suitable place to thank them, so in chronological order, I offer thanks to: William Cook, Ed Zigler, Susan Harter, Pat Jette, Marty Mayman, Bettie Arthur, Al Cain, Irene Fast, Eric Bermann, Tom Cummings, John Mordock, Beatrice Klein, David Crenshaw, Ed Gardner, Libby Barker, Charlie Tsarnas, Carol Eagle, and Susan Coates. These teachers, when combined with my students at City College, have provided an optimal "holding environment" for which I am forever grateful.

The authors and publisher gratefully acknowledge permission for the following excerpts:

Harry Potter and the Sorcerer's Stone by J.K. Rowling, copyright by J.K. Rowling, 1997

The Brooklyn Follies by Paul Auster. Copyright 2006 by Paul Auster. Published by Henry Holt and Company. Reprinted with permission by the Carol Mann agency.

The Runaway Bunny by Margaret Wise Brown. Copyright 1942 by Harper and Row Publishers. Text copyright renewed 1970 by Roberta Brown Rauch. Used by permission of Harper Collins Publishers.

The Maturational Processes and the Facilitating Environment by D.W. Winnicott. Copyright 1965 by International Universities Press. Reprinted by permission of Paterson Marsh on behalf of the Winnicott trust.

Therapeutic Consultations in Child Psychiatry by D.W. Winnicott. Copyright 1971 by Basic Books. Reprinted by permission of BASIC BOOKS, a member of Perseus Books Group. Reprinted by permission of Paterson Marsh on behalf of the Winnicott trust.

Through Pediatrics to Psycho-Analysis: Collected Papers by D.W. Winnicott. Copyright 1975 by Basic Books. Reprinted by permission of BASIC BOOKS, a member of Perseus Books Group. Reprinted by Paterson Marsh on behalf of the Winnicott trust.

Playing and Reality by D.W. Winnicott. Copyright 1971 by D.W. Winnicott. Reprinted by permission of Taylor & Francis Books UK.

Chapter One

─────────○─────────

Overview

CHAPTER 1 PROVIDES A SCHEMATIC overview of many of the often poetic paradoxes that Winnicott suggests lie at the heart of the human experience and therefore at the core of the therapeutic process. Each paradox will have one to three of Winnicott's works attached to it, and these readings will serve as the starting points for our discussion of the value and meaning of Winnicott's work. I will end the chapter with an annotated listing of some of Winnicott's most stirring, even provocative quotes, to whet your appetite for "Winnicottisms" and to provide a flavor of what is to come through a discussion of his work.

Chapter 2 focuses on the following: what mothers do naturally cannot be taught, yet mothers must be helped when things go awry—a model for the skills and challenges facing psychotherapists.

The article read is: "Primitive Emotional Development" (1945).

Winnicott had enormous faith in the "good enough" mother to be just that—to be sufficient in her attunement to help her baby come alive. In parallel fashion, Winnicott repeatedly stressed the therapeutic value of having sufficient faith in the patient to allow her the space to create health. Yet Winnicott was at times quite pessimistic about the capacity to teach mothers how to mother if they weren't already "good enough." Similarly, the "cleverness" of interpretations by poor therapists for their own sake is repeatedly derided by Winnicott as intrusions akin to the mother's maladaptive attempts to have her baby comply with her needs and demands. But how does a therapist know when to intervene or not and at what level? When is the optimal intervention linked to listening and faith, and when must it be active and creative? What is needed in the therapist to allow the patient to develop creatively? For Winnicott, these questions are answered by the assessment of the patient's (child or disturbed adult) and the therapist's (or mother's) capacity to play. What the attainment of the ability to play implies for mother and child and therapist-patient will provide the scaffolding for the depiction of Winnicott's two other pillars of personality development: the authentic nature of the self and the existence of transitional phenomena. This tripartite foundation of human-making—play trueness of self and transitional experience—will be constantly woven together by Winnicott to create the fabric underlying identity formation, therapeutic intervention, and, as we shall see in later chapters, the creation of culture itself.

Chapter 3 presents the next paradox/dilemma: something essential about a person is bound up with bodily aliveness and is thus ultimately unknowable—yet therapy is primarily an interpretive practice.

The article serving as the focus for elaboration of this dilemma is: "Communicating and Not Communicating Leading to a Study of Certain Opposites" (1963).

Here the paradox has several components: (a) human beings are fundamentally, irreducibly alone and secret at the core of their beings, yet (b) they crave being connected and understood by another so that (c) the key balance in life is to tolerate our aloneness (whether in the presence of others or not) yet still desire to connect. The implications of this dilemma and balancing act for the therapeutic process are central to Winnicott's ideas on technique and the therapeutic process.

Chapter 4 speaks to the following dynamic: precocious compliance equals psychic death, yet the child's utter dependence as an infant promotes independence.

The articles that address this conflict are: "Reparation in Respect of a Mother's Organized Defence against Depression" (1948) and "Ego Distortion in Terms of True and False Self" (1960).

Although mothers are typically "good enough" in their infant care, they are never perfectly sufficient, leading to constant mishearings and misreadings of the infant's state of mind and bodily needs. What is to be done with these moments of aloneness by the infant? The profound needs of the infant push him toward compliance, but the Scylla of compliance leads the infant to the False Self–state of psychic surrender and loss of aliveness, while the Charybdis of separateness leaves the infant prone to abandonment and despair. How the infant and mother strive to create a vital balance between these dilemmas will be the focus of this chapter.

Chapter 5 expands upon the previous dilemma: the infant is an isolate who needs its mother to protect the privacy of their mutuality—to be insulated but not isolated is their goal.

The articles that speak to this paradox are: "The Capacity to Be Alone" (1958) and "Mirror-Role of Mother and Family in Child Development" (1967).

The baby is not only a true isolate but in fact needs the protective shielding of her mother in the first months of life to ensure her privacy. Indeed the better the mother can protect the baby from impingement from the outside world, the truer and more alone the baby is, yet simultaneously, the greater the infant's capacity to connect to others in a genuine, desired fashion. How the mother and baby create this state of sufficient insulation to paradoxically prevent the loneliness of isolation will be the crux of the matter in this chapter.

Chapter 6 depicts yet a fifth paradox: an object only becomes real by being hated, implying that the world only feels substantial if one's attempts at destroying it are unsuccessful.

Here we read Winnicott's seminal work: "The Use of an Object and Relating through Identifications" (1971).

The infant's experience of nonperfect mothering allows him to feel distinct and hence alive. This necessary distinguishing process, however, leads to the infant's "obliteration" of the mother. Can the mother survive this obliteration? If she survives without undue retaliation, then and only then can the infant feel distinct and therefore begin the process of becoming a person. Hating and its vicissitudes, particularly the role aggression and instinct play in

Winnicott's conceptualizations of personality development, begin to take full shape here.

Chapter 7 is a synthesizing chapter, primarily through a clinical consultation.

The articles used in this synthesizing process are: "Birth Memories, Birth Trauma and Anxiety" (1949) and "The Case of Bob" from his *Therapeutic Consultations in Child Psychiatry* (1971).

Using the "Case of Bob," a six-year-old boy, we will attempt to synthesize the central concepts we have reviewed up to this point: the capacity to be alone; the relegation of instinct to a secondary role in the first months of life; the power of the infant's spontaneous gesture; the mirror-role of mother in early life; the dangers of annihilation if mother is not available early on and the role mother's mood can play in the development of a false compliance. We also touch on the role of the birth process as the starting point for the potential disruption of the baby's "going on being."

Chapter 8 takes us to the first of Winnicott's two greatest contributions to the field. Here we discuss the role of play. The works to be studied are: "Playing: A Theoretical Statement" (1971), "Group Influences and the Maladjusted Child" (1955), and "The Case of Hesta" in *Therapeutic Consultations in Child Psychiatry* (1971).

The importance of the capacity to play cannot be underestimated in Winnicott's theorizing. Its existence in the child implies the attainment of most of what Winnicott would depict are the major developmental achievements: the capacity to be alone; the capacity to create a potential, intermediate space between inner life and external reality; the capacity to sustain a True Self; and the capacity to use objects. The use of play is also discussed phenomenologically as a means of understanding life from the vantage point of actual experience of the child. It thus provides the most original means for the child to expand and process reality. This, in turn, allows play to be used as the royal road to communication with a child in a therapeutic setting. The Case of Bob vividly portrays the use of play as both a therapeutic process and a diagnostic marker of progress and conflict in development.

Chapter 9 is perhaps the core of the book as it explores Winnicott's most original contribution, the role of transitional phenomena and potential space as a third, intermediate aspect of experience.

The articles reviewed here are: "Mind and Its Relation to the Psyche-Soma" (1949), "Transitional Objects and Transitional Phenomena" (1951) and "The Location of Cultural Experience" (1967).

We begin this chapter by first reviewing Winnicott's treatment of mind, psyche, and body. As an extension of his concepts of the True and False Self and "going on being," Winnicott wrestles with how missteps between mother and baby can lead to the baby experiencing his mind as split from his feelings of visceral vitality and the pathological sequelae of this split. This provides a segue into how the baby creates a third, intermediate arena between inner and outer reality through the use of transitional phenomena. These phenomena are the linchpin of all of Winnicott's theorizing and will be discussed both in their own right and in their linkages to the other central facets of Winnicott's conceptualizations.

Chapter 10 takes us to a more in-depth investigation of the role of aggression in Winnicott's theorizing and, more specifically, to the role and etiology of hate in early life and in the treatment process.

The article reviewed here is: "Hate in the Countertransference" (1949).

Winnicott's "optimistic" view of what the ordinary mother can achieve vis-à-vis her baby is utterly non-Pollyannaish precisely due to the central role that hate and aggression play in his theorizing. What are the necessary preconditions for hate to develop? What must the role of mother be in "using" this hate profitably for the baby? What is the impact on the baby if hate cannot be properly integrated? These are all crucial issues in Winnicott's work. The classic paper "Hate in the Countertransference" addresses all these questions in parallel with questioning how the therapeutic process can only be useful if these same issues are wrestled with by therapists, both internally and with their patients. Distinguishing between "realistic" hate and countertransferential hate is thus a process that must be managed well by both mother and therapist.

Chapter 11 expands on Winnicott's theorizing on aggression and hate, extending it to the realm and meaning of antisocial behavior.

The articles most central to this facet of his work are: "The Antisocial Tendency" (1956) and "Aggression in Relation to Emotional Development" (1950–1955).

As a natural progression from his study of hate, we turn to Winnicott's understanding of the antisocial tendency. He is able to create a hierarchy from healthy, normal deprivations by the mother as a necessary aspect of her baby's developing self to prolonged, chronic deprivations that lead a child to problematic, "nuisance" behavior. Winnicott presents this "nuisance" behavior as an expression of hope, hope that what was once received contingently by the baby from the mother can be retrieved. He then struggles with whether this reparation by the mother can restore the child back to her original state of intactness or whether there is a residue of pathology that cannot be annulled.

Chapter 12 shifts gears somewhat and turns to a view of Winnicott as therapist more than theoretician.

The articles reviewed in this chapter are: "The Aims of Psychoanalytic Treatment" (1962) and "The Case of Ada" from his *Therapeutic Consultations* (1971).

Winnicott synthesizes and operationalizes his theorizing through his clinical cases, while his cases reciprocally inform and expand his theoretical musings. His "Aims" paper vividly depicts what he sees as the meaning of treatment from both the patient's and the therapist's points of view and provides greater clarity on the parallels he constructs between the mother-infant and therapist-patient dyads. The Case of Ada, in turn, links his theoretical discussion of hate, hope, and the antisocial tendency to clinical case material.

Chapter 13, the final chapter, further develops our understanding of Winnicott's conceptions about the treatment process, this time in terms of what characteristics are necessary and sufficient for being a "good enough" therapist and how one defines transference and countertransference as part of this exploration.

The articles that inform chapter 13 are: "Advising Parents" (1957), "Countertransference" (1960), and "The Case of Robert" from his *Therapeutic Consultations* (1971).

This chapter will pay particular attention to how the significant moments in treatment occur when a child or adult is surprised by the material in a treatment hour, creating a release from the compliance Winnicott views as central to neurotic life. It will also focus on the mutuality of the treatment relationship. A sign of great health in the mind of either patient or therapist is the ability of one individual to enter imaginatively and accurately into the thoughts, feelings, hopes, and fears of another person, as well as to allow the other person to do the same to us. Impediments to that process are seen in transferential and countertransferential paradigms that must be explored for treatment to prosper.

THE LANGUAGE OF WINNICOTT

It is essential that any discussion of Winnicott speak early on about his use of language. It has been made clear to me by many colleagues that only two to three of Winnicott's papers are typically read as part of one's training, in part because his language is so evocative that this sampling is felt as sufficient. This book is therefore also an attempt to both stay true to the beauty of his language and yet provide the reader with a more comprehensive depiction of his writings, so that you may be made curious enough to go back and read some more.

With his words, Winnicott evokes a parallel process in which reading his work resonates on multiple levels in what must be at least some approximation of what it would have been like to be in treatment or supervision with him. As Ogden (2001) beautifully puts it, Winnicott uses "language to create experiences in reading that are inseparable from the ideas he is presenting, or more accurately, the ideas he is playing with" (p. 299). It therefore seems essential to me that if we are to play with Winnicott, we must from the start have a vivid sense of his ability to use words to communicate at multiple levels of being. The following collage of quotes from his work is perhaps best viewed as a collection of his "greatest hits," and I present them to make vivid his splendid sandbox of ideas and inspirations. It is also, of course, the best prelude to the fuller discussion of his writings that will serve as the backbone of this book.

Some grand "Winnicottisms" in annotated fashion:

Later I will try to explain why disintegration is frightening, whereas unintegration is not. (Primitive Emotional Development)

The precision of his prose, right down to his subtle distinctions in use of prefixes, will be a repeated motif throughout this book.

The corollary of this is that where playing is not possible then the work done by the therapist is directed towards bringing the patient from a state of not being able to play into a state of being able to play. (Playing: A Theoretical Statement)

To control what is outside one had to do things, not simply to think or to wish, and doing things takes time. Playing is doing. (Playing: A Theoretical Statement)

Playing is immensely exciting. It is exciting not primarily because the instincts are involved, be it understood! (Playing: A Theoretical Statement)

It is good to remember always that playing is itself a therapy. (Playing: A Theoretical Statement)

These quotes speak to the role of play as diagnostic exemplar; as *the* essential facet of child behavior, as fostering health by its repetition, as the means to establish the capacity for vitality, and as the process whereby aliveness is fully attained, making it intrinsically delightful for its own sake and not for instinct's sake.

The significant moment is that at which the child surprises himself or herself, it is not the moment of my clever interpretation that is significant. (Playing: A Theoretical Statement)

This quote speaks concomitantly to the significance of surprise as a moment of potential change in the experience of self, to the necessity of the child surprising himself, as opposed to the surprise being imposed by an outsider, and to Winnicott's contempt for cleverness as part of the therapist's arsenal of technique.

> *Death has no meaning until the arrival of hate and of the concept of the whole human person.* (The Theory of the Parent-Infant Relationship)

> *However much he loves his patients he cannot avoid hating them and fearing them, and the better he knows this the less will hate and fear be the motives determining what he does to his patients.* (Hate in the Countertransference)

> *I suggest that the mother hates the baby before the baby hates the mother and before the baby can know his mother hates him.* (Hate in the Countertransference)

The centrality of hate as a developmental achievement and the placing of both hate and death in a developmental framework are at the core of these three quotations. Note how the therapist's acknowledgment of his hatred of his patient in the second quote is paralleled by the mother's hatred of her baby in the third quote. Parenting and treatment are therefore both dramatically more effective if the therapist/mother is aware of the hate/aggression intrinsic to the human encounter and indeed to the very making of a truly human being.

> *Mothers who do not have it in them to provide good-enough care cannot be made good enough by mere instruction.* (The Theory of the Parent-Infant Relationship)

This quote is among the most pessimistic statements made by Winnicott about mothers, but his use of the word "mere" speaks to the possibility of growth in a mother's capacity to care through treatment, if not by education.

> *The analyst may appear to be very clever, and the patient may express admiration, but in the end the correct interpretation is a trauma, which the patient has to reject, because it is not his.* (The Theory of the Parent-Infant Relationship)

An enormously powerful statement as to what truly promotes change in psychotherapy, speaking to Winnicott's resolute belief that change comes internally and creatively from the patient and not from the therapist. Indeed, if it comes solely from the therapist, it is inherently traumatic in its dire impact on the patient's originality.

> *However, it seems to be usual that mothers who are not distorted by ill-health or by present-day environmental stress do tend on the whole to know accurately enough what their infants need, and further, they like to provide what is needed.* (The Theory of the Parent-Infant Relationship)

This is perhaps his most vivid depiction of the motivation and existence of the "good enough" mother.

> *This was a protest from the core of me to the frightening fantasy of being infinitely exploited.* (Communicating and Not Communicating Leading to a Study of Certain Opposites)

This is a telling example of Winnicott's access to his own inner life, even to its most frightening domains.

> *A good object is no good to the infant unless created by the infant.* (Communicating and Not Communicating Leading to a Study of Certain Opposites)

Defying simplistic, content-focused notions of "good" or "bad" objects, Winnicott is far more concerned with the creative process as the defining characteristic of health or madness.

> *In the artist of all kinds I think one can detect an inherent dilemma, which belongs to the co-existence of two trends, the urgent need to communicate and the still more urgent need not to be found.* (Communicating and Not Communicating . . .)

> *It is a sophisticated game of hide and seek in which it is joy to be hidden but disaster not to be found.* (Communicating and Not Communicating . . .)

Although healthy persons communicate and enjoy communicating, the other fact is equally true, that each individual is an isolate, permanently non-communicating, permanently unknown, in fact unfound. (Communicating and Not Communicating . . .)

These three quotes, all taken from one of his masterpieces, "Communicating and Not Communicating Leading to a Study of Certain Opposites," together speak to the profound dialectic he posits as the centerpiece of the human experience—the simultaneous wish to connect yet remain apart, to avoid exploitation yet to embrace attunement.

Adolescents on the whole eschew psychoanalytic treatment, though they are interested in psychoanalytic theories. (Communicating and Not Communicating . . .)

This follows directly from the three quotes above, as adolescence is a period of special vulnerability to fears of exploitation and hence a great suspiciousness of treatment, and yet a special pull toward knowing oneself, and hence a time for being drawn to theories of how personalities are formed.

Probably I get a specially clear view of this problem in a children's outpatient department because such a department is really a clinic for the management of hypochondria in mothers. (Reparation in Respect of a Mother's Organized Defence against Depression)

This is at first reading a rather provocative stance by Winnicott, but in context, it speaks directly to his notions of the importance of bodily awareness and the relationship of psyche and soma as an index of mental health in mothers and babies.

The good-enough mother meets the omnipotence of the infant and to some extent makes sense of it. She does this repeatedly. (Ego Distortion in Terms of True and False Self)

What is essential in this quote is not only its establishment of infantile omnipotence as a necessary fact of early life but also its emphasis on the repetitive nature of parenting as the key process behind the infant's capacity to become real.

> *Thus the basis of the capacity to be alone is a paradox; it is the experience of being alone while someone else is present.* (The Capacity to Be Alone)

Perhaps Winnicott's most famous phrase is that there is no such thing as a baby, only a mother-baby dyad. The above quote follows directly from this conception: only when the baby is fully assured that he is safely unintruded upon yet looked after can he eventually tolerate the experience of actually being physically alone.

> *I am suggesting that, ordinarily, what the baby sees is himself or herself. In other words the mother is looking at the baby and what she looks like is related to what she sees there.* (Mirror-Role of Mother and Family in Child Development)

This quote predates and yet captures beautifully Kohut's conception of the mirroring object.

> *The baby quickly learns to make a forecast; just now it is safe to forget the mother's mood and to be spontaneous, but any minute the mother's face will become fixed or her mood will dominate and my own personal needs must then be withdrawn otherwise my central self will suffer insult.* (Mirror-Role of Mother . . .)

Here Winnicott aptly describes the process whereby the baby is prone to develop an overly compliant, "False Self" to ensure continuity with a mother overly dominated by her moods, yet keep a "True Self" when mother is sufficiently masterful of her own emotional states to focus on her baby.

> *When I look I am seen so I exist. I can now afford to look and see. I now look creatively and what I apperceive I also perceive. In fact I take care not to see what is not there to be seen.* (Mirror-Role of Mother . . .)

Here, in Winnicott's inimitably succinct, poetic yet enigmatic phrasing, is embedded his belief that the "good enough" mother's attention to the baby allows him the freedom to not just take on the world but to creatively master it and not be thwarted by unnecessary fears and doubts.

> *Psychotherapy is not making clever and apt interpretations; by and large it is a long term giving the patient back what the patient brings. It is not easy and it is emotionally exhausting but we get our rewards.* (Mirror-Role of Mother . . .)

> *I think I interpret mainly to let the patient know the limits of my understanding.* (The Use of an Object and Relating through Identification)

> *We all hope that our patients will finish with us and forget us, and that they will find living itself to be the therapy that makes sense.* (The Use of an Object . . .)

These three quotations are vital to understanding Winnicott, for they speak to his belief in the psychotherapeutic process as a mutually difficult, deep process, to the limitations of words used by the therapist to evoke change and to his beautiful perspective on therapy as work and not as a life in itself.

> *When the analyst knows that the patient carries a revolver, then, it seems to me, this work cannot be done.* (The Use of an Object . . .)

Perhaps only Winnicott could state something this outrageous in this understated a fashion! It certainly provides an outer limit to the prerequisites necessary for an in-depth exploration of a patient's psyche.

> *I realized, however, that play is in fact neither a matter of inner psychic reality nor a matter of external reality.* (Location of Cultural Experience)

A child's capacity to play is treated by Winnicott as the gold standard for health precisely because her nature is defined by the above quotation. Play's status as the quintessential embodiment of transitional phenomena in a transitional space is what allows creativity, originality, and genuineness to flourish—the three aptitudes that together define for Winnicott the best that life has to offer.

> *It is of first importance for us to acknowledge openly that absence of psychoneurotic illness may be health, but it is not life.* (Location of Cultural Experience)

This quotation flows directly from the one before it, because while the absence of neurosis may preclude psychiatric diagnosis, it does imply the availability of creativity, originality, and genuineness, which only full living implies.

> *Needless to say the therapist must have professional reliability as something that happens easily; it is possible for a serious person to maintain a professional standard even when undergoing very severe personal strains in the private life and in the personal growth process which, we hope, never stops.* (Therapeutic Consultations in Child Psychiatry)

> *What the patient meets is surely the professional attitude of the analyst, not the unreliable men and women we happen to be in private life.* (Countertransference)

Winnicott's discussion of what characteristics and behavior are necessary in order to be fully professional speaks volumes to the deep personal integrity he conveys throughout his clinical writings, as well as to his depiction of life as a humble process of continual growth and struggle in which the therapist must rise above his own personal fragility to maintain a professional attitude.

> *In order to use the mutual experience one must have in one's bones a theory of the emotional development of the child and of the relationship of the child to the environmental factors.* (Therapeutic Consultations in Child Psychiatry)

Here is a most vivid example of Winnicott's fundamentally developmental orientation to the treatment of both children and adults and fundamentally phenomenological focus on the interplay between environment and constitution.

> *I suggest that this I AM moment is a raw moment; the new individual feels infinitely exposed. Only if someone has her arms round the infant at this time can the I AM moment be endured, or perhaps, risked.* (Group Influences and the Maladjusted Child)

Winnicott's phenomenological orientation allows him to articulate this utterly in-the-moment point of dramatic meaning in the psychological birth of the baby and what must be provided for by the mother to ensure its possibility.

> *The antisocial child has two alternatives—to annihilate the true self or to shake society up till it provides cover.* (Group Influences and the Maladjusted Child)

> *When a child steals, what is sought is not the object stolen; what is sought is the person, the mother from whom the child has the right to steal because she is the mother.* (The Deprived Child and How He Can Be Compensated . . .)

> *The antisocial tendency implies hope.* (The Antisocial Tendency)

Winnicott suggests here that antisocial qualities are an intrinsic part of being human. He also suggests that the antisocial act is originally an act of protest over something that was once possessed by the child but now perceived as lost. Importantly, this implies that the antisocial tendency is developmentally far more evolved than the experience leading to psychosis of having never viably possessed a "good enough" experience. In Winnicott's view, the tendency to steal implies a refusal to surrender to the despair of never regaining the lost mothering person.

> *What releases the mother from her need to be near-perfect is the infant's understanding.* (Mind and Its Relation to the Psyche-Soma)

Speaking of the slightly older (six months or so) infant, Winnicott again demonstrates the inherently reciprocal, mutual nature of the mother-infant dyad.

> *Integration of a personality does not arrive at a certain time on a certain day. It comes and goes, and even when well attained it can be lost through unfortunate environmental chance.* (Aggression in Relation to Emotional Development)

Yet another depiction by Winnicott of the inherently fluid nature of personality formation, as well as a humble reminder of how traumatic later experiences can undermine even well-established capacities for vividness and vitality.

> *In doing psychoanalysis I aim at: Keeping alive. Keeping well. Keeping awake.* (The Aims of Psychoanalytic Treatment)

> *I never use long sentences unless I am very tired. If I am near exhaustion point I begin teaching. Moreover, in my view an interpretation containing the word "moreover" is a teaching session.* (The Aims of Psychoanalytic Treatment)

Winnicott's deep sense of humor, often at his own expense, his utter belief in the many virtues of simplicity and his abhorrence of "talking at" as opposed to "being with" one's patients are so apparent here.

> *For instance, I got hit by a patient. What I said is not for publication.* (Hate in the Countertransference)

In closing, a last peek at Winnicott's devilish sense of humor and profound genuineness as a therapist and person—what better segue into playing with his work?

Chapter Two

───────────○───────────

Dialectical Meaning-Making in Infancy

Dilemma: A baby has instinctual urges and predatory ideas—how are both possible and where does it leave the mother?

Article reviewed: "Primitive Emotional Development" (1945).

I DON'T KNOW WHETHER WINNICOTT HAD a penchant for rhythm and blues, but I feel quite sure that he would have made a link between a song entitled "Give Me One Reason to Stay Here" by Tracy Chapman and his article "Primitive Emotional Development" (1945). Chapman's soulful distinction between the deadly engulfment caused by an overly intrusive squeeze versus the soothing, repetitive holding that gets her through the night highlights the life-or-death importance of early mothering in a manner that Winnicott would have certainly resonated with. As we will see later on in this chapter, Chapman's distinction also mirrors Winnicott's depiction of the inner dread of twelve psychotic adults he analyzed during World War II. Indeed, these patients' fear of "falling forever" or their dread of human interaction became essential data in Winnicott's depiction of the centrality of early infancy as the cradle for meaning-making.

Winnicott was certainly not the first psychoanalyst to work with psychotic adults. and he certainly rested on Melanie Klein's (1957) shoulders in his focus on the earliest ties between mother and baby as the starting point for a person's psychology. But he does stand first in linking actual mother-infant dialectical interaction (and not solely fantasy) to the genesis of well-being or psychopathology. More fundamentally, he joined with Klein and others in stressing that the making of meaning is not stationed primarily in the Oedipal, three-to-five-year-olds' triad, but in the four-to-ten-month-olds' making distinctions between self and other.

It is essential to stress that Winnicott was first trained as a pediatrician and had thousands of mother-baby interactions in his internal repertoire before he ever became a psychoanalyst. His unique training as baby doctor/analyst thus kept the phenomenology of babyhood at the forefront of his work and made the links between the psychotic regressions of his adult patients and the behaviors of his infant-mother dyads uppermost in his mind. It allowed him to feel certain that there was a psychology of babyhood, and that the baby was an inherently psychological being.

This brings us directly to his paper "Primitive Emotional Development." It's easy to create a fantasy about the historical context of this paper. The war in Europe had ended only months before, and Winnicott had played an important role on a national level, via BBC radio broadcasts, in the attempt to help parents ride out the traumatizing effects of war on their relationships to their children. Whatever weariness such a war effort may have cost him, he now was to present this paper to the British Psychoanalytic Society, summarizing his work with a patient population seen as unsuitable for psychoanalysis. If that wasn't unsettling enough, he was to posit in this paper that Oedipal configurations were not the central organizing means for personality formation and that such an organizing point was instead to be found in the preverbal baby! To make this paper even more potentially heretical, he gave the baby a mind, even a calculating mind. At this moment in time few, if any, in the audience would have found this notion at all likely.

This takes me to the heart of the paper itself, to page 152, where he writes:

In terms of baby and mother's breast, the baby has instinctual urges and predatory ideas. The mother has a breast and the power to produce milk, and the idea that she would like to be attacked by a hungry baby. These two phenomena do not come into relation with each other till the mother and child live an experience together.

What a brilliant, epic three sentences. At this relatively early moment in his thinking, Winnicott integrates two distinct modes of being into a new, essential synthesis. He affirms that there are drives in the baby (instinctual urges), keeping true to his psychoanalytic training. But then he adds that the baby has predatory ideas. Ideas! He gives the baby a mind and a motivational force distinct from his urges. Being predatory, moreover, implies being related and relationship-seeking. He thus establishes himself as a combination of drive/object relations theorist in a single sentence. Still further, he speaks of the infant as predatory, giving the baby an active, life-seeking force and vitality; this view of the infant will persist throughout his writings. The baby's creativity and vitality will serve as the template for mental health and as the standard for judging the degree of pathology in all his patients.

Perhaps even more startling, Winnicott matches the infant's urges and ideas with an equally "charged" mother who has both milk-producing power and the *wish* to be attacked by the baby. This is not a mother fearful of engulfment or dreading the baby's predation, but a strong, vibrant being fully wanting to take this baby on. One almost gets the image of two beings about to begin a jousting tournament, having at each other with reckless abandon. This takes mother-infant interaction firmly into the realm of mutual reciprocity and into a completely "in the moment," experiential dynamic. It is only when mother and child "live an experience together" that the separate phenomena of charged mother and baby become fully alive. Thus, these three sentences in so many ways create a template for object relations theory, empirical mother-infant interaction studies, and the integration of drive and relational theories that will define much of the writing in psychoanalysis for the next sixty years. The mutually, equally energized character of both participants, moreover, brings an intensity to mothering and "babying" right from the start of life, positing a positive, engaged life force as the cauldron from which humanity emerges.

I stress the intensity underlying this first relationship for two reasons. First, the energy involved makes it simpler theoretically and literally to understand how and why a mother can be "good enough" and doesn't have to be, indeed shouldn't be, perfect. That mother and baby are both so voracious means that they will be clumsy and misread each other often. They will both make mistakes reading one another and staying attuned. But baby's literal and ideational hunger will keep it related despite the errors and mother's equal wish to be "attacked" keeps her in the "game," despite her anxieties and weariness. I stress this intense, mutual "life force" also because it fits both with the notion of "the competent infant," actively taking on the world, and with the devoted mother, eager after nine months to "get at" her baby. It is a most parsimonious way to understand maternal devotion in the face of exhaustion and to understand the baby's quest to know about the world despite his marked confusions and complexities. Therefore, the average mother and the average baby stay "good enough" since they both bring enough to the table (remember, he eats and she wants to be eaten) to allow them to muddle through.

Except when they don't muddle through. This paper, after all, derives from his work with twelve adults who most certainly did not have a "good enough" experience. It is important to note that he speaks in this paper of psychosis and not schizophrenia. That is, he speaks to psychotic states, sometimes transient, oftentimes persistent, which he continuously links to the interplay of mother and baby. Given our present knowledge of the role of neurochemical disruption or deficit in schizophrenia and given, even in 1945, the existent knowledge of its role in dementia praecox, it is curious that Winnicott gives these causative agents no role in his theorizing. We can speculate that he would have seen neurotransmitter dysfunction as an important ingredient that would affect the goodness of fit between mother and baby, making it much more difficult for the mother to read the baby's cues and for the baby to make use of the mother's cues. In that sense, he would have most likely viewed physically causative factors as impediments to adequate mother-infant interaction and suggested that from this impoverished or distorted interaction would come the states of mind we call psychosis. This perspective also leaves room for the view that all of us are susceptible to psychotic states if faced with circumstances that are damaging and overwhelming enough. Since we are all mothered to a "good enough" degree (in health) as opposed to a perfect, ironclad degree, it follows that later unfortunate events can disrupt anyone if awful enough. Indeed, it can easily be argued that Winnicott's brilliance is enhanced exponentially by his ever-present awareness of how difficult life can be, so that he never takes for granted how health and pathology can quickly flip in balance, for better or for worse.

Winnicott's primary contribution to the field in this paper can be stated in earnest on pages 146–147. Here he begins by describing psychoanalysis as historically focused on the treatment of neurotic patients, then suggests that, thanks largely to the work of Klein, psychoanalysis can be comfortably extended to work with depressed patients. In this paper, Winnicott adds:

> The same technique can take us to still more primitive elements, provided of course that we take into consideration the changes in the transference situation inherent in such work. (p. 146)

From a teaching point of view, it is the next paragraph, where Winnicott distinguishes between the treatment of neurotics, depressives, and psychotics, that deserves our rapt attention as a "tipping point" toward understanding the main thesis of the present paper.

> I mean by this that a patient needing analysis of ambivalence in external relationships (a "neurotic") has a fantasy of his analyst and the analyst's work that is different from that of one who is depressed. In the former case the analyst's work is thought of as

done out of love for the patient, hate being deflected on to hateful things. (p. 146)

What does this mean? A neurotic patient, as Winnicott defin one here, is troubled by the ambivalence that exists in terms of her whole self in relation to certain key whole others. The Oedipal struggles of such a patient by and large exist outside of the analyst and are only brought into the analysis through transference. Even in such heated, transferential, potentially "teachable" moments, however, the hate expressed comes from a whole person whose reality testing is sufficiently strong to still experience the analyst as a whole person. The analyst is thus most of the time protected from the patient's hate by its being placed on others, with love and gratitude toward the analyst providing a milieu for holding this ambivalence "up to the light." Working with a depressed patient, however, brings a critically different paradigm to the fore, with a resulting greater demand placed on the analyst. Winnicott describes this as such:

> The depressed patient requires of his analyst the understanding that the analyst's work is to some extent his effort to cope with his own (the analyst's) depression, or shall I say guilt and grief resultant from the destructive elements in his own (the analyst's) love. (pp. 146–147)

When a patient is depressed, for Winnicott, his developmental struggles live in the world between the Oedipal configurations of ages three to five and the predepressive relationships of the first six months of life. Here the patient's primary struggles are around the loss of love and the effects of guilt and reparation. As the patient makes manifest these feelings of guilt, lovelessness, and resulting sadness, the task of the analyst is to be able to sit and hold the patient's inevitable need/wish to stir up similar feelings in the analyst. Despite such aroused sadness, the analyst remains available to the patient, therefore stirring up hope in the patient that she will not resuffer the feared loss of love. The analyst's capacity to tolerate his own sadness is thus critical and absolutely necessary to the patient if she is to work through her grief and depression. The analyst must cope with the grief and strain caused by the arousal of the destructive elements in his own soul and in doing so helps forestall a repetition of the patient's early loss of a sufficiently available parenting experience. This in turn mitigates the destructive aspects of the patient's personality structure, easing the depressive experience and paving the way for a fuller working-through of more neurotic configurations.

This leads Winnicott to an extension of analytic work to those patients whose attainment of the depressive relationship was not fully manifest. He describes their dilemma and concomitant task of the analyst as follows:

> To progress further along these lines, the patient who is asking for help in regard to his primitive, pre-depressive relationship to objects needs his analyst to be able to see the analyst's undisplaced and co-incident love and hate of him. In such cases, the end of the hour, the end of the analysis, the rules and regulations, these all come in as important expressions of hate, just as the good interpretations are expressions of love, and symbolical of good food and care. (p. 147)

Winnicott vividly tells us in this paragraph that the fragmented, mistrustful, paranoid world of the predepressive patient cannot help but be relived in the analyst's presence. There is little, if any, ability on the patient's part to protect the analyst or shield him from his (the patient's) primitive life. Without this shield, there is an enormous burden placed on the analyst to be critically aware of his own love and hatred of the patient. We talk today in this regard of the difficulties inherent in working with the regressed borderline patient, who can stir up in us the most primitive retaliatory and loving aspects of our being. A good moment in the work with such a patient never ends easily, a bad moment is feared to be endless. For the loss of the good moment carries with it no guarantee that it can be found again, while the experience of the bad moment carries with it no easily seen avenue of escape. Notice how Winnicott creates a parallel scaffolding for the behavior of the therapist that mirrors the developmental needs of the patient. The higher-level neurotic patient requires scaffolding that tolerates ambivalence; the depressive patient requires scaffolding that tolerates guilt, grief, and loss of love; while the psychotic or predepressive patient requires scaffolding that tolerates bits and pieces of self filled with all-or-none hating and loving expressions. Interestingly, Winnicott prescribes analytic training to proceed toward the more regressed patients only after working with more coalesced patients. Regrettably, this rarely happens in training; it is far more usual for the beginning therapist to be paired with the patients few, especially more senior therapists want, while the most senior therapists often prefer and have access to those patients most firm in their capacity to maintain whole experiences of self and other.

It is also interesting in this regard to note what Winnicott will describe in later papers as a fear of breakdown being a fear of a recurring madness. We all carry with us fragments of those early experiences that were not made whole with meaning and comprehension. If neurotic, such fragments are small and ephemeral and rarely persist in their intrusiveness. What gets stirred up, however, in moments of extreme vulnerability, is the whiff of that feared perfume, that scent of fragmented, disorganized chaos that we do all we can to repair and repress. In patients where predepressive relationships prevail, these fears of fragmentation are omnipresent and the analyst's job becomes akin to the shield-making, ever-reliable role that a mother with an infant strives for.

One further point before we return to the text. Perhaps the most appealing aspect of Winnicott's work is that it relies so fundamentally upon constant diagnosis. If we all contain fragmented aspects, for example, how do we determine if such fragments are mere appendages to a vibrant, solid core or conversely lie at the very core of the patient's experience? Importantly, I don't mean, nor does Winnicott, to look upon diagnosis as a static entity, a label to be derived and hung on the patient. Diagnosis should be a process that is always alive and always dynamic. The patient is shifting states throughout a treatment, often within a session, so that engaging in a diagnostic process means not just assessing the meaning of a particular content of the patient's internal experience, but also assessing what this content says about the underlying levels of organization and structure of the patient. To put it within a statistical metaphor, every patient has a modal level of experience of self and other and concomitant defenses to maintain them and a range of such self and object representations and defenses. Winnicott is describing what the requirements within the analyst should be for dealing with patients as a function of these patients' modal experiences of self and other. Thus, as patients improve or regress developmentally, the analyst must be prepared for these shifts to occur. This preparation is what is meant by constantly thinking about diagnosis.

A related aspect of diagnosis that will be taken up in greater detail in later chapters has to do with the capacity for play as a diagnostic indicator. The capacity for play requires enough of a sense of self and other so that "inside" and "outside" have begun to be consistently discriminated from one another. This allows play to be both real and easily set aside as not real when required. All one has to do is be within earshot of a four-year-old as she elaborates and narrate a play scene and then hear the child immediately respond to mother's call with an "In a minute, Mom!" to know that play is both real and not real to a child. It is the space (the transitional space for Winnicott) between real and not real where play occurs, and thus the capacity to play is a vital diagnostic marker in the assessment of a child's state of mind.

The capacity to play thus implies enough integration of self and other so that external reality is recognized, a state of being taken for granted in the analytic work with neurotics. Winnicott spends the rest of this paper trying to describe what occurs in the earliest moments in life that allows external reality to be recognized in a reliable fashion. He reasons that if he can describe such phenomena in infancy, he can thereby tell us what the inner life of his psychotic patients was like and what an analyst must do to provide treatment for such patients.

Let's go back to the text, to the moment when the "predatory" baby meets the "wish to be attacked" mother.

> I think of the process as if two lines came from opposite directions, (this is probably where I got the jousting tournament image from!) liable to come near each other. If they overlap there is a

moment of illusion—a bit of experience which the infant can take as either his hallucination or a thing belonging to external reality.

In other language, the infant comes to the breast when excited, and ready to hallucinate something fit to be attacked. At that moment the actual nipple appears and he is able to feel it was that nipple that he hallucinated. So his ideas are enriched by actual details of sight, feel, smell, and next time this material is used in the hallucination. In this way he starts to build up a capacity to conjure up what is actually available. (p. 152–153)

This is an enormously evocative depiction of the earliest moments of learning, of instinct, of motivation and of mother-baby interaction. It highlights several core components of Winnicott's view of personality development: (1) the baby comes to a feeding with eagerness and anticipation, not passivity or neutrality; (2) the baby comes to a feeding with her mind, even in its earliest moments, working, *hallucinating* in this case something she wants to devour; (3) the mother's reading of her baby propels her to provide this "something," i.e., she is "good enough" at providing this nipple; (4) biologically, the fact that a baby's mouth and a mother's nipple are ordinarily remarkably well suited in size and form to each other cannot be taken for granted (as Winnicott does) since it allows for the possibility that the baby's hallucination can be fulfilled; (5) the good fit of the nipple and its milk become linked with what the baby's mind hallucinated; (6)the attendant sensations of this good fit increase the baby's mindfulness so that (7) she can begin to create a memory of something that actually exists.

So we begin to have a picture of what the infant's most primitive moments of development are like. What is the mother's role? Winnicott tells us in the next paragraph.

It is especially at the start that mothers are vitally important, and indeed it is a mother's job to protect her infant from complications that cannot yet be understood by the infant, and to go on steadily providing the simplified bit of the world which the infant, through her, comes to know. Only on such a foundation can objectivity or a scientific attitude be built. All failure in objectivity at whatever date relates to failure in this stage of primitive emotional development. Only on a basis of monotony can a mother profitably add richness. (p. 153)

And only Winnicott can leap from what a mother does for a baby in the first days of life to its ramifications for the development of objective science! Just as with the baby, here the mother's role is described in a manner that predicts all other aspects of Winnicott's thinking on the mother's role in personality development: (1) mother is first and foremost a stimulus barrier that blocks out from the baby's perception any sensory stimuli that cannot be assimilated easily; (2) mother must be steady in her reliable provision of sensations that the baby can understand; (3) this regularity must be so good that it becomes monotonous to the baby, i.e., that the baby can take it utterly for granted; (4) taking experiences for granted provides the impetus to try new experiences; (5) failing to provide such regularity calls into question whether anything of reliability exists outside of the infant, leading to failures in the development of objectivity and in the belief that an "outside" of the baby is safe. This causes fundamental confusions for the baby in terms of what is "inside" (i.e., a hallucination) and what is "outside."

We are presented here with a dilemma whose multiplicity is exactly the point. At first Winnicott tells us how important it is that the infant's hallucination be matched by the mother's actual breast so that there is a moment of *illusion*, a point where the infant can either magically think he created the breast or believe it belongs outside of him. At first, presumably the infant can only believe in the illusion, for there is no "outside" yet. So if the mother provides this illusion so perfectly, how does this provide the infant with the basis for objectivity, for reality over fantasy? The answer to this riddle again has to do with his concept of the mother being "good enough," not magical. The mother has to be reliable enough to create a rudimentary sense of coherence for her baby, but not so perfect that there is no lag whatsoever between what a baby feels and what the mother provides. It is in the minute but real lags in time between need and satisfaction that the baby begins to distinguish between what is an internal sensation, a fantasy in Winnicott's terminology, and what is external reality. And what is the payoff for the baby? Winnicott says it beautifully:

> The point is that in fantasy things work by magic; there are no brakes on fantasy, and love and hate cause alarming effects. External reality has brakes on it, and can be studied and known, and, in fact, fantasy is only tolerable at full blast when objective reality is appreciated well. The subjective has tremendous value but is so alarming and magical that it cannot be enjoyed except as a parallel to the objective. (p. 153)

The mother who provides the adequate blend of reliability in just enough time allows the baby to appreciate the objective, indeed to become a "scientist" in his exploration. Anyone who has watched a baby drop a spoon from his high chair and follow its path knows what a scientist a baby is! As we will see later on, the notion of time in this equation is critical: too little time between baby's hallucination and response by mom provides too much magical power; too long a time between wish and response leads to feeling unprotected, leaving one at the mercy of "the alarming effects" of love and hate.

How does Winnicott link these discussions of the first moments of life back to psychosis in adults? Psychotic adults retain this primitive state of development or have been traumatized to the point where they regress back to this state where magic and illusion predominate. As Winnicott puts it:

> The object behaves according to magical laws, i.e. it exists when desired, it approaches when approached, it hurts when hurt. Lastly, it vanishes when not wanted. The last is most terrifying and is the only true annihilation. To not want, as the result of satisfaction, is to annihilate the object. (p. 153)

A patient of mine recently described the behavior of his one-year-old just before bedtime. He drinks some milk from his "sippy cup" each night in a ritualized, pleasurable fashion. But what is most pleasurable for him is to triumphantly yell "Done" and stick out the cup in the direction of his mother to take it at the exact moment when the milk is finished, i.e., it must vanish as it is not wanted. If his mother is not there immediately to take it, the baby immediately hurls it at the mom, ready or not, and the mother is quite appalled, not only at the baby's behavior but at the pleasure he derives from startling her. Indeed, the more she uses a stern, unusual voice to reprimand him for this behavior, the more he smiles and laughs ruthlessly. This older baby's pleasure in annihilation is obvious and the more his mother is appalled (but, crucially, not abandoning or rejecting) the more magical delight he gets from being "done" with her. The monotony of his feeding ritual gives him the platform from which to have magical fantasies without being terrified of them.

This example leads to two final points to be made about this paper. The first deals with the ruthlessness implied in the example above and Winnicott's postulation that the beginnings of life have an early, ruthless stage. He writes:

> The normal child enjoys a ruthless relation to his mother, mostly showing in play, and he needs his mother because only she can be expected to tolerate his ruthless relation to her even in play, because this really hurts her and wears her out. Without this play with her, he can only hide a ruthless self and give it life in a state of dissociation. (p. 154)

The balance of magic and objective reliability a mother and baby establish sets in motion the constant struggle all humans face between what wishes we feel entitled to and those we must earn via the reality principle. Winnicott provides us with the types of interaction in earliest life that set the stage for this life-long struggle. He implies that for those persons who regress back to this primitive point in development, the terrors of subjectivity and magical thinking can be heartbreakingly overwhelming and be set off without notice or regard for conventional notions of time and space. This leads to one final point. Regardless of how disrupted our early life may have been, development proceeds, at least in bits and pieces. Without a steady, positive ratio of reliable "outside" to magical "inside," the infant, child, or adult is always at the mercy of a fear of disintegration, of a return to being nothing but bits and pieces. Disintegration

> means abandonment to impulses, uncontrolled because acting on their own; and further, this conjures up the idea of similarly uncontrolled (because dissociated) impulses directed towards himself. (p. 155)

Winnicott's psychotic patients, subject to these bursts of disintegration, described experiences that resonated with Winnicott's knowledge of the earliest mother-baby experiences. His knowledge of what a good-enough mother provides motivated him to try and produce similar experiences in his patients. His experiences with these patients, integrated with his knowledge of mothers and infants through both pediatrics and psychiatry, provided a firm basis from which to create this paper, a paper that can readily be seen as the platform from which the rest of his clinical and theoretical work could emerge.

Chapter Three

---○---

A Good Object Must Be Found in Order to Be Created

Paradox: "A good object is no good to the infant unless created by the infant. . . . Yet the object must be found in order to be created."

Article reviewed: "Communicating and Not Communicating Leading to a Study of Certain Opposites" (1963).

> *Once there was a little bunny who wanted to run away.*
> *So he said to his mother, "I am running away."*
> *"If you run away," said his mother, "I will run after you.*
> *For you are my little bunny.". . . .*
> *"Shucks," said the bunny, "I might just as well stay where*
> *I am and be your little bunny."*
> *And so he did.*
> *"Have a carrot," said the mother bunny.*
>
> Margaret Wise Brown, *The Runaway Bunny* (1942)

THE RUNAWAY BUNNY SPEAKS BEAUTIFULLY of the wish to run away and create one's own space, to not be one with the mother, to not be found. It also speaks to the disaster inherent in not being found, in not being run after. The crux of the book, to my mind, is when the bunny says "Shucks," realizing that he cannot outlast his mother. With a mild expletive that depicts some aggression, a certain resignation to still being little and the crucial notion that he *might* stay with his mother, connoting some choice in the matter, he re-creates being her little bunny on his own terms. The mother, meanwhile, in her profound wisdom, nonchalantly accepts her bunny's "choice" and offers him "good enough" supplies, a carrot.

Winnicott would certainly have enjoyed this book! For much of what is addressed in his article "Communicating and Not Communicating" mirrors Brown's mother and child bunnies. The bunny's need to destroy his mother by his wish to run away and his mother's indefatigable refusal to be destroyed and constant adaptation to his changing states are a sublime introduction to Winnicott's notion of the "good enough" mother. Yet Brown's marvelous ending is an even more apt depiction of Winnicott's thinking. The mother bunny does not swallow up the baby upon his "choice" to stay with her, nor does she need him to take care of her; she provides her "carrot-breast" while giving him the space to create her on his own terms. She is the "found" object that the baby "creates." Thus Winnicott would agree with Brown that the development of personhood (or rabbithood!), of a self separate from another, derives from acting as if I am *not* your person and from the parent tolerating this "not-ness."

It is my opinion that the paper I focus on in this chapter is Winnicott's masterpiece. It contains as clear a view of the range of his thinking on personality development as anything else he wrote. It accomplishes all this within its first few pages, which would be terrific enough. But it then goes on to poetically address the ultimate existential paradox—how we are first and foremost isolates, utterly alone yet simultaneously subsumed by our wish to connect to others so as to not feel alone. The article is replete with paradox, highlighted by the quote that starts the chapter. Yet it is also replete with his comfort in not solving the paradoxes for us. He creates a process that parallels and thereby amplifies the content of the dilemmas he raises.

This binding of content and process begins with the quote with which Winnicott opens the paper. He quotes the poet Keats, "every point of thought is the center of an intellectual world." With this, he provides the counterpoint to the aloneness that is at the center of his paper, emphasizing the almost infinite richness of a single thought and, by implication, a single individual. He then juxtaposes Keats's observation with the statement that he has only one idea in this paper and a rather obvious one at that! Thus his own idea is both meager/redundant and yet the center of his intellectual world. This implies exactly the juxtaposition of humility and profundity that both typifies his work and is at the core of the infant's and mother's tasks in developing the baby's personhood.

The blending of process and content is further demonstrated in the second paragraph of the paper, where he describes his own process in creating it.

> Starting from no fixed place I soon came, while preparing this paper for a foreign society, to staking a claim, to my surprise, to the right not to communicate. This was a protest from the core of me to the frightening fantasy of being infinitely exploited. . . . In the language of this paper it is the fantasy of being found." (p. 179)

Beginning by telling us of his surprise and of his most profound fear, Winnicott opens a window to his soul at the very moment he reveals how frightening it would be to reveal himself! I am struck by his including the word "foreign" in that first sentence. It is as if the idea of explaining his thinking to such an audience generated a fear of being exposed and hence exploited. He therefore had to stake a mental claim to refuse to communicate, to keep a part of his self protected. Being found in that way would have been akin, he feared, to losing his self entirely and therefore being annihilated.

This paper, perhaps more than any other, resonates with my students when I quote from it. They immediately note how much they wish to be known by their own analysts, for example, but not to be known. Students describe cases where ten-year-olds constantly dart out of the room, roaming our corridors to stay hidden and yet are terrified of not being found. Or they talk of feeling, in their most intimate moments, a comforting lack of complete intimacy, of maintaining a secret interior monologue, of wanting to be known but not owned. How do a mother and baby create that balance? More profoundly, how do they create a balance such that the baby is thriving, as opposed to merely surviving?

Students then describe moments with their cases or in their own treatment where they want to be swallowed up and ask how that fits with Winnicott's notions. I reply that the phrase "I want to be swallowed up, to be known completely" implies both volition and an "I," two interactive achievements that are the focus of Winnicott's "Communicating and Not Communicating" paper. The actions of the *Runaway Bunny* are not those of an infant. Students note that they seem more characteristic of Mahler's practicing subphase of the toddler years. Other students note how the negativity involved in such mother-child interaction feels more "anal" than the first year of life Winnicott focuses on. I add to this the games of "peek-a-boo" and "hide-and-seek," two games intrinsic to every culture. I argue that peek-a-boo occurs at exactly the time in development (the second six months of life) where the dilemma Winnicott describes arises. Hide-and-seek, however, is a much later game, starting at about three years of age and lasting through latency with minor variations. Yet both games have at their core the playing with permanence. Think of the pleasure the infant gets in appearing and reappearing. I remember a series of snapshots my wife took of my then fifteen-month-old son in his crib. He and I are using a blanket to cover and uncover him, and both of us are laughing. In one telling shot, the blanket is off him, but he's covering his eyes and delighting in his belief that I couldn't see *him* because, with his eyes covered, he couldn't see me! Thus even without the cognitive capacity to recognize my existence independent of his, he could still delight in making me "disappear." Think of the delight the child playing hide-and-seek has when, while hidden, the grown-up speaks out loud of wondering where the child is, so that the child has the twin pleasures of not being seen yet knowing the adult is on the lookout for him. Think of the awfulness involved in not being found in that game and of having to announce where one is hiding. For Winnicott, this need to be found while needing to hide trumps psychosexual stages, such that whether one is playing a very "phallic" game of hide-and-seek or even "tag," or the very "anal" game of making one's "pee or poop" disappear down the toilet, or the very "oral" game of peek-a-boo, one is always dealing with the existential dilemma of being lost and found. Indeed, for Winnicott himself, the appearance in front of a foreign audience stirred up that same feeling of being found, this time in its malignant form, of being infinitely exploited. How terrifying is this experience of being found in this way? Winnicott is never more dramatic when he says:

> Rape, and being eaten by cannibals, these are mere bagatelles as compared with the violation of the self's core, the alteration of the self's central elements by communication seeping through the defenses. (p. 187)

How does he get to such a remarkably visceral depiction of the dangers in being found? He begins with a review of his thinking on how self and other are formed.

> Relating to objects is a complex phenomenon and the development of a capacity to relate to objects is by no means a matter simply of the maturational process. As always, maturation requires and depends on the quality of the facilitating environment. Where neither privation nor deprivation dominates the scene and where, therefore, the facilitating environment can be taken for granted in the theory of the earliest and most formative stages of human growth, there gradually develops in the individual a change in the nature of the object. The object being at first a subjective phenomenon becomes an object objectively perceived. This process takes time, and months and even years must pass before privations and deprivations can be accommodated by the individual without distortion of essential processes that are basic to object-relating. (pp. 179–80)

What does he mean by a subjective phenomenon becoming objectively perceived? At first, and for many months, each misattunement between mother and child creates an experience in the baby of "not me," but that meaning is only about its subjective experience of, to use our terminology from the previous chapter, its own illusion or hallucination. Only after the constant repetition of experiences of being deprived and not deprived across many modalities with a given person can the infant begin to recognize these "not me" elements as belonging to a specific person, which heralds the onset of the objectifying process.

What separates Winnicott from many other object relations theorists, even in his own day, is his emphasis on the environment's role in leading the child to experience creativity, not just control, as its most important aim. He notes:

> At this early stage the facilitating environment is giving the infant the experience of omnipotence; by this I mean more than magical control, I mean the term to include the creative aspect of experience. (p. 180)

What is essential for Winnicott is that the baby invents its own mother, indeed makes her come alive from nothingness. In other language, the baby turns the mother into a series of verbal nouns: milk-giver; warm body holder; smiling face maker; the mother becomes an action the baby needs and over time these action states coalesce into a being the baby creates as mother. This is essential to Winnicott's theory because it is the precursor to play. The capacity to create the first "other" becomes the capacity to invent other actions in other contexts and hence other beings in other contexts. It is striking how active the baby is; much as Piaget sees the baby's activity as the ignition switch for cognition, so Winnicott sees activity as the birthplace of eventual relatedness. So unlike Piaget, however, who sees the infant as the atomic unit generating development, Winnicott only sees this verb-creating baby in a dyadic context. Only if mother can rise to the baby's needs to turn her into a verb can the baby's development thrive.

Here Winnicott adds to the equation something he only alluded to in his "Primitive Emotional Development" paper, that which he calls the Primary Maternal Preoccupation. He rejects the notion of "id-satisfactions" as the primary catalytic agent driving development, with mother's role simply being to reduce frustration in the baby. What he called the mother's wish to be attacked in his 1945 paper he now sees as her most basic focus on the child and that notes this preoccupation is willing and deliberate. This is a more parsimonious, ego-driven economy for Winnicott. He implies that drive theory readily accounts for id and superego development, but it leaves to the ego a secondary, mediating role. The mother's willingness to engage the baby and the baby's creation of the mother, however, move ego resources into the equation of personhood from the beginning. This, in turn, more efficiently allows for the creative process of a "me" and a "not me" to arise out of an interactive, mutual unit. Development becomes inherently bidirectional and the "facilitating environment" allows the infant to

> create and re-create the object, and the process gradually becomes built in, and gathers a memory backing. (p. 180)

Why does Winnicott insist that in health the object is created and not found? Even further, why does he insist that an object is only "good" if it is created by the infant? Students repeatedly ask what would be wrong in finding that the mother is there but not created. This is a crucial point. In Winnicott's mind, a found but not created mother would make the infant an essentially passive creature, content to wait and be found. On a grand scale, this would make it much harder to account for the incredibly rapid growth of identity-making in the baby in the first year of life. On a more microanalytic scale, it minimizes the infant's role in the interactive process. Winnicott accentuates the infant's role by telling us that

> the change of the object from subjective to objectively perceived is jogged along less effectually by satisfactions than by dissatisfactions. . . . Instinct gratification gives the infant a personal experience and does but little to the position of the object. (p. 181)

In other words, in its emphasis on instinctual gratification, drive theory certainly gives the child experience but, to use the same expression he used both in this paper and in "Primitive Emotional Development," it leaves the baby "fobbed off" and thus with little awareness of the other. It is therefore in the baby's dissatisfactions, in the typical if erratic shifts in physical tension, that he or she gains over time a sense of the other as a separate being, precisely because the distress keeps the baby alert and immersed with the other in the attempt to mitigate this dissatisfaction. Winnicott's years as a pediatrician are most evident here. Watching thousands of babies with their mothers could not help but make him a witness to infant distress, no matter how preoccupied the mother might adaptively be with her baby.

Is infant distress the same as aggression? Is the infant inherently aggressive? Winnicott adds a crucial element of his thinking here, separating himself from Klein's theorizing in a most important way, and paving the way for his thinking about communicating. He writes:

> In the area of development that is prior to the achievement of fusion, one must allow for the infant's behavior that is reactive to failures of the facilitating environment, or of the environment-mother, and this may look like aggression; actually it is distress. (p. 181)

Aggression cannot occur, in Winnicott's view, unless there is someone to be aggressed upon. There is no "someone" until the fragments of interactive behavior coalesce sufficiently (in "fusion") to create the rudiments of a "me" and a "not me." This takes roughly the first five to six months of life. Prior to this time frame, there can be no true projection either, since there is no "inside" to project out from. The infant can thus be strikingly upset, irritable, or simply needing to move its muscles to meet immovable objects, but it is not aggressing upon anyone, nor projecting its aggression onto anyone. Denial and avoidance can be primary defenses for this age infant, but not projection.

After the baby has achieved fusion, frustration has an enhanced value.

> Adaptation failures have value in so far as the infant can hate the object, that is to say, can retain the idea of the object as potentially satisfying while recognizing its failure to behave satisfactorily. (p. 181)

Needless to say, the briefest review of either our own individual experience or the experience of reading the front page of any newspaper tells us that the human capacity to hate while still maintaining the good object is fragile at best. Nevertheless, the capacity to hate is a landmark achievement in development, one that we will study repeatedly in later chapters.

Notably, Winnicott ends his review of his general theory of personality by noting an intermediate stage in healthy development where

> the patient's most important experience in relation to the good or potentially satisfying object is the refusal of it. The refusal of it is part of the process of creating it. (p 182)

(Margaret Wise Brown felt exactly the same way about her runaway bunny!)

If the baby, in its thousands of moment-to-moment interactions with his mother, feels that he has been reliably and consistently enough tended to, he can do a remarkable thing; he can take the mother for granted. Yes, the baby can want to take in the mother's breast, but now, because he's reasonably sure of her reliability, he can also refuse the breast temporarily, knowing the mother won't take it "personally," i.e., won't be so dysregulated that she won't return. If this refusal process goes awry, as in anorexia, it creates a most terrible dilemma for the therapist. Every attempt by the therapist to "fill" the patient (with a good interpretation or even a supportive comment) runs the risk of it needing to be refused by the patient. The baby is thrown out with the bathwater because refusing or repudiating the mother/ therapist makes the taking in of anything, including food, potentially toxic.

Winnicott's "single idea," that of the purpose and limits of communicating, can now be made explicit.

> In so far as the object is subjective, so far is it unnecessary for communication with it to be explicit. In so far as the object is objectively perceived, communication is either explicit or else dumb. Here there appear two new things, the individual's use and enjoyment of modes of communication, and the individual's noncommunicating self, or the personal core of the self that is a true isolate. (p. 182)

Here, as in anything important that Winnicott avers, paradoxes abound but must not be solved. If mother and baby have been reliably established, the baby has a beginning sense of me and not me. It is, in one sense, a whole person. Yet once whole (even if rudimentary), the baby now has parts; once separate from the baby, the object (mother) becomes a person with part objects. When the mother is being fundamentally reliable, the infant has the ultimate pleasure—she communicates simply by *going on being* (p. 183); she simply is within herself in an almost Zen-like way. Winnicott strikingly notes that this "scarcely deserves the epithet communication"! Communication is thus always a distant second-best. It is far better to be able to take the mother for granted, to be alone in the presence of another, to be concentrating on the tasks personally created by the baby than to have to communicate with another. The acme of one's creativity, of one's vividness, is thus in an alone state while utterly knowing that reliable other(s) surround you and will wait for you to communicate without retaliation or repudiation for your going on being. This is what Winnicott means when he says that the personal core of the self is a true isolate. This experience of self is palpably real and utterly reaffirming and therefore must be protected at all costs.

Conversely, when the "other" is not utterly reliable but is perceived as objectively different, the need for communication arises. Indeed, communication is necessary precisely because self and other are different, and thus a chasm must be bridged. Importantly, because communication is always a distant second-best as a state of being, Winnicott begins his presentation of communication by describing two opposites of communication: simple not communicating and active/reactive not communicating. Simple not communicating is perhaps in second place in Winnicott's hierarchy of vitality. It is the same as resting and as such does not run the risk of losing one's sense of authenticity. However, when interacting with an other who is not sufficiently reliable over time, the infant

> develop[s] a split. By one half of the split the infant relates to the presenting object, and for this purpose there develops what I have called a false or compliant self. By the other half of the split the

infant relates to a subjective object, or to mere phenomena based on bodily experiences, these being scarcely influenced by an objectively perceived world. . . . In this way I am introducing the idea of a communication with subjective objects and at the same time the idea of an active non-communication with that which is objectively perceived by the infant. (p. 183)

The infant is constantly organized around wanting to feel real at all costs and at all times. Such genuineness is most easily garnered in the going-on-being of play and self-discovery. These discoveries include interactions with others, provided that the mother is "good enough," so that attunements are easily maintained and disruptions are minimal and growth inducing. Thus simple resting involves minimal loss of realness; indeed, it can be a vital respite from relating and thus is crucial to a True Self. In health, therefore, the role of the facilitating environment is one of creating sufficient space for the maturing baby to create the world on his own terms, while reliably integrating the idea that there are reality constraints of which one must be aware. In childhood, this allows the child the capacity both to play and to work, and especially allows the creation of an intermediate or transitional space between self and reality because the purity of concentration in all three arenas is the same. In essence, the infant is saying, "I reserve the right to say nothing." In adulthood, this health shows up in culture, in art, and in religion where "communication is made without reference to the object's state of being either subjective or objectively perceived" (p. 184). It exists in the thousands of "mini-monologues" one uses to mediate one's experience of everyday reality.

What happens in simple or more malignant pathology? Here

there must be expected an active non-communication (clinical withdrawal) because of the fact that communication so easily becomes linked with some degree of false or compliant object-relating; silent or secret communication with subjective objects, carrying a sense of real, must periodically take over to restore balance. . . . [I]n the healthy person there is a need for something that corresponds to the state of the split person in whom one part of the split communicates silently with subjective objects. There is room for the idea that significant relating and communicating is silent. (p. 184)

Winnicott's emphasis on creativity/realness as the fundamental core of the human personality serves as the starting point for communication. If things go well between infant and environment, realness is dominant and creativity is paramount. When things go poorly, realness must be preserved so it "goes underground," so to speak, leaving a compliant, False Self to interact with the world, while a "secret garden" is established for ongoing communication with those objects (beings included) that are subjectively configured to ensure vitality. In adulthood, this can be as blatant as daydreams of "Walter Mitty–esque" proportions or expressed by the artist as the urgent need to "communicate and the still more urgent need not to be found" (p. 185). In childhood, where the assaults on realness and demands for conformity may be more unrelenting, solitary play or even autistic-like movements are used to repair overly long bouts of compliance. For all of us, there is a need to balance the loss of a shared tie to others by the replenishment inherent in feeling real, even if this reality has to be subjectively and secretly experienced. Note the last sentence of the Winnicott quote above. What he is saying here is extremely important. He is not arguing for the supremacy of withdrawal or even for self-protection. This may be urgently needed if the environment is very pathological and gives minimal room for living. For most of us, however, he is trumpeting the heuristic value of silence as enhancing our selves *in relation to and in communication with others.* It is in our interior monologues that we practice relatedness with others and that we communicate in ways that develop ourselves in relation to others. It is in our states of rest that we feel the vitality of past and future relations with others, and it is in states of silence that we reaffirm who we would like to be in relation to others.

The creation of a True and a False Self is the means by which Winnicott links health and pathology. In pathology, failures in the facilitating environment create the split in personality we have repeatedly described. In health, despite reliable care, a core part of the self must stay hidden and "never communicate with the world of perceived objects" (p.187). Indeed, he emphatically states that the healthy person knows that this core must never be communicated or be influenced by external reality. This creates a paradox that is truly hard to decipher. If the facilitating environment is reliable enough to allow the baby to go on being, why would a need arise to protect his core self? Wouldn't such reliability lead to maximum openness, maximum self-exposure? Why must this core never be communicated to others, indeed not even be influenced by others? Winnicott creates a "black box" at our core, a box that must be returned to repeatedly in order to maintain vitality and individuality, yet must never be shared. He holds this view strongly, almost religiously, as we see in the following quote:

> In life and living this hard fact is softened by the sharing that belongs to the whole range of cultural experience. At the centre of each person is an incommunicado element, and this is *sacred* and most worthy of preservation. (p. 187)

Winnicott thus turns existentialist notions on their head. Rather than lamenting the human condition, that we are born alone and die alone, Winnicott turns our irreducible aloneness into a sacred preservation. This notion carries with it a profound implication, both in clinical work and in everyday life, for our understanding of trauma. First, it suggests that the ultimate psychological disaster is the penetration of the core self. Since the core cannot be shared except at the cost of its loss, any successful attempt by the outside world to penetrate the core is by definition traumatic. This in turn gives the concept of trauma a heuristically vital starting point. An experience is traumatic exactly because the core self is violated, and thus our underpinnings are irrevocably distorted. To prevent this distortion from literally killing us, we organize primitive defenses to massively defend the core from further impingement. These defenses, however, because they are so "all or none" in nature, further distort our tether to external reality, such that the trauma is experienced as deadening, in both directions: toward the core self, so that we lose genuineness; and away from the core self, so that our connections to others are filled with primitive distortion.

While it is the defenses we employ that make the traumatized subject appear so damaged, it is the altered core self that generates these behaviors and makes the resolution of trauma so difficult to attain.

My students still wonder why the core self must be unfathomable, like a "black box." It certainly appears to be the case that the healthier we are, the greater emotional flexibility and resourcefulness we have. Shouldn't this flexibility imply greater openness of spirit? Why shouldn't this openness be relatively endless? Why should it end at some irreducible place? More importantly, from the perspective of a baby developing in a truly benign facilitating environment, why should it need to be so vehemently protected and remain unshared?

This last question is perhaps the best place to begin to at least address these dilemmas. The good-enough facilitating environment is ideal precisely because it is not perfect. Its very nature implies a balance of accurate and inaccurate child-world interactions. The baby feels sufficiently held but increasingly distinct from those who hold her. The holding allows the baby to feel that the world will be an inherently benign place to explore. Brief failures in being held give the baby her separateness and, with years of practice, her distinctiveness. This distinctiveness is exactly what allows the baby to feel unique and not simply an extension of another. In Winnicott's terminology, it is what makes the baby (now child) feel *real*. To lose this sense of realness, by extension, is to be drawn back to the state before a "me" and a "not me" is firmly established, shattering the experience of a self in a blurred, terrifying diffuseness. Remember from our previous chapter how much of Winnicott's thinking was derived from his analysis of psychotic adults. Think of the vignettes he described from the lives of those patients: one patient could not adopt any routine because she had no sense of the stability of time; another patient thought her twin was herself in her pram; a third patient lived in her head to such a degree that she was not aware of what her feet were doing and thus tripped and fell constantly, while a fourth lived in a box twenty yards above her head, connected to her body by a slender thread. These profound distortions in time and space all speak to a loss of feeling real and to the bizarrely primitive defenses employed to protect some faint remaining tie to living. If the only way we establish realness is by brief misattunements with others, then this separateness is paradoxically exactly what eventually makes us feel comfortable with others.

There is one key element that distinguishes Winnicott's thinking about the importance of aloneness from the *idea* of existential aloneness. Indeed, it provides a comforting antidote to aloneness and gives his work a profoundly optimistic tone. This element is his description of the content of our core self. This content, Winnicott tells us, is our communication with subjectively perceived objects. In other words, our irreducible "atomic unit" is our inner dialogue with others as we subjectively experience them. This uniquely derived "unit" is thus inherently not some barren landscape, some schizoid desert, but a vivid collection of self-other clusters of experiences that give us our distinctiveness. At their best, these experiences inform our understanding of objectively based reality but are never blurred with it.

This line of thought led Winnicott to ask the question,

How to be isolated without having to be insulated? (p. 187)

The solution to this dilemma allows Winnicott to discuss the third pillar of his personality theory. He has already presented communication in the context of the inherent creativity of self-development and in the context of the creation of true and false selves to manage relating to others. His third pillar is his notion of transitional objects and phenomena, a pillar we will only briefly mention here but will come back to repeatedly in subsequent chapters. Between the developmental periods of utter subjectivity and objectively perceived objects lies a transitional period

in which transitional objects and phenomena have a place, and begin to establish for the infant the use of symbols. I suggest that an important basis for ego development lies in this area of the individual's communicating with subjective phenomena, which alone gives the feeling of real. (p. 188)

This transitional period corresponds with the beginning of play, the natural outgrowth of Winnicott's three pillars of personality (the capacity for a True Self, the capacity to be alone, and the capacity to have an intermediate arena between self and other). Play allows children to practice all they have learned from the earlier periods of mother-baby interaction. Play is utterly subjective, yet it is not within one's mind, but with the shared objective reality. It allows the child to make this reality subjective (the spoon that becomes a car, a firefighter, or a baby in succession) but remains outside of the baby so that it can be communicated to others and shared with others. Play is thus "inside-enough" to feel real to the child, yet "outside enough" to not reveal his developing core self. It thereby provides the medium for connecting to others and for experimenting with what others have shown the child. It is simultaneously capable of being steadfastly real (a teddy bear is not a dream or hallucination) yet almost inexhaustibly malleable. This leads the healthy child to eventually have three lines of communication:

> communication that is forever silent, communication that is explicit, indirect and pleasurable, and this third or intermediate form of communication that slides out of playing into cultural experience of every kind. (p. 188)

The idea that we have three lines of communication is so optimistic. If babies were saddled with only the first two lines of communication, there would be too drastic a divide between what they would have to keep secret and what they could share with the world. If adults were similarly limited to these two extremes, experience would be limited to a battle, to use other terminology, between id and superego. The transitional space of the child and its adult equivalent, the creation of culture, soften the blow of our basic aloneness and give both adult and child a playground in which fulfillment of many kinds can occur. It is what allows a person to remain safely isolated but not insulated from others.

Two last points are worth mentioning here before we move on to other articles in other chapters. One has to do with the capacity for work and the other to do with the nature of adolescence.

For Winnicott, the capacity to work is inextricably linked to the positive value attached to the right to not communicate. The right to be alone in the presence of another (facilitated by the good-enough mother) establishes the capacity to have a silent, isolated core. The mother (or the therapist) hears the child (patient) signal his need to not communicate and allows this silence to ensue without withdrawal. The capacity to be alone in the presence of mother leads over time to

> the acquisition of a capacity for withdrawal without loss of identification with that from which withdrawal has occurred. This appears as the capacity to concentrate on a task. (p. 188)

This fruitfully leads Winnicott, as we shall see in other chapters, to link problems in children's capacity to work to difficulties arising from their disrupted ties to significant others (see especially the cases of Ada and Robert).

As a final point, Winnicott makes a connection between his "single idea" of the individual as an isolate and the study of adolescence. He writes:

> At adolescence when the individual is undergoing pubertal changes and is not quite ready to become one of the adult community there is strengthening of the defenses against being found, that is to say being found before being there to be found. That which is truly personal and which feels real must be defended at all cost, and even if this means a temporary blindness to the value of compromise. (p. 190)

I don't think there is any adult who has raised an adolescent who would not resonate with this depiction of adolescence. This resonance provides a last bit of confirmation that Winnicott's exquisite portrait of the underlying aspects of communication is of inestimable heuristic value in the study of personality and a crucial linchpin of his own theorizing about the developmental process.

Chapter Four

―――――――――――○――――――――――

The True Self and False Compliance

Dilemma: Precocious compliance leads to a False Self, yet the baby's utter dependence promotes compliance.

Articles reviewed: "Reparation in Respect of Mother's Organized Defence against Depression" (1948) and "Ego Distortion in Terms of True and False Self" (1960).

I BEGIN WITH AN INCIDENT THAT OCCURRED while I was walking on Broadway in New York City. As I walked north I could see about thirty yards ahead of me a mother with two young children walking toward me. The older child was about six and held his mother's hand. The younger child, also a boy, looked about two and was in a stroller. While mother and six-year-old were chatting amicably, the toddler was clearly talking to himself in an animated way, the kind of performance that in a thirty-year-old would have a warranted a "street diagnosis" of schizophrenia, but in a two-year-old, we take with a smile. As we approached one another, the toddler and I caught each other's eye. As we passed within several feet of one another, he looked up at me and made a huge, snarling roar. I replied, "What a strong lion you are," and he forcibly and delightedly replied, "YES!"

Why do I begin with this anecdote? To me it personified what Winnicott referred to as the *spontaneous gesture*. This child, in his part interior/part exterior monologue of play, was the fierce attacking lion and I, responding to his gesture, was perhaps the fearful hyena on the savanna. The fact that I could tolerate his "attack," survive, and even validate his ferocity delighted this child, moving him to give me a vital, life-affirming reply.

For Winnicott, this child's capacity to play, his capacity to create, and his willingness to spontaneously follow and express his creativity would be ample signs of vitality. To take us back to his writing and theorizing, the incident suggests some important questions that lie at the heart of the two papers to be discussed in this chapter. What are spontaneous gestures, where do they come from, and what happens to the child if mother does or does not respond adequately to them? What does it mean to have a False Self, a True Self? How quickly does one develop a False Self? Is a False or True Self an all-or-none phenomenon or can the concepts be placed on a continuum? What goes on in life to prevent True Selves from flourishing? Are True and False Selves dynamic or static in nature?

It is clear that on many levels—personal, professional, and societal—Winnicott saw the existence of True and False Selves as an integral etiological catalyst to understanding the quality of life. A True Self connoted good-enough mothering, a capacity to have a central, isolated core, and a capacity for creative interaction between self and others. A False Self connoted overcompliance with mother, a need to hide or even dissociate from one's central core, and significant limitations in the capacity to feel real. These selves originate from the baby's spontaneous gestures and thus from the mother's (caretaker's) reactions to her. These two papers speak most directly to these moments, and so they are the focus of the present chapter.

Although the "Reparation" article is tiny (five and a half pages), it is an early gem in Winnicott's work in this area. Students immediately have many questions about the paper, always a good sign, and the first question is often: what does "mother's organized defense against depression" mean? It is important to place this concept on a continuum. We all must work through the depressive experience, as Klein explained and Winnicott strongly believed, because the "good enough" mother never can nor should satisfy all our omnipotent fantasies. We all thus carry the scars of "failed" interactions, of urges and wishes ignored or misinterpreted, but hope that with good-enough mothering, we also carry with us both enough supplies to carry on and the hope that additional or even better supplies will be forthcoming. We all must "do battle" with our "trolls" (Ibsen), our hurts, and our disillusionments. In this context, if one becomes a mother, the question then becomes: to what extent have you come to a place within yourself where you can deal with your own disillusionments well enough to be "good enough" with your baby? Or conversely, to what extent are you dominated by moods such that you must defensively protect yourself from your own disillusion, your own depression? If the mother's moods and depressions predominate too often, too much of the time, the baby becomes bathed in them. Yet for Winnicott, mothers do not want to bathe their babies in their moods and so attempt to create defensive barriers to these experiences. If these barriers, the quality of which we will describe below in greater detail, dominate the mother's experience, then the baby will be forced to act to try to eradicate them.

Why would the baby be moved to such acts of eradication, or, to use Winnicott's title, acts of reparation? Because the baby is seen (after the first few weeks of predominantly self-regulatory acts) first and foremost as an active, creative being who longs for the space to act spontaneously, to generate spontaneous gestures that potentially will expand her knowledge of herself and the world. The child is thus organized around creating the potential space to express these gestures and have them responded to in validating ways. Once the baby is capable of some rudimentary sense of self and other (approximately four to eight months), he has a sense of the mother's mood states. If the mother's mood predominates, the baby attempts to take on the role of chameleon, to take care of the mother's mood, to make reparation, so that she becomes available again for spontaneity. It's as if the baby is saying, "I sense that you're not with me now, so I'll attempt to change my behavior to get you back." As the baby repairs the mother to keep her going, it raises the question, at what cost to the baby does this reparation entail? For Winnicott, the answer is some degree of loss of the True Self and hence some loss of creativity and feeling real.

It is important to stress that this experience is highly dynamic, occurring on multiple levels for both baby and mother. Mothers are always in the process of repairing themselves, as this is part of the human condition. The baby is also always in part in a process of repair, in his case, on a minute-to-minute basis. To use a whimsical metaphor, the baby is trying not to make reparation a full-time job so that there is more time for play than time for work. The mother is simultaneously trying to maximize her True Self experience, trying to make reparation for prior hurts and disillusionments in her life, and trying to keep her reparation efforts from clouding her being in the moment with her baby. All this is done to best enable the baby to spend his time developing the capacity and space to play and not in the work of gauging and responding to the mother's mood. The fact that Winnicott believes that the vast majority of mothers are "good enough" in these Herculean tasks is yet another reason why his theory is so fundamentally optimistic.

With this as an overview, let us turn to the "Reparation" paper. He begins by verifying the vital importance of Klein's (1930) depressive position both in normal development and in the treatment of pathology and the need to understand guilt and aggression in the context of the reparation process. He notes:

> The attainment of a capacity for making reparation in respect of personal guilt is one of the most important steps in the development of the healthy human being, and we now wonder how we did analytic work before we consciously made use of this simple truth. (p. 91)

Winnicott begins this paper validating the depressive position as a landmark attainment for the baby. By *personal guilt* he's referring to the concept that the baby's great hunger for the mother on a multitude of levels is now accompanied by the feeling that this hunger takes something from her. This is perhaps the most fundamental blessing and curse of life. It is a blessing because being aware of the mother's needs creates the cradle for care and concern about others that is the bedrock of civilization. It is the curse of existence because the depressive position carries with it the idea that we are always wrestling with the personal guilt that we have taken too much from the ones we love. We thus all develop a life equation in which we give to others and take from others because we were given to and yet we wrestle with whether this give-and-take feels adequate, induces guilt, or induces resentment. What is essential to note here is that the depressive position implies that the baby knows that the mother is separate from the baby and therefore that mother's needs are not always the same as the baby's. It is in the awareness of this separateness that the give-and-take equation is created.

An example from everyday life makes it clear that this equation is often center stage at any point in development. Last year my then fourteen-year-old son and I were discussing soccer and his love of the English Premier League. He noted that there was a Fox Sports Channel on cable TV that televised many of these games and how great it would be to get this channel. Thinking I was being a "good enough" dad, I found out that the price for obtaining this new channel was "only" five dollars a month. Comparing this cost to the many thousands of dollars I was now spending on my older son's first year in college, I thought this was a great bargain! I therefore ordered this channel and went to tell my son of this "Valentine's Day present." Shockingly, rather than being delighted, he looked hurt, disappointed, and misunderstood. After several moments he blurted out, "I didn't expect you to buy that for me, I've been making my own money [refereeing basketball games]." I had missed his attempt at reparation, at giving back something even while he wished to take something! Had I simply told him the cost of the new channel and asked how he thought we might pay for it, I would have given him the space to make reparation, instead of making him feel more guilt for asking for something valuable (to him) from me.

As a starting point to begin discussing the role mother-child interaction plays in the development of the need for reparation in the child, Winnicott says:

> Early in my career a little boy came to hospital and said to me, "Please Doctor, mother complains of a pain in my stomach" and this drew my attention usefully to the part mother can play. . . . Probably I get a specially clear view of this problem in a children's

outpatient department because such a department is really a clinic for the management of hypochondria in mothers. (p. 92)

Winnicott is not implying that mothers of babies are all hypochondriacs! Instead he is reminding us of the inherent bi-directional nature of the developmental process. How? What does it mean to be hypochondriacal? In this case, it means maintaining a hyperalert interface between mind and body. Since the baby is still predominantly a body and not a mind governing a body in the first months of life, this hyperalertness is really a necessary precondition for good-enough mothering. If the mother were not empathic to most of the baby's bodily movements and expressions, there would be no attunement. Some degree of vital enmeshment is thus necessary for good mothering to occur. Indeed, in what he refers to as a primary maternal preoccupation, the mother begins child rearing with an investment/need to enmesh. In other words, the mother can only know about her baby if she is empathizing with his body. This cannot help but make her critically attuned (sometimes over-attuned) to her own body. This confusion between her worries and her child's body can easily be transplanted into the mind of the sensitive child, as the little boy's complaint to Dr. Winnicott in the quote above easily attests. As Winnicott puts it a bit later,

> There is no sharp dividing line between the frank hypochondria of a depressed mother and a mother's genuine concern for her child. (p. 92)

This lack of dividing line also blurs the boundary between child and maternal depression. Winnicott notes:

> A doctor who knows nothing of psychiatry or knows nothing of the contra-depressive defenses, and who does not know that children get depressed, is liable to tell a mother off when she worries about a child's symptom, and fail to see the very real psychiatric problems that exist. (p. 92)

What does he mean by "contra-depressive" defenses? Here he refers to the extent to which the mother recognizes her own depressive experiences. Does she run from these affects and create a self that must deny them? The purpose of a contra-depressive defense is to move the self into action, to escape from the "La Brea" tar pits of dysphoria. But if mother is driven to deny loss and sadness, to stay "up" and "perky," then what is the baby to do if, because he is sleepy, or ill, or lonely, he cannot stay perky? This mood difference creates a rift between mother and child and potentially truncates the baby's experience of having those feeling-states validated. The baby is thus in a "lose-lose" situation: should he persist in his true feeling, he remains subdued but loses mother; if he complies with mother's need to not remain subdued, he "loses" (buries?) that feeling but acquires a compliant False Self.

Anxiety in the mother is another crucial variable to be added to the dynamic here. Anxiety can certainly be used by the mother to replace sadness, so that instead of perkiness, anxiety predominates as the mechanism of defense, generating the same "lose-lose" situation for the baby but with a difference in the content of what must be complied with.

The "lose-lose" nature of the situation is also why,

> on the other hand, a psycho-analyst fresh from newly discovered understanding of childhood depression could easily fail to notice when it is the mother who is more ill than the child. . . . The child uses the mother's depression as an escape from his or her own; this provides a false restitution and reparation in relation to the mother, and this hampers the development of a personal restitution capacity because the restitution does not relate to the child's own guilt sense. (p. 92)

In this extreme circumstance, the child's development is besieged on two fronts: the difficulties inherent in addressing his own feelings of aggression and resultant guilt, and the difficulties of tending to the dominating moods of his caretaker. Here the child "chooses" the task of making reparation to the mother, presumably because this caretaking produces more immediate results (i.e., the child may be quite good at getting the mother out of her mood, and, in keeping with Robert White's [1981] concept of "effectance motivation," the child wants to continue that which makes him feel most competent). However, the more the child's reparation is aimed at ameliorating the condition of his mother, the fewer resources he has available to engage in understanding the nature and limitations of his own aggression, leaving him vulnerable to neurotic disorder. The child may increasingly look more depressed, or—more typically in childhood—act more irritable, be more withdrawn or aggressive, perform less well academically, etc. At the same time he can make no headway toward understanding his own experience. Should the mother remain overly troubled, the child may never be but a reflection of her own sadness and self-doubt. Should the mother regain her own footing independently of the child's attempts at reparation, there arises the possibility that the child may be able to turn toward wrestling with his own depression, rather than remaining with the mother's. The implications for clinical intervention are enormous in that they impel clinicians to use their clinical acumen in the service of distinguishing levels of disturbance in caretakers as well as the child. Making a further distinction between those children whose parents have indeed worked through their depressive issues but have children who insist on repairing them anyway as a retreat from their own experience is also critical. Winnicott talks about such children in the following way:

> Their task is first to deal with mother's mood. If they succeed in the immediate task, they do no more than succeed in creating an atmosphere in which they can start their own lives. It can be readily understood that this situation can be exploited by the individual as a flight from that acceptance of personal responsibility which is an essential part of individual development. (p. 93)

In other language, the child can stay "preoccupied" with her parents' inner life as a means of avoiding acknowledgment of her own psyche and thereby not having to take responsibility for its limitations and aggressive nature. I am struck here by the link this type of child has to an early paper by Anna Freud in her book *The Ego and the Mechanisms of Defense* (1936) on what she termed "altruistic surrender." Here the child (and adult) gives up the battle to address his own personal guilt and resorts instead to a lifelong devotion (to the welfare of sometimes quite specific, sometimes more generic) a significant other(s). A case of mine involved such an issue. I had seen a boy at the age of five for a three-session consultation. The mother would then call or come in to see me about him every eighteen months or so, and she did so most recently when the child was about eleven. The boy was underachieving a bit in school, seemed poorly motivated in general, and was quite irritable with his younger sisters. Mother spoke of having to help him each night with his homework so he could keep up with his high-achieving peers at a Manhattan private school. She reported that he was doing increasingly poorly and asked whether I could see him again in consultation. The boy came in to my office and remarked that he didn't remember my room so much but did remember my toys, which he looked at longingly but instead went over to the "adult" side of the office and sat down. After at first denying any problems and not knowing really why his mother wanted him to come see me, he did respond to my wondering about his feelings about school. He noted, in a plaintive, exhausted tone, how his mother wanted him to do so *well* and—given how kind she was to him in so many ways, including helping him with his homework—how he so wanted to please her. The work, however, was simply too hard sometimes, and it made him so "restless and bothered" that he only did more poorly, especially recently. It became clear to me that this child's efforts to please his mother did not fit well with his intellectual endowment, which, though ample, was not extraordinary. I saw his irritability and lack of motivation as strengths and efforts on the part of his True Self to disentangle a bit from his mother. Ironically, I thought that if he had been academically more gifted, it would have been easier to comply with the wishes and needs of his mother, making it more likely that he would have become more fully immersed in a False Self compliance. Work thus focused on helping the mother see how her needs were limiting the child, which, to the mother's great credit, could be heard and used well by her to the child's benefit.

Let me now link this conception of Winnicott more directly to the concept of "neurosis." Here neurosis is used as a way of conveying that the mother's "vital balance" (Menninger et al., 1960) is weighted toward the use of defenses that keep her preoccupied with internal issues at the expense of adapting flexibly to the demands of reality, in this case, child rearing. Thus the child's spontaneous gestures are either not predominantly empathically felt by mother or are misconstrued to fit with the defenses mother employs to stay regulated. The gestures of the child are therefore likely to be experienced as empty or furthering disconnection. In the most extreme versions of this type of interaction, "failure to thrive" babies are produced. That is, the baby experiences any or all his gestures of spontaneity as leading to parental withdrawal, chaos, or intrusion. The baby must therefore shrink away from experience so profoundly that even the most basic of its needs, to eat and sleep, are profoundly disrupted. Babies can thus literally die as the hopelessness and helplessness they experience make them akin to the despairing, suicidal adolescent or adult.

The way to avoid this failure to thrive is to have the mother be predisposed to become attuned to her baby, experiencing the primary maternal preoccupation we alluded to earlier. At the risk of being absurd, a baseball metaphor can be applied here. A fielder who is in the proper position to field a ball before it is thrown will obviously not catch every ball hit his way, but he will be far more likely to catch a ball than a fielder who is not ready. A primarily preoccupied mother is therefore a mother in the "ready to field" position to catch the child's next spontaneous gesture. It may often be that a baby's spontaneous gestures are not immediately understood by its mother, and so she engages in a checklist of hypothesis testing. Is the baby cold, hungry, bored, silly, aggressive, etc.? Each hypothesis brings a counterhypothesis or impels an action. If the action doesn't result in reconnecting to the baby, the mother goes down her list until she can come up with a "correct" response. A flexible, less-depressed mother will probably have a longer list of hypotheses to choose from, as her enhanced empathy allows her to create more categories to understand a baby's experience from. Such a mother, perhaps just as importantly, will also have the necessary energy to go through more of her checklist before she succumbs to a less-than-useful exhaustion or irritability or perseveration in response to her baby.

It is important, however, to stress how this "ready to attune" state occurs in the context of time. It's not just whether or not the mother can ascertain the baby's state of mind and have enough emotional availability to attend to the baby, it is also a function of whether she can do this within the framework of the baby's capacity for attention. If the mother is quite closely attuned and active, the lag between the baby's gesture and the mother's reply is almost nonexistent, and the baby can experience the magical illusions we discussed in previous chapters. If the mother's response, though well attuned, comes later in time but is still able to be attended to by the infant, the baby begins to experience the "not me–ness" necessary to reach and maintain the depressive position. But if the mother's response, however well attuned, does not arrive until well after the baby has the capacity to receive and attend to it, then internal chaos is unleashed in the baby. The desperate baby will try anything and everything in her behavioral repertoire to try and regain connection to her heretofore reliable mother. It is here that the seeds of the False Self are sown.

It is in this context that I paired Winnicott's "Reparation" paper with his paper titled "Ego Distortion in Terms of True and False Self." (1960). This paper provides us with Winnicott's most differentiated elaboration of the nature and function of the True and the False Self. It also depicts the creation of a continuum of False Self states and contains some important theoretical distinctions between his theory of personality development and that of "classical" (drive) analytic theory.

Winnicott sets up his thinking on the origin and nature of the False Self by first speaking about the nature of instincts. This is crucial to his theory because False and True Selves can only occur for Winnicott in the context of a dyadic experience. Looking at mother and baby as an indivisible unit leads to the necessity of explaining the motivations for the behaviors of each participant. For the mother, as we have learned, the motivation stems from her primary maternal preoccupation and her capacity to distinguish her needs and moods from her baby's. This role is not particularly distinguishable from the role ascribed to mothers by drive theory. When Winnicott turns to the baby's motivations, however, he makes it clear that he is speaking in a manner quite different from his drive theory colleagues.

> It must be emphasized that in referring to the meeting of infant needs I am not referring to the satisfaction of instincts. In the area that I am examining the instincts are not yet clearly defined as internal to the infant. The instincts can be as much external as can a clap of thunder or a hit. (p. 141)

Winnicott is convinced that an instinct can only be described in the context of its having a purpose and thus can only be said to exist when the infant has created a rudimentary sense of an inside and an outside. As we have seen, this beginning experience coincides with what Klein called the depressive position and begins around the second six months of life. Prior to this achievement the behaviors that drive theorists would call instincts are what Winnicott would call muscle erotisms, spontaneous gestures, or physiologically derived movements in general. They do not seek a state of satisfaction because this term implies a reliable, predictable state the baby knows and remembers that it wants to return to. This is simply beyond the ken of the largely undifferentiated infant in the first months after birth. This is no mere quibbling over semantics to Winnicott. He firmly believes that drive theory places the beginnings of infant life in an overly sophisticated state where instincts can exist because the baby purposefully is trying to impose his id satisfactions upon the mother. Winnicott notes:

> The infant's ego is building up strength and in consequence is getting towards a state in which id-demands will be felt as part of the self, and not as environmental. When this development occurs, then id-satisfaction becomes a very important strengthener of the ego . . . but id-excitements can be traumatic when the ego is not yet able to include them. (p. 141)

Several key elements of Winnicott's thinking are involved here and need to be identified. When he notes the baby's ego is building strength, he implies the holding function created by the attuned, "good enough" mother that serves as a stimulus barrier for the infant. Her adequate handling allows the baby to experience enough stimulation to let maturation proceed at its correct pace without overwhelming him to the point where overly intense stimulation (id-excitements) bring the child to chaos and hence trauma. If the demands of the infant are met in an attuned, modulated way by the mother, these experiences strengthen the baby's capacity to handle newer and more-intense stimuli. Eventually, these stimuli are not only processed by the baby but can be accepted by the baby as part of the broader construct of "me." This is the infant-based side of the model that Winnicott in prior chapters was describing in terms of mother. Thus, her adequate balance of attunement and misattunement creating the first experiences in the baby of "not me" are matched by infant behavior that helps create a "me." Once the baby has a firm "me" and "not me," then he can behave as if he truly wants something gratified, which for Winnicott is the apt time to call these wishes for satisfaction instincts. The visceral sensations that infants experience prior to this consolidating "tipping point" are certainly real, but only after multiple repetitions can they be subsumed into a self that can contain them and begin to experience them as coming from inside.

As we have seen from the "Reparation" paper, False Self organization occurs in the context of failures of maternal attunement. These failures consist of overly developed compliant behaviors by the infant serve to prevent the loss of the feeling of being real and alive. In this paper, the False Self is placed on a continuum in its relation to the True Self that it defensively protects. At one extreme, the False Self is so pervasive that the True Self is hidden to the person himself and all everyone sees is the False Self organization. Here,

> in situations in which what is expected is a whole person the False Self has some essential lacking. (pp. 142–143)

On a second, less extreme level, the person is aware that a potential True Self exists and is permitted a secret life. Within this category are persons for whom psychological or medical illness has as its positive aim the preservation of the True Self, so that symptoms keep the True Self protected.

On a third level, Winnicott creates a fascinating duality. On the one hand, this next point on the continuum is deemed healthier than the first two points because

> the False Self has as its main concern a search for conditions which will make it possible for the True Self to come into its own. (p. 143)

The fact that conditions in the environment may exist that would allow the True Self to surface obviously implies a more benign psychological milieu and a profound sense of hopefulness on the part of the True Self that it may emerge. This hopefulness, however, is precarious and fraught with danger, for if these conditions cannot be found, the person risks exposing the True Self without assurance that it will be safe. As we have seen from the prior chapter, this lack of protection for the True Self risks its annihilation and faced with that possibility, Winnicott believes the only solution is suicide. This provides a fascinating window through which to understand suicidal behavior, especially the common feelings in those who were close to the deceased who simply cannot comprehend how the person could get to such a state of despair. For Winnicott, it is not despair as much as it is self-protection from a fate worse than death that prompts a suicide.

Just short of health and therefore in the range of most "neurotic" or "normal" persons (remember, Winnicott does not equate health with normality but with a capacity for creativity) are those whose False Self is built on overly close idealizations and identifications with significant others in their home or environment. Within this category fall those who act primarily according to a role that can shift somewhat in differing contexts, a role that has substantiality and continuity, unlike the chameleon-like nature of the False Self at early points on the continuum.

Importantly, Winnicott also describes what the False Self looks like in health. He makes it clear that the True Self, while the only way to feel authentic and vital, could not survive in "mannered" society on a full-time basis. It would clash too readily with the needs for genuineness of other True Selves as well as the demands for conformity from those with False Self organizations at whatever level. The healthy person with a True Self must therefore keep it reserved for those reliable enough to accept it in certain contexts, including its expression as cultural or artistic expression. The limitations to its expression may cause suffering but allow the person to function in society.

We can now use Winnicott's words to summarize the role of the mother in creating either a True or a False Self in her baby. This would allow us to add a final component to the process that we have not yet discussed, i.e., the role of language in the mother-baby relationship.

Winnicott dichotomizes the two types of mothers who create the true and false selves respectively. Quite simply, the good-enough mother helps create a True Self in the baby, while the not good-enough mother helps create a False Self organization.

> The good enough mother meets the omnipotence of the infant and to some extent makes sense of it. She does this repeatedly. A True Self begins to have life, through the strength given to the infant's weak ego by the mother's implementation of the infant's omnipotent expressions. (p. 145)

So far, we are on safe, repeated ground here.

> The mother who is not good enough is not able to implement the infant's omnipotence and so she repeatedly fails to meet the infant gesture; instead she substitutes her own gesture which is to be given sense by the omnipotence of the infant. This compliance on the part of the infant is the earliest stage of the False Self and belongs to the mother's inability to sense her infant's needs. (p. 145)

Once again, we are staying with repeated themes. The good-enough mother allows the very new baby to feel omnipotent repeatedly so that his first experiences with the world are filled far more with the illusion of omnipotence (I would call it the beginnings of competence) than with chaos or confusion. This allows the baby to slowly accept limitations to his omnipotence and, much as a seesaw can steadily shift with increasing weight on one end, the baby slowly moves toward accepting reality constraints as its "heavier" end, while never giving up its "lighter" but more authentic True Self. As Winnicott beautifully puts it,

> The True Self has a spontaneity, and this has been joined with the world's events. (p. 146)

It is important to now at least briefly consider the important link to the role of symbolization and language in this process. As the infant comes to balance what is illusory with what is real, he can begin to imagine and play with what he wishes for but may not actually get. The first initial symbol is both the baby's magical wish (I want mother's breast) and the external object (e.g., the breast) wished for. As the baby comes to increasingly distinguish between the two, he feels good enough about the object even if it doesn't arrive magically or instantly as soon as it is wished for. The ability to delay is thus created and is based on the fact that the infant has enough memory traces of the object to still survive without it, if only for a very short time at first.

Thus the good-enough mother provides yet one more splendid component of living. She provides a link between symbol formation and object (person) relating. The baby is essentially saying: *You have been available to me in a good enough way so that I can create symbols of parts of you in my mind to comfort me for a period of time.* It is then a relatively short step for the baby to jump to: *Because symbol formation reminds me of you (mother), I will generalize symbol-making to a broader and broader context until the cognitive process takes on a life of its own.* Thus, for Winnicott the capacity for symbolization flows directly from the process of relatedness. This implies that if there is not good-enough mothering, then the first attempts at symbolizing are not as successful and have an aspect to them of fragmentation or disruption. This is consistent with a feeling-state in which the beginnings of a sense of self don't feel sufficiently real, and the beginnings of experiencing the other are felt as a matter of compliance and not spontaneity.

The greatest symbolizing function available to humans is obviously language. At first the sounds made and heard by the baby are things, no different than a breast, a bottle, or a toy. As the capacity for language expression coexists with the time frame for the depressive position to occur, the baby begins to link certain repetitive sounds with objects that are used as symbols. Language is thus connected to things, at first things related to the first object (mother) but quickly to a whole host of nouns that repeatedly give the baby and mother a whole new arena for understanding and connection. Eventually, this use of symbols permits the capacity to play, the capacity to be alone with one's self, and over time creates a link to both cultural life and the use of inner monologues to guide the balance between the True Self and its relation to the external world.

Winnicott makes one final point in this paper regarding the use of symbols that has great heuristic value, although it has not, to my knowledge, been operationalized in clinical work to any systematic degree. He notes:

> By contrast, where there is a high degree of split between the True Self and the False Self which hides the True Self, there is found a poor capacity for using symbols, and a poverty of cultural living. Instead of cultural pursuits one observes in such persons extreme restlessness, an inability to concentrate, and a need to collect impingements from external reality so that the living-time of the individual can be filled by reactions to these impingements.

This description is remarkably consistent with the behavioral description of children and adults with what we now call Attention Deficit Disorder, with or without hyperactivity. Without minimizing the potential role of neurophsyiological factors in the etiology of ADHD, Winnicott's link of these behaviors to False Self experience should become a part of the discussion of this range of disorders to a more explicit degree.

Now that we have an exposition of how infants develop authenticity, we will further develop in the next chapter how the mother helps create the optimal environment for this authenticity to emerge. This will then lead (in chapter 6) to how the infant uses these maternal behaviors to move away from and eventually "hate" the mother in order to thrive, yet another truly "Winnicottian" paradox.

Chapter Five

―――――――――――○―――――――――――

We Are Essentially Isolates, with the Capacity to Be Alone

Dilemma: If we are essentially isolates, how do we develop the capacity to be alone?

Articles reviewed: "The Capacity to Be Alone" (1958) and "Mirror-Role of Mother and Family in Child Development" (1967).

> *"What is REAL?" asked the rabbit one day. . . .*
> *"Real isn't how you are made," said the Skin Horse. "It's a thing that happens to you. When a child loves you for a long, long time, not just to play with, but REALLY loves you, then you become Real. . . ."*
> *Nana grumbled, . . . "You must have your old Bunny!" she said. "Fancy all that fuss for a toy!"*
> *"Give me my bunny!" he said. "You mustn't say that. He isn't a toy. He's REAL!"*
>
> Margery Williams, *The Velveteen Rabbit*

LIKE THE RUNAWAY BUNNY, *The Velveteen Rabbit* is a classic of children's literature precisely because it captures something essential about the way children experience the world. It also exemplifies Winnicott's belief that we are not born real, but that genuineness is achieved through the hard work of living and being in the moment. Winnicott would also certainly endorse Williams's notion that the work of becoming real only comes through intimacy, takes a great deal of time to accomplish, and for the purposes of the present chapter, allows one, much like the old Skin Horse in the book, to truly be alone.

We have come a considerable way in four chapters toward elucidating key elements of Winnicott's theorizing. Winnicott first described, via "Primitive Emotional Development," the early days, weeks, and months of life as a two-body cauldron within which humanity is created or stultified. Winnicott notes the strikingly vivid parallel between the almost mystical, but not-to-be-magical good-enough psychoanalyst with his or her patient and the "good enough" mother with her baby. At the most fundamental of levels, neither analyst nor mother can be taught the ineffable ways to be with their partners, but if both do their jobs well enough, the baby (patient) develops a sense of being held and, from this holding, a sense of the world as a vivid, predictable place.

Winnicott then teaches us, in "Communicating and Not Communicating," that the essence of being human is first and foremost a sense of body aliveness. Winnicott distinguishes this aliveness from mere normality and views creativity as a crucial diagnostic indicator of health. As much as aliveness is exalted in its diagnostic value, it is obtained most directly without the use of words alone. Thus, just as a therapist is repeatedly cautioned against using clever interpretations, a parent is cautioned against using compliance, verbal or otherwise, as a benchmark for the developmental progress of the baby. Indeed, the creation of a True Self is the antithesis of compliance and this True Self includes the pivotally important ability to *not* communicate. The aloneness that results from the ability to *not* have to communicate is basic to being fully human, and it is this primary aloneness that paradoxically allows true communication to proceed.

Winnicott then explored, in both the "Reparation" and "Ego Distortion" papers, what goes wrong if this True Self is not obtained. He described how a precocious compliance is engendered in the baby if he has to be too much of a "weather forecaster" in terms of reading mother's moods and having to match them. Attending too much to mothers' moods and needs disrupts the child's capacity for "going on being." It then leads to having to hide the True Self. In the most benign of circumstances, the True Self is hidden until mother's predominating moods pass and then is capable of being restored to its central place in the child's life. In more pathological situations, the True Self is hidden away more pervasively or buried to the point of nonawareness, resulting in a loss of realness and a deadening of inner vivacity or creativity, regardless of how the person may function on the "outside."

The child is utterly dependent on her caretakers in the first weeks of life. There is thus a primary need on the baby's part to figure out how to get along with his caretaker, without her becoming impossibly frustrated. There is also a vital role, largely pushed to the side by Winnicott, to be played by the baby's temperament, or to put it in his terminology, of the baby also being "good enough" to be easily enough "read" by the mother to allow his survival. Winnicott instead emphasizes the ways in which the mother is primarily preoccupied with her baby, placing the sole onus on her to be predictable and available. Her preoccupation allows the baby's spontaneous gestures to be met by her illusory attunement, creating an experience of omnipotence in the baby that serves as a bridge, over many months, to the balancing of fantasy and reality that allows for a unique sense of competence and purpose to be created.

This process allows Winnicott to create two benchmarks of mental health: the capacity to play and the creation of a True Self. These serve as his main diagnostic indicators. As we shall see when we review several of his clinical consultations, these indices largely determine his mode of entry into work with the child and his degree of satisfaction with their outcome. Up until now I have spent a good deal of time enlarging upon his concept of the True and False Selves and less time on understanding the origins of the capacity to play. Before I can adequately address the capacity to play, however, we must discuss its critical forerunner, the capacity to be alone. How the baby develops this capacity, how and why it occurs out of interaction with mother, and how it serves as a prerequisite for play is the subject of the papers reviewed in the present chapter.

Winnicott begins his "Alone" paper with a need to address the positive aspects of such a capacity. He posits:

> It will be appreciated that actually to be alone is not what I am discussing. A person may be in solitary confinement and yet not be able to be alone. How greatly he must suffer is beyond imagination. However, many people do become able to enjoy solitude before they are out of childhood, and they may even value solitude as a most precious possession. (p. 30)

Winnicott sees his task in this paper as walking us through his concept of the capacity to be alone, first via drive theory, then via Kleinian terminology, and last in his own language. He begins with the quote above, distinguishing being literally alone from having the capacity to be alone. It is worth taking a moment to expand on his comment about solitary confinement, as it is obviously the most extreme form of aloneness. We can imagine that if we had the ability to relate meaningfully to others, solitary confinement would be a most terrible—but bearable—deprivation. In the language of object relations, our ties to others would mitigate the physical deprivation from others, while for those without such enduring ties, the lack of others to actively bounce off of would prove catastrophic . . . I am reminded of the great Chekhov short story "The Bet," where a young man chooses solitary confinement, is able to fill his time in admirable ways, but "loses" the bet intentionally at the story's end. The loss of ongoing contact with one's loved ones would be profound, but these past relationships would presumably fill our mind, making it at least possible to endure. For someone without meaningful ties to others, it would be much harder to maintain a past, become that much harder to keep oneself alive in time and space, and make confinement truly interminable.

Thus Winnicott begins his musings about aloneness by placing its origins in our ties to others, but when?

> The capacity to be alone is either a highly sophisticated phenomenon, one that may arrive in a person's development after the establishment of three-body relationships, or else it is a phenome-

non of early life which deserves special study because it is the foundation on which sophisticated aloneness is built. (p. 30)

For the only time I can see in his work, he hedges a bit as to the origins of this capacity to be alone. He wrestles with whether such a capacity begins as an Oedipal (three-body) phenomenon whose origins lie in the working through of the primal scene or begins in the second six months of life. He gives us a brief hint a bit earlier in the paper as to how he decides if this capacity is pre- or post-Oedipal in origin. He notes:

After thinking of three- and two-body relationships, how natural that one should go a stage further back and speak of a one-body relationship! (p. 30)

Strikingly, he discounts the notion of a primary narcissism, i.e., that a person should begin as a one-body phenomenon. This sort of narcissism would be a

violation of a great deal that we know through our analytic work and through direct observation of mothers and infants. (p. 30)

This rejection of an infant's primary narcissism sets the stage for the basic point of his paper.

Although many types of experience go to the establishment of the capacity to be alone, there is one that is basic, and without a sufficiency of it the capacity to be alone does not come about; this experience is that of being alone, as an infant and small child, in the presence of mother. Thus the basis of the capacity to be alone is a paradox; it is the experience of being alone while someone else is present. (p. 30)

The elegance of his prose here is augmented by the nonlinear nature of his thinking. For what he is saying is that a one-body relationship (i.e., the capacity to be alone) arises out of a two-body (i.e., mother-infant) relationship and not the other way around. This is quite distinct from other psychoanalytic positions (both Freud's and Mahler's, for example) that stress the beginning state as one of primary narcissism that evolves into a two-person and then an Oedipal (three-body) paradigm over the first three to five years of life. As we shall see shortly, this is another way of saying that the first unit of life is mother-baby and that out of this unit comes the capacity to fashion a separate unit called "baby." The simultaneous living of these two units is what is being thought through here. Thus, this paper outlines the underlying basis for what we have been describing in terms of True and False Selves in earlier chapters. What he will do later in the chapter is provide the crucial phenomenology of the mother-baby unit that allows the baby-as-unit to flourish. This will solidify the theoretical constructs he has presented up until this point and set the stage for later discussions of play and transitional phenomena.

Winnicott coins a new term to describe the relationship between the baby-as-unit and the mother-baby-unit. He calls it ego-relatedness.

> Ego-relatedness refers to the relationship between two people, one of whom at any rate is alone; perhaps both are alone, yet the presence of each is important to the other. I consider that if one compares the meaning of the word "like" with that of the word "love, one can see that liking is a matter of ego-relatedness, whereas loving is more a matter of id-relationships, either crude or in sublimated form. (p. 31)

Before he expands on this concept, Winnicott struggles with a natural obstacle to his thinking. If the baby is first off a part of a two-body relationship and is utterly dependent on mother for basic survival at any level, then how can we talk of the baby being alone in any usual sense of the word? This is what he means by distinguishing between a more sophisticated sense of aloneness that occurs through the working through of the Oedipal experience and a more unsophisticated aloneness that can occur in the second half of the first year of life. He notes:

> Being alone in the presence of someone can take place at a very early stage, when the ego immaturity is naturally balanced by ego-support from the mother. In the course of time the individual in-

trojects the ego-supportive mother and in this way becomes able to be alone without frequent reference to the mother or mother symbol. (p. 32)

Now Winnicott gets down to business! For his thinking here to move forward, he must tease out the nature of what the young infant is actually doing within the mother-baby unit so that we can understand how developmentally the baby-as-unit comes to be. He does this in an ingenious way, by parsing out the phrase "I am alone" developmentally. He begins with "I."

First there is the word 'I,' implying much emotional growth. The individual is established as a unit. Integration is a fact. The external world is repudiated and an internal world has become possible. . . . At this point no reference is made to living. (p. 33)

This point in development is akin to the beginning of Klein's depressive position. It also relates to Winnicott's thinking (described earlier) that the "omnipotent" baby who has been met by a "good enough" mother has had sufficient experiences of attunement spiced with misattunement to experience herself as separate from the mother, and with the beginnings of a "me" and a "not me." Winnicott goes on:

Next comes the words 'I am.' . . . By these words the individual not only has shape but also life. . . . The individual can only achieve the 'I am' stage because there exists an environment which is protective; the protective environment is in fact the mother preoccupied with her own infant and orientated to the infant's ego requirements through her identification with her own infant. (p. 33)

Here we have a vivid depiction of the mother's role in giving the child a sense of vitality, of making him a verb and not just a pronoun. Her empathic identification with her baby leads her to provide an appropriate stimulus barrier so as to protect the child from feeling chaotic or overwhelmed. She therefore provides the space in which the baby may feel alive and able to take on the world. Importantly, Winnicott notes that the baby at this stage does not have to be aware of the mother as a specific other; rather it is her function as a protective shield that is primary. This leads him to the last stage of his parsing.

> Next I come to the words 'I am alone.' I consider, however, that 'I am alone' is a development from 'I am,' dependent on the infant's awareness of the continued existence of a reliable mother whose reliability makes it possible for the infant to be alone and to enjoy being alone, for a limited period. (p. 33)

The infant has moved from a mere verb ('I am') to a verb that can count on another to be available such that she can tell the difference (at least for a short time) between when she is alone but in the presence of someone from being alone in a timeless, terrifying way. What a stupendous achievement! I stress the notion of time because, however brief these moments of tolerated aloneness may be at first for the baby, they are qualitatively distinct from prior experience. They are not simply "me" versus "not me," they are "me" in the presence of "not me" for a time. This implies that it is now more a matter of building up longer periods of aloneness, through practice, that spurs development forward. This is a development in quantity not quality, again giving the earliest months with mother the ultimate priority in the humanization process.

What Winnicott does next in this paper is remarkable. He links drive theory with object relations theory in a uniquely, integrative, "Winnicottian" way. He first restates his paradox.

> The capacity to be alone is based on the experience of being alone in the presence of someone, and . . . without a sufficiency of this experience the capacity to be alone cannot develop. (p. 33)

He then speaks of id experiences or, as he calls them, id-impulses. He notes that they are only useful if they can be given a meaning, i.e., that they are contained in "ego living" and not experienced as foreign, overwhelming stimuli. If the ego is not strong enough to contain the impulse, the baby is disturbed, if the impulse can be contained, the baby is enlivened by it. He notes:

> Id relationships strengthen the ego when they occur in a framework of ego relatedness. (p. 34)

This simple phrase is a crucial tenet of Winnicott's thinking. It allows him to acknowledge the vital importance of id experiences and therefore of drive theory in early development. Indeed, by using the phrase "id relationships" and not simply id-impulses, he is validating the ways in which drives are not simply stimuli but occur in relationship to an experience of self. But he takes the importance of drives one enormous step further by noting that they strengthen the baby if and only if they occur when the baby is alone in the presence of another. I will quote extensively from the paper at this point because I believe this point cannot be overstated.

> It is only when alone (that is to say, in the presence of someone) that the infant can discover his personal life. The pathological alternative is a false life built on reactions to external stimuli. When alone in the sense that I am using this term, and only when alone, the infant is able to do the equivalent of what in an adult would be called relaxing. The infant is able to become unintegrated, to flounder, to be in a state in which there is no orientation, to be able to exist for a time without being either a reactor to an external impingement or an active person with a direction of interest or movement. The stage is set for an id impulse. In the course of time there arrives a sensation or an impulse. In this setting the sensation or impulse will feel real and be truly a personal experience. (p. 34)

I trust you can see why I quoted this comment in such detail! It gives a phenomenological context for all of his thinking up to this point. Being alone with a reliable mother nearby provides a temporal and spatial place for the baby to exist in a state of "going on being." The infant is not driven by biological need at that moment, nor does he need to grope for mother in some desperate, but unspecified manner because of her past reliability. With "no needs to do, no promises to keep" as it were, the infant can relax. If a need or sensation or drive then comes along, it can be experienced as deeply as possible. This deeply felt experience strengthens the baby and motivates her to repeat and expand on these deeply felt, but not overpowering experiences. As Winnicott puts it:

> It is only under these conditions that the infant can have an experience which feels real. A large number of such experiences form the basis for a life that has reality in it instead of futility. The individual who has developed the capacity to be alone is constantly able to rediscover the personal impulse, and the personal impulse is not wasted because the state of being alone is something which always implies that someone else is there. (p. 34)

This passage also speaks to the exquisite balancing act between mother and baby. If the relaxed baby experiences an impulse with a mother nearby who is not only available but intrusive, the baby cannot experience the impulse on in his own terms nor engender a reaction to it on his own terms. The boundary between infant experience as its own unit and his experience within a baby-mother unit is blurred. The infant experiences something, but it is not fully his own. This puts a strain, over time, on the ratio of False Self to True Self experience, making it more likely that the baby must hide his personal life more routinely. If, on the other hand, the mother is not reliably enough present, should the id-impulse be too strong, the baby is likely to be overwhelmed by the experience, as the mother's shield-bearing role is too haphazard to allow the baby to count on it. The baby then experiences life as full of potential chaos and is prone to trauma. If, however, the good-enough balance between mother and baby is achieved most of the time, the baby can count on intense, vividly felt internal experience to be accompanied by a nearby, reliable "other." Over time, the presence of the actual mother becomes less and less necessary for the same vitality to be experienced.

This conceptualization allows us to reconfigure many aspects of later anxiety and to see them as further manifestations of this early phenomenology. Stranger anxiety, for example, can now also be seen as the baby's reaction to a new, unreliable "other" that cannot be counted on to be predictably available should an impulse be too strong; or, similarly, the stranger can be the overly abrupt stimulus that prevents the baby from maintaining his relaxed state. The presence of the reassuring mother at that point can mitigate the stranger's intrusion. Separation anxiety can also be viewed within the context of the capacity to be alone. The further the infant feels from the mother in terms of an internal perception that she will be reliably available if need be, the more vulnerable the capacity to be alone. This provokes the need to reestablish the mother's presence if an id-impulse (internal) or external, intrusive stimulus is forthcoming. If the mother (or, as we shall see when we discuss transitional phenomena, a mother-symbol) is not readily procured, intense anxiety is experienced.

This paper also makes it easier to understand Winnicott's discussion of the essential need *not* to communicate. If the capacity to be alone is absolutely essential to the discovery of one's personal life, then it follows that the right *not* to communicate is at first really the relaxed state of being self-contained in mother's presence. The silence of that moment is simply the maintenance of the alone state, which further allows new, deeply felt sensations to be experienced in a reciprocal, expanding manner. Over time, as symbolization and language develop, the right not to communicate becomes more intentional; nevertheless, it still preserves the child's capacity to be alone and hence original and creative.

A critical aspect of the "Capacity to Be Alone" paper is augmented by Winnicott's later (1967) paper titled "Mirror-Role of Mother and Family in Child Development." The "Alone" paper provides the most comprehensive depiction of the actual experience (in Escalona's use of the phrase, 1967) of the infant in his balancing of drive and relatedness. What the "Mirror-Role" paper adds is the specific role of the mother in this process.

Winnicott begins this paper as he often does, by summarizing his past theorizing up to a point and then using that point as his jumping-off place. So he begins:

A baby is held, and handled satisfactorily, and with this taken for granted is presented with an object in such a way that the baby's legitimate experience of omnipotence is not violated. . . . All this belongs to the beginning, and out of all this come the immense complexities that comprise the emotional and mental development of the infant and child. (p. 112)

Always invested in the baby's phenomenological experience, Winnicott takes this summary and asks,

Now, at some point the baby takes a look round. What does the baby see when he or she looks at the mother's face? (p. 112)

He then goes to the heart of this paper.

I am suggesting that, ordinarily, what the baby sees is himself or herself. In other words the mother is looking at the baby and what she looks like is related to what she sees there. (p. 112)

This is not a simple point. Winnicott is saying that the baby (here almost at the very beginning of life) has no conception of "me" or "not me" yet. Therefore what he experiences when he scans mother's face is some preliminary attempt to make sense of his blurred internal/external sensations. What the baby "sees" is therefore his first estimation of what the world is about, and since there is no "other" yet, he sees himself without recognition that he is a "self" or an "other" that he perceives. But what is this mirror? Here the mother's role becomes explicit. If the mother is attempting to empathize (Winnicott would use the term identify) with the baby's experience, if she is preoccupied in a "good enough" way, then her face is an "accurate enough" mirror of the baby's state. Therefore "what she sees there" (in her looking at her baby) is a good-enough approximation to what the baby experiences viscerally. In our language today we would note that mother and baby are attuned or that the mother's reflective functioning is apt enough to read the state of mind of her baby in an appropriate fashion. If she is looking accurately, then her facial expression will presumably match what she sees, which will match what her baby experiences. The baby will then get an accurate "mirroring" of his internal state. This leads to a significant exchange with the world, a two-way process in which self-enrichment alternates with the discovery of meaning in the world of seen things. (p. 113)

This last quote highlights the inherently reciprocal meaning-making process that thrives in later life if these earliest beginnings between mother and child are accurately experienced from the baby's point of view. Mother's mandate is to keep her own moods from predominating and clouding the baby's mirroring. Here Winnicott provides a bit more data on when and how mothers' moods may predominate and their differential impact on their babies. He writes:

Many babies, however, do have to have a long experience of not getting back what they are giving. They look and they do not see themselves. . . . [T]heir own creative capacity begins to atrophy, and in some way or other they look around for other ways of getting something of themselves back from the environment. . . . Second, the baby gets settled in to the idea that when he or she looks, what is seen is the mother's face. The mother's face is not then a mirror. (p. 112)

Here there is a further refinement of how a False Self is developed and how the capacity to be alone can be limited. Not being mirrored reduces the felt experience of the world-making sense of the baby's inner life and indeed serves as an illusory extension of the infant's inner states. Without such a sense-making mirror, the infant retreats from further omnipotent illusion making, losing the ability to create the world on his own terms. This prevents the infant from slowly giving up this illusory process in the balancing of fantasy and reality described in earlier chapters.

Winnicott also suggests some interesting implications of what can happen to babies dependent upon what they find when they "look for other ways of getting something of themselves back from the environment." He speaks of how mothers "can respond when the baby is in trouble or is aggressive, and especially when the baby is ill" (p. 112). We can then easily extrapolate from these differential patterns of maternal response and wonder if the baby could then only feel most real, or even develop the capacity to be alone, when troubled, being aggressive, or being ill. The implications for distorted development along the lines of attention, conduct disorder, or hypochondriacal dimensions are striking and worthy of attending to in our history taking in clinical consultations. He also stresses the active meaning-making characteristics of the infant who will

> do all that is possible to see in the object some meaning that ought to be there if only it could be felt. Some babies, tantalized by this type of relative maternal failure, study the variable maternal visage in an attempt to predict the mother's mood, just exactly as we all study the weather. The baby quickly learns to make a forecast: 'Just now it is safe to forget the mother's mood and be spontaneous, but any minute the mother's face will become fixed or her mood will dominate, and my own personal needs must then be withdrawn otherwise my central self may suffer insult.' (p. 113)

This quote provides the clearest image yet of what lengths the baby will go to create a True Self of spontaneous creativity and how alert the baby must be to protect this True Self from "insult." Although this alertness allows a True Self both to exist and to stay protected, it comes at the cost of the installation of a "radar detection" system that could serve in another framework as the prototypical depiction of a "neurotic" paradigm. If this radar construction becomes too predominant, then the baby's prime focus becomes one of prediction and not living. She becomes always on the lookout for predictability to disappear and fears chaos and disruption around every turn. The more pervasive this chaos-avoidance paradigm becomes, the more likely the person's diagnostic classification in later life shifts from "neurotic" to more profound disruptions in selfhood, such as borderline or even largely psychotic conditions.

Winnicott uses an explicitly free-verse poetic style to summarize his thinking about the need to be mirrored. He writes:

> When I look I am seen, so I exist.
> I can now afford to look and see.

I now look creatively and what I apperceive I also perceive
In fact I take care not to see what is not there to be seen (unless
I am tired). (p. 114)

The four lines encapsulate his thinking beautifully. Line one
speaks to the "good-enough mother" reflecting back her infant's
gaze, thereby validating his sense of being. This in turn, given line
two, engenders in the baby enough trust in the world to want to see
more of it. This "mirrored" taking on of the world, in line three, allows the child the omnipotence of having wishes (apperceptions)
become actualities (perceptions), making the world still more benign and inviting. Finally, the balance of omnipotence and dawning
reality testing allows the baby to minimize persecutory anxiety so
that the world becomes "good enough" (unless the baby is overtired
and needs respite).

Winnicott concludes this paper by linking the mirroring function of the mother to the psychotherapeutic process. In the following quote, this linkage both repeats several of his core notions of
what therapy is about and adds a key component derived from his
thinking in this paper. He notes:

> This glimpse of the baby's and child's seeing the self in the
> mother's face, and afterwards in a mirror, gives a way of looking
> at analysis and at the psychotherapeutic task. Psychotherapy is
> not making clever and apt interpretations; by and large it is a
> long-term giving the patient back what the patient brings. It is a
> complex derivative of the face that reflects what is there to be
> seen. (p. 117)

His mistrust of "clever and apt" interpretations is an oft-
repeated mantra for Winnicott. It speaks to his discrediting of the
use of the "forehead up" as the prime vehicle for therapeutic intervention (although in later chapters when we review his "Consultations," we see his remarkable use of interpretation) and of his enormous faith in patiently being "good enough" in the here and now
with his patients as the vehicle for therapeutic growth. What he
adds here is how "good enough" therapy is derived from that original paradigm of the appropriately preoccupied mother (therapist)

being able to reflect back to the infant (patient) what the infant is bringing to the interaction. It is a direct and vivid endorsement for empathy as the prime vehicle for interpersonal and therapeutic growth.

Winnicott adds one final element to this depiction of psychotherapy and, interestingly, he then ends with a remarkably personal evocation of what it means to him to be a therapist. He concludes:

> I like to think of my work this way, and to think that if I do this well enough the patient will find his or her own self, and will be able to exist and to feel real. Feeling real is more than existing; it is finding a way to exist as oneself, and to relate to objects as oneself, and to have a self into which to retreat for relaxation. (p. 117)

Note again how authenticity and originality are the hallmarks of mental health for Winnicott and how this capacity for "realness," by definition, implies the creation and existence of a solitary, noncommunicating place of solitude for the person to retreat to that is not just safe, but optimally relaxing.

What is the impact on Winnicott of being this type of therapist? He tells us with typical eloquence and grace,

> But I would not like to give the impression that I think this task of reflecting what the patient brings is easy. It is not easy, and it is emotionally exhausting. But we get our rewards. Even when our patients do not get cured they are grateful to us for seeing them as they are, and this gives us a satisfaction of a deep kind. (p. 118)

Phrased in this way, his personal comments on being a therapist are strikingly similar to those of a mother with her baby. The task of being a "good enough" mother is emotionally exhausting, no matter how "easy" a baby may be, although parenting certainly gives us our "rewards." It is the last sentence, however, that is most striking. I am reminded of Freud's quote about the purpose of treatment being the replacement of neurotic misery with the misery of everyday life in the sense that even the best of treatment cannot overcome the difficulties inherent in being human. Not every patient, not even every one of Winnicott's patients, gets cured. But in keeping with the intrinsically optimistic core of Winnicott's writings, he states that the empathic reflecting back to the patient—what he brings to the analytic hour—is *in and of itself* vitalizing and evokes gratitude on the part of the patient. Thus even when treatment is not optimally successful, the empathic process remains the "royal road" to generating intimacy and connection and thus evokes not only gratitude in the patient, but also a deep satisfaction in the therapist. That Winnicott could speak so openly about this satisfaction speaks volumes about both his deeply embedded capacity for pleasure derived from work and his understanding of how important it is for this satisfaction to be expressed publicly. As always, the humanity of his writing speaks as meaningfully to the reader as does its content.

With a thorough understanding of Winnicott's theorizing on connection, solitude, and attunement, we can now turn to the role that hate plays in his assessment of the humanizing process.

Chapter Six

———————○———————

Using Objects and the Capacity to Hate

Dilemma: A mother only becomes real to her baby by being hated, thus the world only feels substantial if the baby's attempts to destroy mother are survived, so how does she do it?

Article reviewed: "The Use of an Object and Relating through Identification" (1969).

> *If you're lost you can look and you will find me*
> *Time after time*
> *If you fall I will catch you, I will be waiting*
> *Time after time*

> Cyndi Lauper, "Time after Time"

THE ELOQUENT CHORUS OF CYNDI LAUPER'S song "Time after Time" puts to music the words of a "good enough" mother to her baby. In the papers reviewed so far Winnicott makes clear how this "good enough" mother operates. We have yet to understand, however, a profound aspect of mother-infant interaction, the role of aggression. As even the most cursory, naive look at world affairs tells us, we will have a very limited understanding indeed of personality development if we cannot account for aggression. Fortunately, Winnicott is perhaps at his most brilliant in his discussion of hate, whether it be of mother and baby for each other as in this paper, or between therapist and patient as in his paper "Hate in the Countertransference," to be reviewed in a later chapter.

Winnicott begins this paper with a sweeping relegation of object relations to the sidelines as he propels us directly into looking at object usage instead. He begins:

> I propose to put forward for discussion the idea of the use of an object. The allied subject of relating to objects seems to me to have had our full attention. The idea of the use of an object has not, however, been so much examined, and it may not even have been specifically studied. (p. 86)

Winnicott at first states his argument with utter simplicity.

> To use an object the subject must have developed a capacity to use objects. This is part of the change to the reality principle. (p. 89)

How do we understand this statement? This may be one of those rare times where he is using language so simply that it is too simple for its own good. I think what he's trying to tell us is that the capacity to use objects is not a given. Monumental, environmentally complex mother-baby interactions have to occur for the baby to fully develop that capacity. Importantly, it is an incredibly dynamic, active set of phenomena that creates this capacity. The active, reciprocal process of mother-infant interaction is the blacksmith's shop through which this capacity is forged. As we have noted, through the back-and-forth of mother-baby interaction, a spontaneous gesture occurs on the baby's part. The mother stays by and large the same in the midst of this spontaneous gesture. Over time, the baby increasingly has the experience that even when he does something that feels viscerally distinct, mother *stays the same*. If the mother stays the same while the baby feels different, then she over time increasingly feels, from the baby's point of view, outside of the baby. Being outside of the baby means that for that moment, the mother has been "destroyed" as an extension of the baby. Multiply these mini-distinctions by the thousands and "suddenly" it's that cataclysmic moment when, as Winnicott puts,

"Hullo object! I destroyed you. I love you. You have value for me because of your survival of my destruction of you. While I am loving you, I am all the time destroying you in (unconscious) fantasy" (p. 90)

It's the most sublime kind of joy; the discovery that the "thing" survived because it was so real.

One core theme Winnicott does not address explicitly (but should have, I believe) is the notion of faith. For what comes out of being able to use an object is that the baby has faith in that object. The baby comes to trust that that object is going to be there, and that is where the very notion of faith comes from. And what is faith? Faith from the baby's point of view is the knowledge that the mother is going to be there even if she is not needed at a given moment. The baby is creating mother and baby in the context of the future tense. Even if the future is just a few seconds away for the baby. Faith is the obverse of what Winnicott talks about when he describes how the worst catastrophe in the world is the psychotics' feeling that they'll fall and fall forever. It's instead the fundamental belief that someone will be caught at a soon-enough point. Thus, Cyndi Lauper's chorus: "If you're lost you can look and you will find me. If you fall I will catch you, I will be waiting." That is the absolute essence of a usable mother, a mother who is waiting to be used.

Another way of describing this aspect of the mother-child bond is to note the interesting parallel between the baby's illusory sense of omnipotence and the notion of faith. While the baby is developing the sense that the mother will be there when he cries or the mother will pick something up when he drops it—it's at once a sense of magical omnipotence, but it is also a matter of faith. In Winnicott's language, internalizing the object has to do with believing in the illusion that someone will always physically be there for you; the admixture of this faith and its gradual relinquishment is the backbone of the humanizing process.

To put this far less abstractly: A year-old baby is placed in his high chair to have supper. You, the parent, have been harried and rushed but in taking care of your baby, you put the "just-right" food down in front of her. The baby goes BAM, and right on to the floor goes the food! There's an immediate wish to retaliate at that moment, and yet your baby's having this perfectly spontaneous gesture at your expense! For the baby, part of what makes her relish the experience is the physical sensation of "BAM." The baby is also saying, What are you going to do with my gesture, mommy or daddy? Are you going to allow me to destroy this food? Are you going to change your mood? And if you do, because I have come to know my mommy or daddy across a certain range of behaviors, is the mommy or daddy I have a sense of going to survive? Is he or she going to stay within that range or will he or she become some other person? Depending on the parent's frame of mind at that moment and therefore what the infant's behavior means to him, the parent can "lose it" and act outside her range or can stay poised and familiar to the baby, despite how irritable she might feel. That's the moment where the baby has potentially "destroyed" the parent. What comes next helps determine the nature of object usage and puts into place another affective experience that the child can or cannot make sense of. At its best, the moment can be the vital, yet nonmagical moment of object usage. Because then I the parent am real, and I the baby become equally real and yet not identical. To put this back in Winnicott's language, the "BAM" of knocking over a food tray is akin to an "id satisfaction," and if the mother and baby survive this id satisfaction in the context of relatedness, it makes their relationship stronger.

At this point, students often link the tolerance of the baby's "BAM" with working with parents and helping them to understand better both their children's behaviors and their own "mistakes" in parenting. In that context, when parents tell their child's therapist about their doubts and their loss of faith in their child's psychological and/or behavioral status, they're really seeing whether or not they can *use* the therapist in Winnicott's sense of that word. Their admission of lack of faith in their child/themselves is an enormously vulnerable state of mind. Will the therapist be able to "hold" that fragile state of mind even if, as a beginning therapist, she is not sure if their conceptualization of the problem is accurate?

This engenders another part of the paradox inherent in object usage. As a therapist, one has to muster up a sense of faith in the patient to demonstrate one's belief that they will not destroy you and will not be destroyed by you. At the same time, the therapist has to have a flexible and a true-enough vision of the patient that the interaction between them feels real.

In a later chapter, I will be addressing the "antisocial tendency" more directly, but in the present context, it is essentially a state of mind in which the infant is unable to use objects. A kind of ruthlessness then develops and the infant discovers that there's really almost no limit to his aggression. Over time, the child finds that she can say and/or do things to people in an almost infinitely exploitative fashion. The more she exploits, the more terrified the child becomes, and the more terrified she becomes the more she exploits. This becomes such a locked-in, reciprocal phenomenon that the person's psyche contains little, if any, room for trust in another. Reciprocally, this is exactly the feeling engendered in others by the antisocial child, the feeling that we have no faith in her capacity for "ruth." There's no capacity to use objects in Winnicott's sense, and so all that remains is the exploitation of objects. Here it is important to keep in mind the distinction between using objects and exploiting objects. Winnicott is not talking about use as a manipulation. He's talking about it as exactly the opposite. When the baby is capable of true object usage, it is because she has internalized enough good object experiences that she actually has created a respect for the sanctity of the other. She therefore wants to preserve that other. She simultaneously keeps in mind the sanctity of the other's sense of self *and* the wish to preserve herself. That is the antidote to antisocial experience.

There's a very important paragraph on page 88 of the "Use of the Object" paper that allows an even deeper understanding of the crucial distinctions between object relating and object use. Winnicott begins:

> It is perhaps necessary to prevaricate a little longer to give my own view on the difference between object relating and object usage. In object relating the subject allows certain alterations in the self to take place, of a kind that has caused us to invent the term cathexis. The object has become meaningful. Projection mechanisms and

identifications have been operating and the subject is depleted to
the extent that something of the subject is found in the object
though enriched by feeling. (p. 88)

What he is essentially saying is that object relatedness is the
precursor stage to object usage. In the very first hours and days after birth, the infant is drawn to relate because the need to get nurturance, bodily warmth, and milk from the mother is so vital that
object relating starts incredibly early. With this initial object relating (but not yet usage) comes a type of generalizing and extension
that looks like an early form of projection. There is then a constant
blurring of what the baby/mother is feeling. The boundaries are
completely permeable. When Winnicott says that "the subject is
depleted to the extent that something of the subject is found in the
object" (p. 88), what he's saying is that at that point in time, infant
and mother are in a zero-sum game. But because there is a time lag
between events, because the "good enough" is not infallible in time
and space, the baby does feel the shift of interaction back and forth.
It is almost as if (entirely from the baby's and a bit of the mother's
points of view) mother and baby are two pieces of Jello; they have
a kind of blubbery feeling to them and they're kind of blubbering
against each other. When one partner gives some of its "blubber" to
the other, therefore, one gets a little "heavier" and the other a little
depleted.

Winnicott continues:

> Object relating is an experience of the subject that can be de-
> scribed in terms of the subject as an isolate. (p. 88)

In other words, the infant is alone in some basic way because it
is still incapable of recognizing the separateness of the other despite
his need for and movement toward this increasingly more reliable
mother. However, when Winnicott speaks of the use of the object,
he implies that the baby has come to take object relating for granted
and

> adds new features that involve the nature and the behavior of the
> object. For instance, the object, if it is to be used, must neces-

sarily be real in the sense of being part of shared reality, not a bundle of projections. It is this I think that makes for the world of difference that there is between relating and usage. (p. 88)

In object usage the baby can recognize that in fact the mother is different from him. It is important to link this concept to last chapter's "Mirror-Role" paper. When the very young baby looks up, what does he see? He sees in the mother's face what he is supposed to look like. That would now be called object relating in the language of "Use of the Object," because mother and baby only exist at that time based on mother's smiling at the baby and not in her own right. Object usage would imply that, from the baby's point of view, the mother he looks at actually looks different from himself. Think now of a moment a bit later in time, to a twenty-four-month-old who knocks her food off the high chair. She can know that it's naughty of her to knock over the food. Now the fact that she knows it is naughty is dramatically different from the merely object-relating baby. Because if she knows it is naughty, it means that she knows that she and her parent actually have a different set of standards about "proper" behavior. Indeed, one of the major things about being two years old is that when you are a healthy two, you want to exploit the fact that you are different. The essence of "two-ness" is that the toddler is exploiting her capacity to make use of the parent. She is exploiting the fact that she is different. Indeed, she relishes the fact that she is different and feels sublimely powerful because she can thrive as a function of these differences.

As we struggle to tease apart object relating from object usage, it's important to keep in mind that the movement from object relating to object usage never fully implies the end of relating. Thus the capacity to relate to people implies that relationships are going to be filled with projections and introjections at any given moment. But at the same time, those aspects of self that are capable of object usage contain a part of the self that is objectively real, and understand that the other is different and has real characteristics that are not just itself and/or extensions of itself. In a different arena, as we shall see when Winnicott discusses transference and countertransference in later chapters, the distinction

between object relating and object usage implies that not all behavior in life or in the consulting room is transference. If everything
were transference, no one would have gotten to the level of object
usage. The mélange of transference/countertransference with the
real characteristics of the therapist/patient is therefore the repetition, in this distinct format, of the balance of object relating and object usage for both patient and therapist. This places the conception of psychotherapy as always a combination of something that's
real and distinct and something that is projected and full of distortion into the new language of object usage versus object relatedness. In parallel fashion, all human interchange becomes a combination of relatedness and usage except if one has been so devas-
tated by poor early experience that one never grabs a firm hold of
object usage. That person is in a world in which almost everything
is transferential. Winnicott would argue that if one were psychotic
for long periods of time, one would always be in an object-relating
mode. There would never have been a sustained period of object
usage, and therefore everything would be a projection or a projected
identification or an introjection. Always. There would be no personal characteristics that are unique and separate.

The "Use of the Object" paper also suggests a different way to
approach identity formation by allowing us to view one aspect of the
writings of Descartes through a Winnicottian lens. Instead of "I
think therefore I am," it could be "I destroy therefore I am." Winnicott would retranslate Descartes' maxim in this fashion because
with the capacity for object usage comes the awareness that others
are not just a collection of dreamlike transferences and projections,
but have some distinct reality components. That, in turn, solidifies
the capacity for the self to feel real. Conversely, when the capacity
for object usage is lost or never found, life experience is completely
mired in one's own projections and introjections, and life takes on
nightmarish proportions that preclude the capacity to realistically
experience a bounded self with "I am" properties. In this context,
Winnicott's depiction of object usage can be more precisely viewed
as an affect theory version of Descartes. He would rephrase
Descartes to say: "I have the capacity to destroy; therefore I am. I
can use objects; therefore I am. I feel, therefore I am."

To go a bit further with the "Use of the Object," Winnicott notes:

> In the sequence one can say that first there's object relating, then in the end there's object use; in between, however, is the most difficult thing perhaps in human development; or the most irksome of all the early failures that come from mending. This thing that there is in between relating and use is the subject's placing of the object outside the area of the subject's omnipotent control; that is the subject's perception of the object as an external phenomenon, not as a projective entity, in fact recognition of it as an entity in its own right. (p. 89)

Here Winnicott is describing the bridge between relating and usage. When the infant can recognize that the object (mother) exists independently, that is the logical precursor to the infant trying her (it) out and seeing if she (it) can be used.

Students at this point usually want me to connect Winnicott's notions of object usage to Klein's depressive position. In this light, it is relatively simple to note that the capacity to use an object is really the capacity to reach the depressive position. But Winnicott is, in a sense, providing us with the phenomenology of how the baby gets from point A (relating) to point B (usage). How do you go from A to B? Let me give a silly analogy. When I teach Winnicott, my students are all (hopefully) listening to me and even nodding their heads occasionally, and it's wonderfully gratifying and a lot of fun, and so in a way that's a very object-related experience for me. The class is fulfilling my needs to be smart and clever until a student, let's call him Alex, raises a question. And that question makes me think—I hadn't thought about Winnicott that way before. So the newness of Alex's question implies to me that he actually has an independent existence. He had thought about this differently and so what do I do with that? If I'm lucky enough to not be so narcissistically absorbed at that moment, as opposed to other times, then I hope that I can actually use that. So I can hear what Alex says and start to think about it and play with it. And I then want to ask Alex a question in reply or make a comment back to Alex, addressing his question. I'm now saying I recognize that he's Alex and Alex is not

Steve, and in fact, now I'm going to explore this distinction. So then the next step would be, if I say something different or if I challenge Alex, will he survive my playing with him? So when Alex says, well, I think it's part of the depressive position and I say object usage explains the process creating the position, and Alex nods his head, it suggests that he's now using me in the Winnicottian sense. The fact that we're now "playing" means that I can use Alex and Alex can use me. We're separate but we feel a connection in our very separateness. Indeed, that connection is forged because we understood each other. I felt enhanced, hopefully Alex felt enhanced, and now we can go back and play some more.

I do want to stress the "feedback loop" quality of the means by which object relating becomes object usage. Moving from relating to usage back to a more enriching form of relating is a cycle precisely because object usage alone is an insufficient explanation of human experience. Critically, the baby also wants to use mother because he wants to feel connected to her. That's the relating part of the baby over time. The toddler wants to be able to knock his food tray over and have mother survive because if mother survives, the baby still has further access. It is not that the baby just wants to use mother, because as primary as the urge to "BAM" the food tray might be, the baby simultaneously also does not want his mother to disappear. Indeed, that would be the worst calamity of all if mother disappeared. So that's the paradigm. Baby relates, which is only full of projection and need, but then the mother's survival in recognizable form after the baby relates begins to help create separation in the baby. The baby then tests this separation. Mother survives this test as well and tens of thousands more. The baby now uses the mother. But the fact that mother survives means the baby is also even more grateful and wants to relate to mother even more in a cyclical fashion. The cycle constantly augments the baby's conception of self as each time he feels more firm and more alive because he is expanding his sense of "me" and "not me." The more reliable the interaction, the more the baby can tolerate its separateness. The baby is now starting to feel *good enough*. The "good enough" mother makes the baby feel good enough. And if the baby feels good enough, he can actually have greater tolerance for its differentness from the mother.

To broaden this paradigm a bit, it is object usage that also gives the baby the fuel to take on learning about the world and its physical properties as well as the fuel to want to keep on relating and enhance her relationships. It is in the very act of using people and having self and other survive that the baby becomes interested in making more sense both of those kinds of relationships and of the physical properties of the world that serve as the context for interaction.

One can also think about this expanding vista in the context of having more than one child. If parents have been lucky enough with their first child that the child feels like they're "good enough," then she can survive the fact that her parents have brought in this new baby. The older child may not like it, and this new "thing" gets a lot of attention, but the first child gets "enough" so that the new arrival can be tolerated. If parents are really fortunate, not only can the first-born tolerate it, the fact that she does tolerate it allows the older child to be nice to the baby without excessive falseness. The new baby can even be experienced as fun or curious at times. I'm reminded of the popular T-shirt that says, "I'm the big brother" or "I'm the big sister." Part of why kids love that shirt is because it defines them better. Here's another whole series of labels and ways of being that enhance the older sibling. Let's suppose one is coming to visit a new baby. What is one of the first things to do in this circumstance if you're a good clinician? You say to the older sib, "Are you the big brother (sister)?" The older sib takes on the distinct feeling of this "bigness" and uses it to enhance and broaden its representation of self and that allows him to tolerate the intrusion of this little "usurper" that's come along and ruined his life!

A last point about the role of language in the passage from relating to usage is appropriate here. Because language and symbolization create the milieu that allows us to more easily make all things separate, less immediate, and more capable of being categorized, it is the most vital tool in allowing relationships with people and things to multiply exponentially. Because by symbolizing, the baby obviously doesn't need to have everything be directly in front of her concretely. She can use words to make all kinds of connections to things that are one step removed from literally being with that thing. As the baby starts to develop language, she thus adds an almost infinitely useful tool to enhance her capacity to relate and to use objects. I say almost infinite because we also know so fully, more than we could ever express, how the deepest of feelings often elude capture solely by words.

This statement on the limitation of words provides a useful segue into the implications of this paper for clinical work. Winnicott notes:

> For instance it is only in recent years that I've become able to wait and wait for the natural evolution of the transference arising out of the patient's growing trust and the psychoanalytic technique and setting and to avoid breaking up this natural process by making interpretations. It will be noticed I am talking about the making of interpretations and not about interpretations as such. It appalls me to think how much deep change I have prevented or delayed in patients in a certain classification category by my personal need to interpret. (p. 86)

This is certainly a most recognizable experience in the evolution of any therapist who has been treating patients in an intensive, long-term fashion. His "certain classification category" once again goes back to those patients who are really quite fragile underneath, even if they may sometimes come across as being neurotic, and that their needs and what they need to change is very deep in the core of their being in terms of a sense of true identity. Therefore rushing in to interpret with patients like this goes back to creating a false self.

> If we only can wait, the patient arrives at understanding creatively and with immense joy and I now enjoy this joy more than I used to enjoy the sense of having been clever. (p. 86)

In the same vein, Winnicott adds:

I think I interpret mainly to let the patient know the limits of my understanding. The principle that it is the patient and only the patient who has the answers. We may or may not enable him or her to encompass what is known or become aware of it with acceptance. (p. 87)

A recent interaction with a patient of mine is directly relevant here. The patient is a fifteen-year-old girl I've been seeing for about two years, and she came to me originally because she was terrified at the thought of being away from her parents for even two or three hours. She is a person of many strengths; she is bright, funny, warm, a good student, and has intimate friends. Nevertheless, she still she has this very powerful symptom. I've often wondered how troubled she is. Is she someone who has a deficit of selfhood and uses a False Self facade to carry on with life? Her parents were very concerned about how depressed she was. They sent her to a psychiatrist, who was convinced that she was profoundly troubled and placed her on antidepressant medication. I kept thinking that she wasn't that troubled. As time went by, the symptom diminished in significant ways. Yet an upcoming trip away from home sent her into a regressed tailspin. Two days before the trip she had a full-blown panic attack in my office, crying hysterically, "I can't do it." She had never "lost it" like that before. I sat very, very quietly through almost all of it, barely saying very much other than to say how scared she was and how she was really convincing herself that it would not be possible for her to make it through this very long weekend. She eventually left the session, in a somewhat more composed way but still very fragile. I had arranged to see her the next day. I then received a phone message that next morning asking me to call her. I called and she said: "I can't talk a lot, I'm in between classes, but I'm definitely not going and I'm absolutely terrified. It didn't work. I'm not going. Good-bye. And not only that, I'm not coming to see you tonight," and she hung up. So I called her back and said: "I don't know whether you're going or not but you're coming to see me tonight. At 6:45 you're going to be here."

Later that evening my patient arrived and said: "My mom said that if I don't go on the trip, then I'm going to have to change, you know, change what—you know, what we've been doing." I was suddenly struck by the thought that much of her not going away was also an attempt to "destroy" both the therapy and her parents. To *use* us in this way. On the one hand she couldn't leave, but on the other hand she was also saying that all of her good parenting is fake because she's really "off" in a core way and, similarly, all of our "good enough" therapy is really useless because she's incapable of being comforted. It's only if she destroys her ties to me and to her parents that she can actually be her own person. What a tortuous decision that was! Because if she didn't go on the trip, she could feel as if she could destroy her parents at the very moment she was clinging to them! So when she said to me, "So I guess if I don't go, then we're over. I looked at her and decided to say, "That sounds very real to me. Ah, and you know, I'm so torn by it." She looked at me and said, "What do you mean you're torn?" And I said, "Well, I'm really torn because there's a part of me that knows that I will always care about you, but I'm also feeling that if you can't go this weekend, that it says that this is a problem that may be beyond my being able to help you. If it is, then this would be really important for the two of us to acknowledge." She became very quiet for a long time and had a look on her face that was sadder than I've ever seen her look. Finally, she quietly said, "I really know I can go." Then right before the end of the session, I said, "I do want to ask you about yesterday, because yesterday you were really in an incredible panic. I didn't say very much at all to you during that session and I wondered what you thought of that." She immediately said, "Yes, you didn't say a word!" I replied that I didn't say a word because "I couldn't think of a thing to say and there was nothing else to say or do but live through it with you."

This was an especially poignant rendition of reaching the limits of one's understanding. I think that I was trying to say to her that I didn't fully understand the nature and power of her phobic behavior, that it was okay for me not to know, and that both of us would survive my not knowing. To get back to Winnicott's terminology, when the patient is consistently at the level of object usage, he or she can survive the therapist not knowing and if anything, there's something centrally necessary about the therapist not knowing. The therapist's not knowing provides confirmation of the True, private Self of the patient. It thereby allows the patient to feel like they're not going to be retaliated against—that's what Winnicott means when he says to survive means not to retaliate. It means that the therapist is fully aware that there's a place inside the patient that is inviolate, the private space Winnicott depicts for us in his "Capacity to Be Alone" paper.

With a large portion of Winnicott's theorizing now in place, it seems an appropriate moment to review a clinical consultation of his, so that we can view his theory in its clinical context. In the next chapter, therefore, I review "The Case of Bob" from his *Therapeutic Consultations in Child Psychiatry*.

Chapter Seven

———————————○———————————

Integrating Theory with Therapy: The Case of Bob

Dilemma: How can Winnicott's theorizing be understood in the context of clinical work?

Articles reviewed: "The Case of Bob" from *Therapeutic Consultations in Child Psychiatry* (1971) and "Birth Memories, Birth Trauma, and Anxiety" (1949).

UP TO THIS POINT, OUR "PLAYING" with Winnicott has taken place solely at the level of theory. But for Winnicott, theory and clinical work were indelibly intertwined; thus it seems a particularly good moment to examine some of his clinical contributions. While we have yet to play with all of his key constructs—namely, play and transitional experience—we have come well enough along that an immersion into one of his "therapeutic consultations" will provide ample clinical resonance for the theory we have reviewed thus far. I have chosen "The Case of Bob" to begin a review of his clinical work because it embodies a number of Winnicott's core constructs: (a) the capacity to be alone, (b) the relegation of instinct (drive theory) to a later, secondary role in the creation of human personality, (c) the role of spontaneous gestures in the interaction between mother (therapist) and baby (patient), (d) the mirror-role of mothering, (e) the development of archaic (annihilation) anxiety in the baby as an interactional failure, and especially (f) the role of mother's mood in the

101

disruption of "going on being" crucial to the infant's capacity for creativity and a sense of feeling real and alive.

Before we turn to the case, a more general word is needed about the nature of these cases, each taken from his remarkable book, *Therapeutic Consultations in Child Psychiatry*. This is a book of "magic," or rather a book of intakes, and is neither a set of instructions on how to conduct therapy nor a guide to establishing a therapeutic relationship. It can be remarkably intimidating to beginning clinicians because he appears able to induce psychological change, often of a lasting kind, from one or two sessions. More dramatically, he is able to make connections with a child that touch him or her at a very deep level in very few words, hence my flip use of the word magic in describing the book. Winnicott is very aware of the special nature of these consultations, as he notes in his introduction to the book:

> My conception of the special place of the therapeutic consultation and the exploitation of the first interview arose gradually in the course of time in my clinic and private practice. . . . I was struck by the frequency with which the children had dreamed of me the night before attending. This dream of the doctor that they were going to see obviously reflected their own imaginative equipment in regard to doctors and dentists and other people who are supposed to be helpful. . . . The children who had dreamed in this way were able to tell me that it was of me that they had dreamed. In language which I now use but which I had no equipment for using at that time I found myself in the role of subjective object. What I now feel is that in this role of subjective object, which rarely outlasts the first or first few interviews, the doctor has a great opportunity for being in touch with the child. (p. 4)

This comment again speaks to the inherent optimism in Winnicott's conception of the child. The child is told of his upcoming visit to a doctor (as a result of his writings, I for many years have specifically asked parents to tell their children that they are about to visit a "feelings" or "worry" doctor), and this sets into motion a wish to communicate with a "preconceived notion" of what this doctor will be about. The preconceived notion (or subjective object in Winnicott's terminology) is a positive expectation at some level that the child can be understood, precisely because their initial fantasy is that the therapist is *a part of themselves that they wish to understand*. This readiness to engage the consultation, if deftly exploited by the clinician, can lead to the results Winnicott demonstrates in his *Consultations*.

On a more personal note, in teaching graduate students to become child clinicians, I am repeatedly struck by how little emphasis is placed on this moment just before the consultation. In many families, the child's symptomatic behavior has often been presented to the child negatively (you have to start behaving better in school, or stop hitting your younger sister, etc.) and/or empathized with but with little effect (e.g., honey, I'm sorry you're so worried). The idea that a parent has consulted with a *doctor*, an outsider, is often enormously powerful to the child on many levels of hope and fear. Even further, for many children, the idea that their behaviors have a link to their internal states of mind and that another, strange adult can enter that state of mind with them can be a revelation. This is especially true if the parents have had a positive experience in their consultation with the therapist, so that on some level, they are less frightened by their own fears and doubts and convey some sense of confidence in the therapist to their child. All of this does lend the initial consultation a special, if ephemeral, opportunity to allow the child to be creative in expressing her inner turmoil and creativity, which, as we know from Winnicott, is the prime antidote to compliance and pathology.

Two interrelated quotes are relevant here. They both speak to the integration of theory with practice that is at the core of every consultation Winnicott describes. He notes:

> In order to use the mutual experience one must have in one's bones a theory of the emotional development of the child and of the relationship of the child to the environmental factors. (p. 3)

And

> The only companion that I have in exploring the unknown territory of the new case is the theory that I carry around with me and

that has become part of me and that I do not even have to think about in a deliberate way. This is the theory of the emotional development of the individual which includes for me the total history of the individual child's relationship to the child's specific environment. One could compare my position with that of a cellist who first slogs away at technique and then actually becomes able to play music, taking the technique for granted. (p. 6)

While these two quotes are hardly comforting to a beginning clinician (I can always imagine their discomfort at the analogy of *slogging away at technique!*), they do stress how theory and hence diagnosis are inseparable from technique for Winnicott. They also stress his emphasis on understanding the phenomenology of a child's specific interaction with her specific environment and not simply on forcing the child to fit his theory.

We are now (at last!) ready to take on the case of Bob. We are told that Bob, age six, has a very depressed mother and somewhat depressed father, both of whom have been treated by a psychiatric colleague of Winnicott's. Winnicott meets briefly with mother, father, and Bob together. Although he does not speak to this explicitly, it is in keeping with Winnicott's theorizing that he would want this brief family contact to give him a taste of what the child is like in the context of his parents. He tells us that Bob has a significant articulation problem and is difficult to understand.

Importantly, we are told:

Nevertheless he communicated freely. He had come in in an excited state and he took up his position in one of the little chairs, eager for whatever should happen. It could be said that he was full of some vague kind of hope. . . . He expected friendliness and helpfulness.

Thus Bob is a prime example of that "wish " to be understood that Winnicott describes as often prevailing in a one-time consultation.

Winnicott begins the consultation with Bob by suggesting his famous "squiggle game." He comments elsewhere:

There is nothing original of course about the squiggle game and it would not be right for somebody to learn how to use the squiggle game and then to feel equipped to do what I call a therapeutic consultation. The squiggle game is simply one way of getting into contact with the child. (p. 3)

I think he minimizes one key aspect of the game that needs highlighting. The game is inherently interactive, in that one player draws something for the other to amend or add to. This makes the game far more like a mother-baby dyadic interaction than simply a game of taking turns or parallel play. It is therefore a breeding ground for issues of separateness, aloneness, and togetherness, issues that lie at the core of Winnicott's theorizing on how development proceeds. Thus the very capacity to play this game is of importance to him and not simply the content of the drawings. It implies some capacity for mutuality, hopefulness, and symbolizing.

Bob's capacity to engage in the squiggle game, coupled with his very first drawing of a ball, are therefore of crucial diagnostic significance to Winnicott. He says:

I made a mental note of this boy's capacity to conceive of a whole object and I also began to doubt the diagnosis that had been assumed to be correct, Primary Defect. (p. 65)

Primary Defect implies retardation and profound cognitive/emotional limitations but the immediate willingness of Bob to relate to a whole object (Winnicott draws a roundish-shape and Bob immediately wants to fill it all in, giving it texture and fullness) places him, in Winnicott's etiology, further along the developmental continuum.

Three drawings follow—a car, a hand, and a sun—and Winnicott summarizes them as

the end of a very cautious first phase in which he used the aspect of his self that tries to comply and to conform, but which does not carry feeling nor does it employ impulse. (p. 67)

We are thus getting in clinical form what we have been describing as a False Self theoretically. It is at this point that a spontaneous gesture arises and Winnicott makes brilliant use of it. Drawing five is

> his version of a squiggle. It was a drawing by use of a wavy line, and it may have been a person or a ghost. I added the moon. (p. 68)

This drawing was the key to the consultation and a marvel of brilliant simplicity in the integration of technique and theory. Why? The child had heretofore been in a state of inhibition and constriction and given his entering diagnosis, Winnicott did not know whether this constriction was a permanent blockage or had the potential to be broken through. So at that moment (drawing number five) the child suddenly makes a drawing filled with fearful content and tentative, possibly harrowing form. The child is thus communicating (without awareness) something far more alive and indicative of profound duress. So what does Winnicott do? Remember, this is an interactive game, and it is Winnicott's turn to make something of Bob's squiggle. It would have been easy to alter the drawing in some profound way, thereby risking a profound misattunement to this spontaneous gesture of Bob's. It would've been just as easy to add nothing to the drawing, missing an opportunity to communicate to Bob that he is capable of being understood, even in this scary place. So Winnicott adds a moon! A simple, nonintrusive response that not only does not get in the way of the communication (drawing), it even resonates with it, as a full moon fits in smoothly with the ghostlike portrait. The addition of the moon is thus to me a compelling example of a confirming, validating communication. In Winnicott's language, it recognizes Bob's capacity to be alone and allows him to be alone in Winnicott's presence. It thus is a statement in a clinical milieu of what Winnicott has stressed is the bedrock of early human achievement—the baby's capacity to be alone in the mother's presence.

Drawing number six offers a validation of this line of reasoning. Winnicott makes a squiggle, and Bob puts in the eyes and calls it Humpty Dumpty. Winnicott adds:

> The theme of Humpty Dumpty alerted me to the idea of disintegration, related to premature reliance on an ego organization. At

this stage I had no idea that his putting in the eyes had significance, but in the critical drawing (number twenty-six) this Humpty Dumpty theme and the eyes came to make clinical sense. (pp. 68–69)

Bob responds to Winnicott's validation of drawing number five by using a shared cultural symbol (the nursery rhyme of Humpty Dumpty) to depict his fragility and hopelessness, his fear of never being able to be repaired. This is what Winnicott refers to in his mentioning of disintegration and he links the conformity of the first four drawings (and perhaps even his entire presentation as a "Primary Defect") to his "premature" reliance on a False Self to stave off this disintegration.

Bob now is more fully invested in the squiggle game, and he gives another wavy line, which he turns into a very dangerous, stinging snake. He also becomes interested in Winnicott's numbering of the drawings and tells each number to all subsequent drawings. Both the snake and the numbering are notable. The fact that he can, on his own, draw a wavy snake suggests a further breakup of the conformity that characterized his first four drawings. The fact that he can become invested in the numbering suggests the availability of obsessive-compulsive defenses to balance the potential expression of highly conflictual material.

Drawing nine reveals more profoundly the archaic fears Bob wrestles with. He draws what Winnicott eventually realizes is a maze, and the drawing stirs up a memory in Bob of a visit to such a maze with his father, a visit that was "horrid" and anxiety-provoking. Winnicott notes:

Here I made another mental note of the idea of a reaction to environmental failure. In this case the idea was of a failure on the part of the father, who would seem to have not realized that a maze would touch on archaic anxiety in Bob. I had got into touch with Bob's threatened confusional state, his potential disorientation. Naturally I was building up in my mind an idea of his illness as one of infantile schizophrenia, showing a tendency to recover spontaneously. (p. 70)

Although Winnicott blithely states that he "naturally" saw Bob's illness as infantile schizophrenia, there is nothing obvious in that statement except if we see this diagnosis in Winnicottian terms. By schizophrenia, Winnicott is referring to the periods in the first year of life where persistent disruptions in the continuity of self leave the baby at the mercy of the most primitive of fears (annihilation), what he has called elsewhere the fear of falling forever. The fact that he could present these fears through a mere nine drawings emboldened Winnicott to believe that further communications could lead Bob to recover and reintegrate.

Drawing number eleven constitutes a shift for Bob that is in keeping with his attempts at reintegration. He abandons the interactive nature of the squiggle game for a moment and wants to draw a complete picture. He starts with his wavy drawings (vulnerable self) but then evokes a different way of being. Winnicott describes it as follows:

> Bob now chose to draw. He drew the sun in his characteristic way and a jet plane by the other technique. Bob said: 'Twelve comes after it." He was now numbering the drawings and was correctly using the words 'he' and 'me' which I put next to the numbers to denote the order of events. He was able to call himself he, and me me, allowing for my having my own point of view, or identifying himself with me in the game. Talking about number 11, I asked Bob if he would like to go in a jet plane. He said: "No, because they may go upside down." From this I gathered that Bob was letting me know of his experience of environmental unreliability during the period of his own near-absolute dependence. (p. 72)

We are thus witnessing Bob, even in the midst of depicting profoundly early disruptions in his quest for continuity and coherence, generating evidence for awareness of self and other, showing clearer and more sophisticated use of language (getting his pronouns correct) and being able to correctly use numbers in an anticipatory fashion. It is clear that Winnicott could see this remarkable duality of illuminating profound disturbance in the context of expressing greater clarity and capability in the moment. In drawing number thirteen moreover, Bob can comment on the nature of his drawing process (he notes in response to his drawing of a boat going to Australia, that his lines are "all wiggly, wiggly"). His capacity for self-reflection is thus also presenting itself in the context of the profound early disturbances he is describing.

Drawings fourteen and fifteen are remarkable depictions of two distinct yet related aspects of Winnicott's theorizing. In drawing four, Winnicott's squiggle goes off the page onto another sheet of paper, and Bob is greatly amused. This speaks to Winnicott's own use of the spontaneous gesture and of their being able to enjoy the gesture together. To use Winnicott's previously discussed paper on the "mirror-role" of mother, Winnicott and Bob are "seeing themselves in the other." This permits Bob to once again delve into his own psychological muddle, in the presence of Winnicott, on drawing fifteen. They delight in mutually making a "hopeless mess and muddle." Bob thus feels that he is no longer alone with his own disorganization and so he does a remarkable thing: he sees the muddle as Donald Duck and puts in the eyes of the "duck." Eyes are his way out of the muddle! This again speaks to the mirroring process between mother and baby as the route to coherence and clarity between inside and outside (or "me" and "not me" in Winnicott's words). If baby sees what the mother looks like, and if what mother looks like is an accurate reflection of the baby's state, then baby feels confirmed. Bob shows us in this drawing how the placing of open eyes permits him to make sense of his now shared muddle with Winnicott.

Being seen by Winnicott allows Bob in the next three drawings to reveal what Winnicott would expect theoretically from a child whose earliest months included periods of discontinuity. He would expect that such "failures" in "good-enough holding" by his environment would leave Bob struggling with fears of retaliation for his anger at not being "held." Drawings sixteen and especially eighteen reveal these fears in the form of an elephant with a beak coming to catch him and a spiked animal that will eat him. Fascinatingly, Winnicott notes Bob's putting his hand to his penis in the midst of his drawing, as a way of letting Bob know that Winnicott understands that such drawings reveal his fears of retaliation, even specifically castration fears. The fact that such castration anxiety is but a mere aside in Winnicott's depiction of the root causes of Bob's difficulties is a striking example of Winnicott's turn away from the Oedipal paradigm as the prime cauldron for psychopathology.

The drawing of three menacing creatures (he added a tiger in number nineteen) leads Bob to a brief "doldrums phase," where he once again uses counting as a defense ("Shall we go up to one hundred?" he asks Winnicott) to consolidate his sense of self after the expression of such primitive aggression.

Drawing twenty-one returns to the muddle, as it were, as Bob draws "a mountain; you walk all around it and get lost." Winnicott notes:

> Now we had entered the third phase, and we began to get down to the significant detail. The content of number 21 made me prepared for a new version of environmental failure producing threat of primitive anxiety of the type of falling, depersonalization, confusion, disorientation etc. (p. 77)

Winnicott must feel Bob coming to something still more viscerally felt because he does something rather striking in drawing twenty-two. He makes a squiggle and then says, *in a challenging voice,* "I'll bet you can't make anything of that." Bob says he'll try and turns it into a glove. Why does Winnicott use this challenging voice? He seems to be resonating with the growing excitement in Bob and so he "stirs up the pot," as it were, arousing Bob, who rises to the challenge and, indeed, raises the ante by asking for a larger sheet of paper for his next drawing. He once again draws a mountain, even bigger than before, and adds that it is slippery and icy. Winnicott takes this as indicative of Bob himself reexperiencing having slipped off of something big (breast? mother?) early in life. He then links this conceptually (but not explicitly to Bob) for the first time to Bob's mother's depression, as an indication that Bob once had something (mother) but now has lost it.

Importantly, and in keeping with his prohibition against the making of "clever" interpretations as opposed to letting the patient reach the material on his own, Winnicott does not yet comment to

Bob about his mother. Instead, he provides Bob with another arena to express his inner experience. He asks Bob if he dreams about "this sort of thing" (i.e., slippery, icy mountains [mothers]). Bob responds by telling him of "horrid" dreams where a witch makes you disappear. He then draws (number twenty-four) a disorganized scribble "dramatizing horror" and then (number twenty-five) draws himself in bed having the nightmare. Think how far he has come in self-representation from the filled-in ball of drawing one to a self-portrait in bed having a nightmare in drawing twenty-five! Drawing stairs to complete his bedroom scene, he

> was very much in the event he was describing. He now told me that the drawing was about two things. The awful one was the nightmare; but there was a real incident which was not horrid, it was nice. He really fell downstairs, and there was Daddy at the bottom of the stairs, and he cried, and Daddy carried him to Mummy, and she took him and made him well. I now had the clearest possible evidence of Bob's wish to tell me about a lapse in the environmental provision which had been 'good' in a general way. (p. 82)

Winnicott is certainly enough of a well-trained psychoanalyst to treasure the primacy of dream material as the royal road to the unconscious! He takes these two "dreams" as confirming evidence of his thinking that Bob's mother was indeed once "good enough" but that her depression had derailed her capacity to maintain her availability to him at an early age (one wonders whether the birth of a new sibling when Bob was only one could have also engendered this "loss").

Now feeling confident, Winnicott is ready to present his "findings" to Bob but brilliantly does not rely largely on words to convey this understanding. Instead he concretely draws a mother with a baby in her arms and then *scribbles out the baby*. At the moment of this "interpretation"

> Bob took the paper and *smudged in the woman's eyes*. As he smudged in the eyes he said: "She goes to sleep." This was the significant detail in the total communication. I now had his

drawing illustrating the holding mother's withdrawal of cathexis. (p. 82)

This is a formidable moment. No sooner does Winnicott begin to formulate an interpretation in words to match his drawing, than Bob takes over (truly making this a stunning rendition of the squiggle game!) and makes an even more specific interpretation! Winnicott focuses on the baby's feeling erased, which naturally makes sense from an adult perspective. But from the child's perspective, indeed from the very sight line of the child, what he sees is the loss of the mother's eyes, the loss of contact. This is probably as close as we can ever get to an infant's rendering of its actual experience with mother from the vantage point of a baby in its mother's arms.

Winnicott is not content to end the interpretive moment there, although the prime moment in the consultation had been reached. He tries to see if Bob can find words to speak to the unspeakable horror of being decathected by his mother. He writes:

> I now put the baby on the floor in my drawing, wondering how Bob would deal with the archaic anxiety associated with falling forever. (p. 83)

Bob responds instead with a fantasy (dream?) in which a witch comes along when his mother shut her eyes. The mother is awakened by the child's screams, and Bob avers that the mother will get the witch but it is the father who takes out his knife and stabs the witch in her tummy, preventing her from ever making people disappear again. Winnicott responds to the dream as follows:

> In this fantasy can be seen the material for a psycho-neurotic organization set up and maintained in defense against the unthinkable or archaic or psychotic anxiety produced in the child by the failure of the mother's holding function. The recovery from the trauma depends on the father's help. (p. 83)

What is left unstated by Winnicott in the above passage is noteworthy. It is certainly apparent that Bob's fantasy allows his mother to not simply be lost in her depression (and therefore not be the witch who makes him disappear by withdrawing) but to be actively awakened by his screaming. He can then hold on to the wish that she would be strong enough to "get" (kill) this witch. He brings in his daddy who, phallically enough, takes out his penknife and kills the witch. The use of displacement onto a witch to protect the mother from his own rage, the reparative fantasy that he can arouse his mother from her depression as opposed to being helplessly abandoned, and his rescue by his phallic father are all important manifestations of his need to place everyone in the triad in action. This "counter-depressive" fantasy, it must be remembered, sits side by side with the more "horrid" fantasy of losing his mother and being lost. It is thus for Winnicott a telling example of a False Self "Oedipal" fantasy used to mask a much earlier, pre-Oedipal experience. Winnicott tells us in his brief history of the case at the end of the consultation that the mother began to deteriorate into depression when Bob was fourteen months old, shortly after the birth of her second son. He notes:

> I asked; "How did you first become ill? In what way did your depression show itself?" She answered: "I kept finding myself going to sleep while I was engaged in doing something." . . . As Bob left my house he said to his mother: "Did you see how I rubbed in the lady's eyes?" This had obviously been the highlight, for him, of the therapeutic interview. (pp. 85–86)

The dramatic congruence between her symptomatology and her son's drawing is uncanny. What is still more powerful is the investment Bob had in wanting to speak of his "rubbing in the lady's eyes." This is a boldly persuasive demonstration of the "curative" impact of turning a passive, helpless-making experience into an active, mastery-filled "working through" process.

One last thought about the case. Although Winnicott is striking in his failure to discuss the actual impact of the birth of Bob's sibling on both his mother and himself, two compelling points bring us back to its salience as an important variable in the process. The first is in the particular mention Bob makes in his "witch" fantasy that his Daddy stabs her in the stomach to kill her. While this may be, in an overdetermined way, related to impregnation fantasies, it is also quite likely related to his wish to kill whatever was in his "mummy's" tummy, that is, get rid of his sibling. The second, related, piece of information is in the "sequel" to the consultation. Bob decides, one year after the consultation, to return to see Winnicott because "I would like to take my brother to see him" (p. 87). He then proceeds to have a "couples session" with Winnicott and his brother, and to take his brother on a complete tour of the four floors of Winnicott's house! I can't help but think that some sort of reparation fantasy, in which Bob returns to the "scene of the crime" (where, in fantasy, he killed off his brother), is occurring. By having his brother meet Winnicott and explore his home, he gets to "undo" the part of his aggressive fantasy of "doing in" his brother.

There is a short reference Winnicott makes in the middle of his consultation with Bob that leads me to a brief discussion of his (1949) paper titled "Birth Memories, Birth Trauma, and Anxiety." After Bob finishes drawing number eleven (a jet plane) and notes that he would not want to fly in one because it may go upside down, Winnicott notes:

> I seem to have asked at this point: "Do you remember being born?" He replied: "Well, that was a long time ago" (!). Then he added: "Mummy showed me where I did be a baby." I found out afterwards that his mother had recently taken him to see the house where he was born. (p. 72)

Although Winnicott doesn't seem to know where his question to Bob came from, his musing on the psychic significance of the birth process and the potential for children and adults to remember the birth process can be traced back to his "Birth Memories" paper and thus warrant some discussion in this context.

Winnicott believed that the relaxed, "good enough" mother is fully capable, in most circumstances, of being ready to engage her baby, whatever the baby's particular rhythms are. This allows the baby, over time, to balance engagement with the ability to be alone while counting on the mother's reliable presence. Thus a relaxed mother interacts with a relaxed, "going on being" baby to produce a healthy outcome. What this, now oft-repeated, equation lacks, however, is the answer to the question, at what point does this process begin? If we assume the mother is ready to begin this process on the right foot and is motivated to do so by her available "primary maternal preoccupation," it becomes more accurate to ask what is the circumstance, for the baby, that begins her orientation to the mother.

Strikingly enough, this orientation occurs in the context of a potentially severe break in "going on being," the birth process itself. If life in utero is so regular, we can state that in Winnicott's terms, the baby is free from having to "react." Yet the birth process is often, at least for a period of minutes or hours, a huge impingement on the baby's experience. The pressure on the baby's head through the birth canal, the shift in temperature once outside the mother, the change in sound, light, and so on in the hospital room all run the risk of forcing the baby to react to completely novel experiences he cannot assimilate. Because the baby's nascent ego has minimal capacities to mitigate any sort of external impingement, the neonate is at his most vulnerable and is most in need of a "holding environment." It is easy to think of the baby's first cry as the most dramatic rendition of this need to stop impingement, and indeed, a newborn's cry is qualitatively more shrill than even a several weeks' older baby, who has presumably begun to count on a reliable mother to be attuned to his needs. I am reminded of the obstetrician Frederick LeBoyer and his insistence on creating a birth process that most dramatically copied intrauterine life precisely because he wanted to avoid birth trauma in the Winnicottian sense. Although a good deal has been done in the average "first-world" hospital to make the birthing experience a less toxic atmosphere for mother and baby, we have by and large abandoned the briefly popular "LeBoyer method," a method Winnicott would certainly have championed.

In a completely different realm, I am also struck by the remarkable staying power that one particular painting, by an artist not particularly well known for his other works, has had for almost one hundred years. I am referring to the Norwegian painter Edvard Munch and his painting *The Scream*. While this scream comes from an adult in the painting, and can certainly speak to the utter, primal alienation generated by day-to-day adult life, is it not possible that it evokes the experience of our entry into the world?

It is almost a given that the vast majority of births, despite the existence of an initially screaming newborn, are benign events, in which the quickly swaddled, warmly held newborn is either awake and alert or fast asleep. But what if the birth experience is so noxious to the newborn that the break in his continuity of being, in the adept rhythms of intrauterine life, is too profound for the newborn, what if he is overwhelmed, and there is an insufficient reaction on the part of the surrounding adult(s) to quell the newborn's distress? Here birth trauma replaces birth experience. Winnicott begins to address this question in the following statement:

> We can postulate a certain state of mind of the unborn. I think we can say that things are going well if the personal development of the infant ego has been as undisturbed in its emotional as in its physical aspect. There is certainly before birth the beginning of an emotional development, and it is likely that there is before birth a capacity for false and unhealthy forward movement in emotional development; in health environmental disturbances of a certain degree are valuable stimuli, but beyond a certain degree these disturbances are unhelpful in that they bring about a reaction. At this very early stage of development there is not sufficient ego strength for there to be a reaction without loss of identity. (p. 182)

Winnicott is thus extending his concept of the need to avoid compliant reaction on the baby's part to the baby's experience in utero. He is suggesting that should any sort of environmental impingement on the baby occur at this time, there is nothing that the baby is equipped with that can counter this impingement. He goes on to note:

> As I see it, the trauma of birth is the break in the continuity of the infant's going on being. (p. 189)

While in health

the interference with the personal 'going along,' (is) not so powerful or so prolonged as to snap the thread of the infant's continuous personal process. (p. 183)

It is in this context that we can understand why Winnicott
asked Bob if he remembered being born. In part, perhaps, his asso-
ciative process was triggered by Bob's noting that he didn't like
planes going upside down, which may have reminded Winnicott of
the baby in the birth canal. Regardless of why Winnicott asked the
question, it is striking to note Bob's reaction. He concretely replies
"Well, that was a long time ago" and has no further associations, except to link his birth to the house where he grew up, as opposed to
anything having to do with the birth process. This is in keeping with
what we come to understand of the etiology of his difficulties and
of his having had a "good enough" experience with his mother until
roughly the beginning of his second year of life. The fact that his
first year of life was presumably "good enough" renders the question
meaningless on a deep emotional level to Bob, so that he can
blithely brush it off. Although, to be fair, the fact that his next two
drawings are of a fish and a boat might, with a bit of "wild analysis"
be linked to life in utero and going through the birth canal!

Bob's capacity to play the squiggle game, as we have seen, was
a significant benchmark in Winnicott's assessment of his condition.
The content of Bob's play, moreover, allowed Winnicott to help him
reintegrate earlier disruptive elements in his life. Having such ample data on its usefulness as diagnostic indicator and therapeutic
tool, we are ready to play directly with Winnicott's conceptions
about play.

Chapter Eight

The Meaning and Power of Play

Dilemma: How does learning to play enable life to proceed?

Articles reviewed: "Playing: A Theoretical Statement" (1962); "Group Influences and the Maladjusted Child" (1955); and "The Case of Hesta" in *Therapeutic Consultations in Child Psychiatry* (1971).

> *But there's things that will knock you down you don't even see coming*
> *And send you crawling like a baby back home . . .*
> *When you're alone you're alone*
> *When you're alone you ain't nothing but alone*

> Bruce Springsteen, "When You're Alone"

WE HAVE NOW COME TO THE POINT OF EXAMINING Winnicott's views on play. As we shall see below, Winnicott believes that the ability to play is the benchmark for the entrance into a life of health and vitality. All that goes right in child development leads to play, and play, in turn, allows every subsequent task and obstacle of the humanizing process to be accomplished. Without further ado, therefore, let's play with play.

In "Playing: A Theoretical Statement," Winnicott sets the stage for play in his conceptualizations. He notes:

> It is possible to describe a sequence of relationships related to the developmental process and to look and see where the playing belongs. A) Baby and object are merged in with one another. Baby's view of the object is subjective and the mother is oriented towards the making actual of what the baby is ready to find. B) The object is repudiated, re-accepted, and perceived objectively. This complex process is highly dependent on there being a mother or mother-figure prepared to participate and to give back what is handed out. This means that the mother (or part of mother) is in a 'to and fro' between being that which the baby has a capacity to find and (alternatively) being herself waiting to be found. If the mother can play this part over a length of time without admitting impediment (so to speak) then the baby has some experience of magical control, that is, experience of that which is called 'omnipotence' in the description of intrapsychic processes (cf. Winnicott, 1962). (p.47)

So far we are on familiar ground, the place where illusion and reality comingle so that the child can both generate omnipotence and cede it back to the world gradually. Winnicott continues:

> In this state of confidence that grows up when a mother can do this difficult thing well (not if she is unable to do it), the baby begins to enjoy experiences based on a 'marriage' of the omnipotence of intrapsychic processes with the baby's control of the actual. Confidence in the mother makes an intermediate playground here, where the idea of magic originates, since the baby does to some extent experience omnipotence. (p.47)

As the mother continues to be attuned enough in this way, the baby starts to feel increasingly confident. The baby feels that in fact she is the one magically having these fantasies of making mommy appear and reappear and do what she wants. Importantly, as the baby develops a sense of physical causation, there is a shift from "Mommy appears and it's a miracle," to "Mommy appears and it's my miracle, I'm creating this miracle." Now if the baby has experienced that control, that beginning capacity to feel life as play, it's wonderfully exciting.

Winnicott adds:

> Play is immensely exciting. It is exciting not primarily because the instincts are involved, be it understood! (p. 47)

Remember, for Winnicott, it's imperative that this is not about instinctual gratification. It's not that play is good because drives are being met. Play is good because the baby delights in the magical control, the omnipotent feelings, the incredible confidence he derives from his "magical" to-and-fro with his mother. Critically, the good-enough mother "gets it"; she goes along with the baby's illusory omnipotence, that he's pulling the strings.

Winnicott then shifts to what mother has to bring to the interaction for the capacity to play to germinate.

> The thing about playing is always the precariousness of the interplay of personal psychic reality and the experience of control of actual objects. This is the precariousness of magic itself, magic that arises in intimacy, in a relationship that is being found to be reliable. To be reliable the relationship is necessarily motivated by the mother's love, or her love-hate, or her object-relating, not by reaction-formations. (p. 47)

How can we understand this? The good-enough mother is not driven primarily by neurosis, but by her having enough healthy, creative space that she and the baby can play in that space primarily. She may have neurotic aspects, but for Winnicott, the definition of "good enough" is that the mother is primarily not driven by neurotic phenomena when it comes to her and her baby. And if the mother can avoid being "reaction-formation driven" in the first year of her baby's life, then she has helped create the foundation for living, the foundation for creativity, the foundation for play, the foundation for optimism, all of those things are there in that good-enough first year.

Winnicott now adds the capacity to be alone to the mixture that allows play to blossom.

> The next stage is being alone in the presence of someone. The child is now playing on the basis of the assumption that the person who loves and who is therefore reliable is available and continues to be available when remembered after being forgotten. This person is felt to reflect back what happens in the playing. (pp. 47–48)

These last two sentences reflect stunning progress in child development. The mother has been so reliable that the baby has developed the exquisite freedom to be able to concentrate on an activity for a few moments, knowing that when his mother returns to mind, she will be physically there as well. Even further, the mother will be there and able to reflect back to the infant a confirmation of what he had been doing while absent from the mother.

Critically, Winnicott then takes playing to an even more sublime level, past notions of concentration or creativity or optimism, by adding the following:

> The child is now ready for the next stage, which is to allow and to enjoy an overlap of two play areas. First, surely, it is the mother who plays with the baby, but she is rather careful to fit in with the baby's play activities. Sooner or later, however, she introduces her own playing, and she finds that babies vary according to their capacity to like or dislike the introduction of ideas that are not their own. Thus the way is paved for a playing together in a relationship. (p. 48)

Playing is therefore inherently object-related at one and the same time that it allows and ensures privacy; it is the milieu in which the baby discovers her True and hence utterly private Self and yet the means by which she engages others and develops rapport. It is the inherent duality of play, that it at once creates privacy yet counts on relatedness, that leads Winnicott to place play in a transitional third area, a place that is not inside by any use of the word. Nor is it outside, that is to say, it is not a part of the repudiated world, the not-me, that which the individual has decided to recognize (with whatever difficulty and even pain) as truly external, which is outside magical control. To control what is outside one has to do things, not simply to think or wish, and doing things takes time. Playing is doing. (p. 41)

Play is thus the prime medium by which this third, transitional play space is created and maintained. As we shall see in subsequent chapters, this transitional play space is then linked by Winnicott to the formations of culture, religion, art, and so on. Play is also about repetition; it is in the endless repetitions of play themes that

> the child gathers objects or phenomena from external reality and uses these in the service of some sample derived from inner or personal reality. Without hallucinating the child puts out a sample of dream potential and lives with this sample in a chosen setting of fragments from external reality. In playing, the child manipulates external phenomena in the service of the dream and invests chosen external phenomena with dream meaning and feeling. (p. 51)

Playing thereby allows the child to consistently work on the boundary between illusory omnipotence and helplessness and thus has at its essence the quest for mastery over the inner and outer chaotic (that is, not yet understood) aspects of its experience. The fact that the baby has internalized mother as a precursor to this process means that his play is always simultaneously related in an equally primary vein even while he hones selfhood.

Winnicott is also pointing out that playing is almost by definition a remarkably fragile phenomenon. Its precariousness is part of what makes it so precious. Therefore when he talks about the "relationship that is being found to be reliable," it is no accident that he uses active verb tenses there because the baby's finding that even if his mother breaks down a little bit, she is much more reliable than not. In a good situation the baby can count on mother to keep going, and if she keeps going "enough," the baby can tolerate it when she occasionally loses her focus or spirit.

At this point students often ask about how a mother "hangs in there" with the play of her child if it is too repetitive or boring and how the parent avoids puncturing the baby's capacity to play. I think the answer to that is really very much in the day-to-day living. To what extent is the mother's ending of a particular segment of play at all consistent with the baby's desire to play? So much of what is learned as a parent is how to make those transitions and how difficult they are. It makes me think immediately of what it is like to be a child therapist when the patient doesn't want to leave at the end of a session. These moments speak to how difficult it is to end the magic of play, to end the magic of relating, and for children who have had parents who have been experienced as unreliable, how frightening and/or depriving it is to end the therapy session. These children expect that the ending of the session will also not be reliably done, such that they won't get back to the pleasure of playing and the pleasure of relating. Ending a session easily is like "going gently into that good night"; it is surrendering, a false compliance. So the child not wanting to end is really a sign in child therapy of hope and a wish to continue the good object and a fear that the good object will not come back, that it is not going to be reliable enough. As Winnicott describes it, the very nature of child's play is such that

> to get to the idea of playing it is helpful to think of the *preoccu-pation* that characterizes the playing of a young child. The content does not matter. What matters is the near-withdrawal state, akin to the concentration of older children and adults. The playing child inhabits an area that cannot be easily left, nor can it easily admit intrusions. (p. 51)

Given this level of concentration, it is easy to understand why leaving a play therapy space, even with the highest-functioning of child patients, is no simple task.

In Winnicott's paper "Group Influences and the Maladjusted Child," he provides several key definitions of terms that expand our understanding of his conceptualizations of play. For example, in the

"Group Influences" paper, he gives perhaps his most direct definition of a False Self.

> If we look at the earlier stages of this process we see the infant very dependent on the mother's management, and on her continued presence and her survival. She must make a good-enough adaptation to the infant's needs, else the infant cannot avoid developing defenses that distort the process; for instance, the infant must take over the environmental function if the environment is not reliable, so that there is a hidden true self, and all that we can see is a false self engaged in the double task of hiding the true self and of complying with the demands that the world makes from moment to moment. (p. 147)

He then provides us with a similarly precise definition of *holding* and the functions it serves.

> Still earlier, the infant is held by the mother, and only understands love that is expressed in physical terms, that is to say, by live, human holding. Here is absolute dependence, and environmental failure at this very early stage cannot be defended against, except by a hold-up of the developmental process, and by infantile psychosis. (p. 147)

Here is the most clear explication of Winnicott's idea that the first way of being is the physical being, for it is in that literal holding that the baby feels like he or she will not fall forever and annihilation anxiety is quelled. We have thus arrived at a series of links in which play is both the ultimate outcome and the process whereby this outcome is attained: (1) physical holding and its resultant internalized state of reliability leads to (2) the creation of a core True Self, which leads to (3) the expression of this True Self through spontaneity which is repeated and held often enough so that (4) the capacity to play is established both with mother and without mother, leading to (5) the creation of an intermediate third place, not fully internal nor external, that is the further breeding ground for creativity, mastery, and aliveness.

We will conclude this chapter later on by tracing the linkage from holding to play through another consultation of Winnicott's,

"The Case of Hesta," a vivid clinical illustration of the power of play.
Before we turn to Hesta, however, there are several important
points to be further derived from his "Group Influences" paper that
both speak to the concept of play and set the stage for his consultation with Hesta. Winnicott notes that this linkage is established
through an integrative process.

> Of all that we find, that which chiefly concerns us here is that
> part of the process which we call integration. Before integration
> the individual is unorganized, a mere collection of sensory-motor
> phenomena, collected by the holding environment. After integra-
> tion the individual IS, that is to say, the infant human being has
> achieved unit status, can say I AM (except for not being able to
> talk). The individual now has a limiting membrane, so that what
> is not-he or not-she is repudiated, and is external. The he or the
> she has now an inside, and here can be collected memories of ex-
> periences, and can be built up the infinitely complex structure
> that belongs to the human being. (p. 148)

He adds one more necessary piece to this process.

> I suggest that this I AM moment is a raw moment; the new indi-
> vidual feels infinitely exposed. Only if someone has her arms
> round the infant at this time can the I AM moment be endured,
> or rather, perhaps, risked. (p. 148)

These two passages tell us that the creation of a "unit" takes
time and that the "I am" unit is utterly vulnerable, because the baby
has put its mother outside of himself. If the baby is not held sufficiently in that process, then he is going to be infinitely exposed.
What a great phrase that is, infinitely exposed, because that is truly
what it seems like. It is timeless, the baby is timelessly vulnerable,
and it is only in the holding that the baby feels that he can mitigate
and control that sense of time and space. It is in the being cradled
that space is contained, and when space is contained, time can be
contained. Babies tolerate time passing by virtue of the experience
of their space being contained by the holding functions of the parent. The baby can now wait (at least a little while) for things because she has an "I," and an "I" implies a holding environment. This
is where the capacity for delay begins: the baby is willing to risk

waiting because she feels like the "not me" is going to be reliable. This ability to delay and the confidence that creates it are really the absolute foundations of humanity, of humanness: if the baby can wait, then she begins to be convinced that space is not infinite and engulfing, and that time alone is not endless and overwhelming. She can thus afford to play, both alone and with others.

It should be clear that this feeling of being fully human is not ever fully complete, nor does it remain static in content over time. One could argue, moreover, that every phase of being, from cradle to grave, is really all about the recapitulation of this humanizing process as a balance between holding and being alone. When one is in one's early twenties, the content of this balance may be leaning heavily toward trying to find a mate who will be able to help create a holding environment. That time period is also organized around finding a "work self" that is fitting yet allows the retention of one's autonomy. When one becomes a parent, the task turns to holding this other being. In middle age, the worry shifts to one's longevity and adaptation to the aging process. So in so many ways we constantly replay at every stage of development this notion of the rawness of an "I am" moment.

If we combine the rawness of "I am" with Winnicott's notion of how we are first and fundamentally isolates, then saying "I am" is an affirmation reifying one's isolation and that is potentially terrifying. Thus, at the same time that the baby says "I am," she is also saying "I am alone." There is also implicit in that affirmation the desire to connect with someone else to ease somewhat the awfulness of that aloneness. The capacity to be alone thus implies the need for relatedness. To the extent that the baby can evoke treasured people in its play, and use the play to engage imaginatively with these people in interactions that explore every type of affect the baby knows, then the baby can tolerate the aloneness and indeed come to thrive despite—actually because of—its awareness. We can also say that the capacity to create symbols allows the child to cognitively "hold" her parent more easily, creating a salve to combat aloneness.

In this context, Winnicott adds the enigmatic sentence,

A group is an I am achievement, and it is a dangerous achievement. (p. 149)

How does this follow? Just before that sentence, he writes:

The newly integrated infant is, then, in the first group. (p. 149)

With integration, the baby comes to feel that she is not infinitely alone; thus by wonderful logic then the baby-mother form a group. So therefore the integrated infant has a self, and it has an other, and that self and other are the first group. Because the baby now has an inside and an outside, and the very notion of inside and outside implies group and nongroup identities, the "I am" moment is also the first group-achievement moment. At the same time, the ability to become integrated carries with it the ultimate danger. Before integration, as it were, the baby doesn't know what she is missing should disaster (loss) occur; she has no self to lose. But, conversely,

only after integration can we say that if the mother fails the infant dies of cold, or falls infinitely down, or flies off and away, or bursts like a hydrogen bomb and destroys the self and the world in one and the same moment. (p. 149)

Winnicott uses these utterly destructive metaphors because he wants to highlight the incredible fragility of the baby at this point in time. This allows him, by inference, to tell us of the profound perils in the inner lives of those adult psychotic patients he analyzed, who presumably had severe environmental failures at that perilous point in their infancies.

It is important to stress that simply being held to the point where an integrated True Self is established does not give the child a lifetime "free pass." At every phase of life where the "I am" question comes up, the child (adult) is essentially putting her integrated True Self to the test, and the more solid the True Self she has, the greater the repertoire of "holding experiences" and "I am" states the person has available to handle the next phase of "I am." But this still doesn't preclude catastrophe. The poignant lines in the Bruce Springsteen song quoted at the beginning of this chapter speak to the absence of a "free pass." At every phase in life you can get blindsided in your "I am" status in a manner that then puts one's level of integration, one's True Self, at risk. Think about healthy people who get kidnapped or put in concentration camps, or a hurricane that wipes out an entire family but one. This puts the concepts of a True Self and a holding environment face-to-face with the consequences of trauma.

Let us now put Winnicott's theoretical discussion of play and its relationship to integration in a clinical context. We take a look at his consultation with Hesta, a sixteen-year-old girl.

> Hesta, now 16, had been nervous since her first menstrual flow, which happened when she was 14. . . . She feared she was a lesbian. . . . At 16 she was acutely ill, with bizarre symptoms. There was a fear she would kill herself. She refused hospitalization. Nursed at home she gradually lost her generalized hostility and she became fat; it was felt that she was behaving as if she were 10 years old, making faces and talking to persons not present. The IQ had already been estimated at about 130. (pp. 176–77)

So this is clearly a very troubled person; this is not someone acting neurotically. Importantly, Winnicott begins his discussion of this troubled adolescent by noting:

> The work that the girl and I did together did not lead to a clearing up of her symptomatology. What did happen was that the parents and the family doctor, who was actively in charge of her case, felt that following the consultation they were now at last in a position to do what they felt they needed to do. They had been hampered previously by the girl's inability to accept the fact that she was ill. After the consultation she seemed to want, as well as to need, help. Hesta had now become able to let herself be an ill person. (p. 176)

In our present language, we would say that Winnicott helped Hesta shift from an ego-syntonic to an ego-alien position vis-à-vis her symptomatology. How does he help produce this shift?

He begins the consultation by meeting briefly with Hesta and her mother and adds:

> Hesta and her mother seemed friendly, and after a few minutes . . . the mother decided to go for a walk in the district. I was left then with a rather heavy 16-year-old girl, potentially hostile and a

bit dressed up, so that one felt she had been told to put on her best things because she was to see the doctor. (p. 177)

He has begun to paint a rather dismal picture and adds to it his mood.

It was a very hot day. I was in a mood just after my holidays in which I was reluctant to work; I let her know this and it seemed to suit her very well. (p. 177)

What I loved about this particular case is that from the start, he wasn't going to paint this lovely nice picture, full of reaction formations. She was fat, she was hostile, she was potentially obnoxious, and meanwhile her mother walks out and goes into town, leaving him stuck with this girl just after his holidays ended! And then he does this striking thing, he tells her of his mood! There he's saying to us how important it is to recognize where you are and to link that state of mind with what you feel the patient is bringing to the setting. By saying to Hesta right off the bat, I don't want to be here either, he immediately aligns himself with her state of mind. *"That seemed to suit her very well,"* he notes, so you can make an argument that at that moment they began therapy. Note that up to this point she "had been told to put on her best things because she was to see the doctor." This was going to be a belligerent, hostile act of False Self compliance that she was about to engage in. So what does he do? He essentially says, I don't want to be here either, it's a beautiful day, why am I stuck cooped up in here? This provides a dramatic True Self depiction, thereby inviting her to eventually speak in a less False Self way. It also allows him to set the diagnostic frame, for in this invitation to a more genuine mode of relating, he can assess whether she has that capacity and to what extent.

He begins with the squiggle game. Notably, her first verbalized comment is that her response "will take time" (p. 178) and she produces a mouse-dog. Winnicott notes:

It was significant that Hesta applied herself to the job, being interested and at ease in her relation to herself. She could work. (p. 178)

Winnicott is immediately impressed with her diagnostically. This gives him the fortitude to address head-on whether she could see her troubles in an acknowledged way. When she draws, in two phases (we'll return to this two-step process in a moment), a circle and a V-shape, he immediately makes them into a girl crying "Help." Although this turns whimsically into a discussion of the Beatles (the key line in the chorus of the song, "Help," being "Help me if you can, I'm feeling down!"), her use of whimsy in the face of this placing "Help" on the table, is again striking in regard to her state of mind prior to the consultation. He is already seeing many strengths in her, most especially the capacity to play.

These strengths are magnified in her third drawing. Winnicott describes the process as follows:

> She turned into a fish springing out of the sea. Eventually she labeled this Dancing Fish. This showed Hesta's capacity for creative imaginative play. She used some of the strength of my squiggle for giving strength to the fish. This drawing made me feel that Hesta had courage of the kind that would enable her, in the course of time, to use her instinctual experiences rather than to be scared of them. (p. 178)

How quickly he has developed a positive conception of her core being! We are reminded of his discussion of the ways in which instincts can be used to strengthen the ego if experienced in a holding environment. The fact that she could take his strong, "phallic" squiggle and add an even bolder "phallic" thrust to it gave him crucial diagnostic evidence of her potential not just to play, but to play to make herself stronger.

Next Winnicott begins to get a sense of the content of her concerns. She draws a squiggle and then finishes it herself, drawing a "sinister man." True to his word about not making interpretations to be "clever," and to his fundamental belief that the patient's getting to the interpretation is infinitely more useful than the therapist presenting it to the patient, he says nothing to Hesta about the potential "meanings" of this drawing. Allowing her to make a squiggle, he turns it into a telephone and notes:

> She and I were playing together and I felt we were at ease. I said at some point, as if we were a bit naughty, I expect mother thinks we are working! (p. 181)

This is a marvelous means of "joining" with Hesta, placing her mother with the rest of adults who want forced compliance and work, and aligning himself firmly with Hesta in their mutual enjoyment of the process of play. He thus acknowledges the primacy of play, as if by making this ego-syntonic, he can help "free" her to address what is ego-syntonic to her in terms of symptomatology. She seems readily to acknowledge this playfulness, as she continues with her theme of drawings of men, but this time makes the man into

> a rugger [rugby] man with freckles, later she added American. She was persevering with the idea of a man, this time allowing comicality and derision. (p. 181)

The "sinister" man who might make her comply has been turned into a comical, foreign, athletic, freckled American. Her "freed-up" drawing emboldens him to take on the question of male-ness vs. femaleness directly, as he asked her

> whether she would have chosen to have been a boy or a girl and she seemed to know the problem, and talked about it rather philosophically . . . and this left open the idea of fantasy and she said to me: which would you rather have been? (p. 181)

She is now showing Winnicott the capacity for fantasy in words as well as playfulness in drawings and makes clear to him that she has thought about her gender identity. In their next two drawings, a baby dinosaur with a large, phallic tail and Jack and the Beanstalk with a large, phallic snout, she is clearly depicting the power of a phallus and doing so in a creative way. Although Winnicott again makes no interpretation to her, he appears convinced that speaking directly to the issue of men and women and what they might do together is of paramount importance and so he startlingly takes her two-part squiggle and draws a very passionate embrace of a boy and a girl. Hesta thought "this 'very good' and at the end labeled it "Tango" (p. 182). This must have represented a stunning achievement by Hesta to Winnicott. He supplies an openly sexualized drawing and she not only can acknowledge it, she can enjoy it and give it a supremely sublimated title that completely fits the drawing on many levels. He must have, by this time, become convinced that there was enormous potential for Hesta to take on the tasks of adolescence. He notes:

> It could be said that my theme was a kind of interpretation, an observation on the two-part nature of her squiggle. (p. 184)

It is useful to speak directly here once again about how to define an interpretation for Winnicott. It goes back to the nature and meaning of play. Play is meaningful precisely because it is an original production of the child or a spontaneous duality between two partners. It does not have a specific end goal, nor is it a means of conformity or compliance. It is bound to the need for surprise and mastery and can thus be potentially frightening as well as potentially satisfying. Interpretation from the therapist, if it is in a directed, forced form, is thus the obverse of play. Winnicott therefore may present themes for Hesta to play with, which can shape her play in the direction of conflicts he wants to see if she can address, but he will leave the meaning-making to her, so that it remains *her* play, thus respecting her boundaries and her True Self.

This respect and appreciation of her integrity led Hesta to her most remarkable drawing. Winnicott made a squiggle and she

> knew immediately what she wanted to do with this and she turned it into a schoolgirl with a hat. Eventually she said that it might be herself, and when I looked at it I could see that it was a rather good self-portrait. I was astonished at the way in which together somehow or other we had achieved a portrait of this girl. (p. 184)

I have never seen Winnicott use the word "astonished" in any other paper, and given his precise use of language, it is notable. Winnicott is convinced, after ten drawings in a squiggle game, that Hesta has come to find the beginnings of herself. She has put the play of male vs. female to great use, enabling her to come to a self-portrait that she finds acceptable and he sees as accurate, so that her self-acceptance seems solid and genuine. This leads us back to a telling diagnostic phrase used to describe her by her family doctor:

> It felt like she was behaving as if she were 10 years old. (p. 177)

In other words, she was incapable or refusing to take on the tasks of gender consolidation of adolescence. With her self-portrait with a hat, Winnicott now felt that she had the potential to do so; indeed, he notes:

> At this point I felt myself becoming convinced of Hesta's capacity to accept puberty and to grow to be an adult woman. (p. 185)

He even sees her as physically different from what others have depicted her as. Where once she was "fat," now he notes:

> There was a link between these curves (in her drawings) and the curves of her own body, taking into consideration the fact that she is very large and plump and yet not really fat. I felt she was aware of her physical self in a quite natural way and in a way that indicated self-acceptance. (p. 185)

Having come to see Hesta's gender identity concerns as part of a two-phase struggle, (one phase referring to early mother-child difficulties and the other to Oedipal concerns), and having seen this two-part struggle reflected in her drawings, Winnicott sought to address this concern with "two-ness" more directly. Fortuitously, as he paused before responding to Hesta's squiggle in drawing eleven, she created a rule.

> If you can't make the other person's squiggle into something you challenge them and it is up to them to make it into something. So I challenged her and she made this two-phase squiggle of hers into a person with a child in a canoe. The person is obviously happy but the child is indifferent. (p. 186)

Winnicott takes this drawing in two directions. First, he links it to Hesta's relationship with her mother, the mother being happy while her child is "left out and alone." But second, he views her frustration with his pausing to draw as a reenactment of her reaction to her mother's detachment, so that she is the happy person in the canoe and Winnicott is the lonely observer. She is eager to continue to play with Winnicott, and he then links her play with psychotherapy.

> Here are conditions to which I have referred in my paper on Playing, in which I claim that psychotherapy is done in the area of overlap between the playing of the patient and the playing of the therapist. (p. 187)

Thus playing takes on an even more exalted status for Winnicott in that its very existence is the milieu where treatment occurs, so that without the capacity for play (for both parties) therapy cannot occur.

Winnicott's willingness to play with Hesta allows her next drawings to speak even more directly to her concerns about her adequacy to be a woman. She turns the next drawing (of her own squiggle) into a woman drying herself off at the very beach where Winnicott had just returned from holiday. Her being pleased with her "Lady at Plymouth" suggests both an attempt to take on the role of a sexual woman and her attempt to take on this role vis-à-vis Winnicott himself, as we can assume that at some level, she was drying "herself" in relation to Winnnicott watching her at this beach.

Her next two drawings speak further to her addressing her sexual concerns. One involves Harpo Marx, whose "dumbness" Winnicott suggests may be an identification Hesta adopts as a means of communicating to him the

> remnants of her sense of inadequacy at the phallic phase, a trouble with school which had also showed up in her school work in spite of her superior intelligence. (p. 188)

The next drawing, they both left as unfinished and labeled as male and female "principles," her most direct rendering of her sexual/physical concerns. The fact that they could both acknowledge these and let them be speaks to a further acceptance by Hesta of her need to work on the sexual issues stirred up by adolescence and her pathological decision to stay stuck in a time before these struggles begin (ten years of age). This takes her to the need to end the time with Winnicott, so she draws a clock and he acknowledges after this "hint" that they have time for one final drawing.

She is notably stuck with what to draw, creating a final problem with a choice between "two" here noting that it could either be a camel or a Negro lady. Not wanting to choose she draws a third choice, a "hippopotamus puppy." Winnicott sees this third alternative as indicative of two possibilities:

> In one sense she had solved the problem by producing a baby. In another sense she had avoided the problem by grasping at a distraction. (p. 192)

Winnicott thus leaves this consultation with the feeling that she now clearly has a path ahead of her that allows for the prospect of solution (she will have children, "two or four," she says) and thus an addressing of her problem. At the same time he is letting us know that she may still choose avoidance if not properly helped through the adolescent passage. He does note at his follow-up that Hesta returns to see him "on demand" six times over the next year and that, although much improved, she still wrestles with a "manageable depression" as her chief clinical feature.

One last point may serve as an "appetizer" to a more thorough discussion of his technique in our final chapters. Winnicott subtly shows his clinical savvy at the very end of the first interview with Hesta. Knowing full well the transferential importance of Winnicott choosing Hesta over her mother, he makes a striking tactical decision as he and Hesta part company. He writes:

> She rather expected me to see her mother and she was very relieved when I said that I was going to tell her mother that I did not want to see her. I said: Of course I can hear mother's point of view and it will be very different from yours, but at the moment I am interested in your point of view. (p. 192)

Having thus validated Hesta's primacy, Winnicott makes a last gesture, complimenting Hesta's mother on the necklace she was wearing. As he puts it,

And so we parted with mother perhaps feeling she had had some personal attention from myself, although she would have to wait before my being able to give her a personal interview. (p. 192)

Having "taken care" of both women, the work proceeded smoothly over time, and so we can leave Hesta and move on to the next chapter and its theoretical and clinical concerns.

Chapter Nine

―――――――――○―――――――――

The Mind, the Body, and the World of Traditional Phenomena

Dilemma: The search for an intermediate area of experience as the centerpiece of Winnicott's work.

Articles reviewed: "Mind and Its Relation to the Psyche-Soma" (1949), "Transitional Objects and Transitional Phenomena" (1958), and "The Location of Cultural Experience" (1967).

One day, they run into a little girl in tears. sobbing her heart out. Kafka asks her what's wrong, and she tells him that she's lost her doll. He immediately starts inventing a story to explain what happened. "Your doll has gone off on a trip," he says. "How do you know that?" the girl asks. "Because she's written me a letter," Kafka says. The girl seems suspicious. "Do you have it on you?" she asks. "No, I'm sorry," he says. "I left it at home by mistake, but I'll bring it along with me tomorrow." He's so convincing, the girl doesn't know what to think anymore. Can it be possible that this mysterious man is telling the truth?

Kafka goes straight home to write the letter. He sits down at his desk, and as Dora watches him write, she notices the same seriousness and tension he displays when composing his own work. He isn't about to cheat the little girl. This is a real literary labor, and he's determined to get it right. If he can come up with a beautiful and persuasive lie, it will

supplant the girl's loss with a different reality—a false one,
maybe, but something true and believable according to the
laws of fiction.

Paul Auster, *The Brooklyn Follies*

PAUL AUSTER'S INVENTION OF A MOMENT in the last months of the
life of Franz Kafka accurately portrays a child's grief and restitution.
The little girl's loss of her treasured doll is devastating. Only a story
created with the deepest seriousness and hence presumably the
fullest empathy can mitigate this loss. It is a story of invention and
creative reparation, and it works. It also provides a perfect segue
into the crucial importance of the transitional object in the developmental process and into a discussion of two of Winnicott's central works. The first, "Mind and Its Relation to the Psyche-Soma,"
is a truly masterful work both in its synthesis of most of his major
conceptions and in its consideration of the mind-body dilemma
from his unique perspective. The second, "Transitional Objects and
Transitional Phenomena," provides a systematic depiction of his
most well-known and perhaps most original concept and connects
it to the rest of his theorizing.

Let's begin with his "Mind" paper, as it fills in an important gap
in his conception of the baby. Winnicott begins:

> The body scheme with its temporal and spatial aspects provides
> a valuable statement of the individual's diagram of himself, and in
> it I believe there is no obvious place for the mind. Yet in clinical
> practice we do meet with the mind as an entity localized some-
> where by the patient; a further study of the paradox that 'mind
> does not really exist as an entity' is therefore necessary. (p. 243)

Where does our thinking take place? If we go back to Piaget's in-
terviews with children in the preoperational period, it is striking to
see how children answer this question. They believe, indeed insist,
that ideas come from outside or at best from somewhere in their
heads where they exist in a preformed way, as if they were physical
objects. In this scheme, there is thus no need for the child under six
to have a concept of mind. He would take them a step further and
suggest that not needing a mind is the essence of mental health in

the child. Adults, by contrast, whether mentally healthy or not, do need to believe in the existence of their minds and would be horrified to be deprived, even theoretically, of this sacred arena. This paradox is therefore the subject of the first part of this chapter.

Interestingly, Winnicott has already given us a number of hints as to how he will address this paradox. We have seen how we come to exist in space and time. Our first location in space is the development of what Winnicott calls "me" and "not me." This boundary, arising in roughly the second six months of life, brings with it our first awareness that the world is not simply an extension of the mind or the body. We exist in time in a similar manner; as our needs are not met instantaneously but come to be met in a "good enough" period of time, our fledgling capacity to wait and to delay creates a sense of time. This is true only if we do not have to wait too long. At various points in his writings, Winnicott describes the role id, ego, and superego take vis-à-vis time. The id's instinctual urges know no time; if we are hungry, for example, the urge is increasingly timeless and overpowering. The superego (a later developmental construct and thus not high on Winnicott's priority list) is equally relentless and timeless, as we can never do enough quickly enough to satisfy it. Finally, the ego and its defenses construct parameters in space and time to strengthen our capacity to tolerate our urges and recriminations.

So what does Winnicott add to this discussion in his "Mind" paper? He seeks to provide a model of health in which the mind plays no consequential role.

> The mind does not exist as an entity in the individual's scheme of things provided the individual psyche-soma or body scheme has come satisfactorily through the very early developmental stages; mind is then no more than a special case of the functioning of the psyche-soma. (p. 244)

For Winnicott, as we have seen, health is defined as the capacity for "going on being," for being in the moment and not experiencing the world in a reactive, self-conscious way. The "good enough" mother's attentiveness allows the baby to exist in his body, attuning to psyche (thought) and soma (body) in a way that creates a hyphenated, conjoint, seamless entity without a mind getting in the way. It is the reactive focus on mother's "moods" that forces the child to experience pockets of being outside of his initiative, creating a place outside of his psyche and soma that must be attended to.

Winnicott goes on to suggest that we must look first at the pathological forms of mind formation.

> In the study of the developing individual the mind will often be found to be developing a false entity, and a false localization. A study of these abnormal tendencies must precede the more direct examination of the mind-specialization of the healthy or normal psyche. (p. 244)

He then attempts to re-create his theory of the developing baby, this time by describing how a longed-for sense of aliveness is located and made permanent.

> Let us attempt, therefore, to think of the developing individual, starting at the beginning. Here is a body, and the psyche and the soma are not to be distinguished except according to the direction from which one is looking. One can look at the developing body or the developing psyche. I suppose the word psyche here means the imaginative elaboration of somatic parts, feelings, and functions, that is, of physical aliveness. We know that this imaginative elaboration is dependent on the existence and the healthy functioning of the brain, especially certain parts of it. The psyche is not, however, felt by the individual to be localized in the brain, or indeed to be localized anywhere. (p. 244)

This is akin to Hoffer's (1949) notion that the first ego is a body ego. The psyche, the mental apparatus, is therefore a collection and reflection of bodily states. Winnicott breaks new ground in creating a "theory of mind" by describing what must occur to ensure the baby's body ego and what can go wrong in the mother-baby interaction to obscure and distort this body ego. He writes:

> Let us assume that health in the early development of the individual entails *continuity of being*. The early psyche-soma proceeds

along a certain line of development provided its continuity of being is not disturbed; in other words, for the healthy development of the early psyche-soma there is a need for a perfect environment. At first the need is absolute. (p. 245)

This is the only place in his writings where Winnicott describes the mother's (environment's) need to be perfect as opposed to "good enough." This may be his way of emphasizing the absolute needs of the baby in the first hours after birth, but it is striking nonetheless. He mitigates this need for perfection, however, in the very next paragraph, as he states:

The perfect environment is one which actively adapts to the needs of the newly formed psyche-soma, that which we as observers know to be the infant at the start. A bad environment is bad because by failure to adapt it becomes an impingement to which the psyche-soma (i.e., the infant) must react. (p. 245)

Thus Winnicott implies a two-stage process for the mother: at first she must carry the entire burden for the baby, as his needs are absolute and resources negligible. In a sense, he is merely restating the enormous role he places on the facilitating environment, except that here he is speaking most directly to the bodily needs of the newborn, before the newborn has even become a baby. It is as if he is creating a "sensitive period" in the biological sense, in which absolute maternal adaptation is necessary if the newborn is to begin down the path of feeling her continuity and aliveness. The second stage is when the newborn has become a baby and the "good enough" mother concept emerges. He spells this out clearly in the following passage:

In its beginnings the good (psychological) environment is a physical one, with the child in the womb or being held and gradually tended; only in the course of time does the environment develop a new characteristic which necessitates a new descriptive term, such as emotional or psychological or social. Out of this emerges the ordinary good mother with her ability to make active adaptation to her infant's needs arising out of her devotion, made possible by her narcissism, her imagination and her memories, which enable her to know through identification what are her baby's needs. (p. 245)

Why does he suddenly make this distinction between perfect vs. good-enough mothering? It is in the very next paragraph that we get the clarity we need to address the question. He writes:

The need for a good environment, which is absolute at first, rapidly becomes relative. The ordinary good mother is good enough. If she is good enough the infant becomes able to allow for her deficiencies by mental activity. . . . The mental activity of the infant turns a good-enough environment into a perfect environment, that is to say, turns relative failure of adaptation into adaptive success. What releases the mother from her need to be near-perfect is the infant's understanding. (p. 245)

This is a powerful statement. Here is the delicate balance: the infant's mental activity (to use Winnicott's exquisite phraseology, the infant's understanding) is precisely what is necessary to make the mother-baby dyad work, yet if this activity is initiated too soon or too pervasively, it quickly becomes an impingement on the baby and places his eventual psychology at great risk. Let me return to the Kafka vignette with which I opened this chapter. It is in Kafka's (as told by Auster) ability to replace the girl's lost doll by a story that gives the doll a new life that we see the process by which an induced mental activity by the mother (Kafka) into the baby (the girl) provides the continuity of being that allows the girl to survive the "deficiencies" of life and make the environment "perfect." Winnicott's depiction of this shift from near-perfection on the mother's part to an interactive dyad in which attunement, misattunement, and reparation is the order of the day also provides the conceptual paradigm that has been replicated in countless research endeavors on the dance between mother and baby (cf. Tronick, Stern, Gergely et al.).

Winnicott then makes a point of establishing even greater room for the mother to "fail" her growing infant by inexact adaptation, indeed establishing these "failures" as the paradigm for good-enough parenting.

In infant care it is vitally important that mothers, at first physically, and soon also imaginatively, can start off by supplying this
active adaptation, but also it is a characteristic maternal function
to provide graduated failure of adaptation, according to the growing ability of the individual infant to allow for relative failure by
mental activity or by understanding. Thus there appears in the infant a tolerance in respect of both ego need and instinctual tension. (p. 246)

This is Winnicott's most explicit reference to the competent infant who can, *in health,* use her mental activity and capacity for delay to help the mother remain "good enough." This is a crucial, if
relatively underemphasized aspect of his theorizing, for without
such an explicit reference to the baby's healthy competence, we are
left with a theory with too great a reliance on the attuned mother
for enabling the baby's aliveness to thrive. He returns quickly (too
quickly for my tastes) to pathology, however, and makes the following explicit declaration of how maternal failures specifically create
a mind-body split in the infant. He notes:

Certain kinds of failure on the part of the mother, especially erratic behavior, produce over-activity of the mental functioning.
Here, in the overgrowth of the mental function reactive to erratic
mothering, we see that there can develop an opposition between
the mind and the psyche-soma, since in reaction to this abnormal
environmental state the thinking of the individual begins to take
over and organize the caring for the psyche-soma, whereas in
health it is the function of the environment to do so. In health the
mind does not usurp the environment's function, but makes possible an understanding and eventually a making use of its relative
failure. (p. 246)

This is the crux of this paper. The overly impinged-upon baby
must use his mind to avoid the loss of his mother and to "recapture"
her. This mental activity is too pervasive and too premature for the
infant to tolerate seamlessly. He therefore becomes a thinker, creating a split between "going on being" and that relaxed, vibrant state
of mind, and a "mood forecaster" having to be preoccupied with his
mother's state of mind. This is reminiscent of Winnicott's writing on

the creation of a False Self from chapter 4. The split between mind and psyche-soma thus becomes another way of his equating the psyche-soma with the beginnings of the True Self and the overly precocious mind with the False Self. Although at times he speaks to differing cognitive endowments as playing a role in the ease with which a mother's mood can be forecast, Winnicott for the most part views precocious mind development as an impediment to health. It is interesting to note the parallel between the exalted status he places on "going on being" and a similar priority he gives to the therapist who can be in the moment with his or her patient. Conversely, he places the overly precocious baby in the same category as the overly "clever" therapist, whose interpretations strip the patient of autonomy in much the same way an overly moody mother strips her baby of its aliveness. I will discuss this parallel more fully in the final chapters on transference and countertransference.

Winnicott then takes the paradigm of excessive mind functioning to the next level. He writes:

> To go a stage further, one might ask what happens if the strain that is put on mental functioning organized in defense against a tantalizing early environment is greater and greater? One would expect confusional states, and in the extreme, mental defect of the kind that is not dependent on brain-tissue deficiency. As a more common result of the lesser degrees of tantalizing infant care in the earliest stages we find mental functioning becoming a thing in itself, practically replacing the good mother and making her unnecessary. . . . This is a most uncomfortable state of affairs, especially because the psyche of the individual gets 'seduced' away into this mind from the intimate relationship which the psyche originally had with the soma. The result is a mind-psyche, which is pathological. (pp. 246–47)

This passage places the cases of Bob and Hesta in a clearer light. Bob can now be seen as an example of the confusional states and "mental defect" development he describes earlier in the passage. Hesta is a prime example of the latter part of the passage, where her experience of her body as an emerging woman was "seduced" away from her psyche, resulting in a girl arrested in a preadolescent, underachieving state.

Winnicott presents one final clinical variation on his theme of the pathology that arises from the premature splitting of psyche and soma. He describes a person who turns this splitting into an over-identification with those who provide care to those with primitive needs. For short, intense periods of time, such persons can be almost magical in the intensity with which they can provide help to people they perceive as in need. It is not coincidental that he uses the word magical to describe these people, as they are viewed as attempting to resurrect the magical behavior of the mother in earliest interaction with her young infant.

> The falsity of these patterns for expression of the personality, however, becomes evident in practice. Breakdown threatens or occurs, because what the individual is all the time needing is to find someone else who will make real this 'good environment' concept, so that the individual may return to the dependent psyche-soma which forms the only place to live from. In this case, 'without mind' becomes a desired state. (p. 247)

This is a most telling, even provocative passage. Its implications for a variety of clinical states are noteworthy. Certainly many "borderline" and severe narcissistic conditions would fall into this category, and the resulting patient rage or numbness in a session when the patient's primitive needs are not met is a common, painful occurrence. It also makes me think of the sometimes unerring accuracy of Tarot card or "palm" readers, in their almost magical, intense, time-limited capacity to meet their clients' needs and wishes. In its most provocative aspect, the qualities he describes above may also be very apt for the therapist who can be "magically" available to his or her patients, as long as the forty-five-minute session is the maximum amount of time the therapist needs to be with them. Such persons, across all three categories, presumably feel quickly depleted by the amount of "reading" of the other that goes along with their intense attunement capabilities. If persons with this kind of fragility and "magical" attunement don't quickly get back the requisite amount of praise or allegiance expected, their depletion becomes manifest, and withdrawal or rage is the only option, again much like that of the infant's behavior they are replicating in an adult format.

I am particularly struck in this context by the role chronic boredom may play in such persons. Boredom at such moments is the "without mind" state Winnicott alludes to in the above passage. The underlying anxiety, rage, and/or confusion must be wiped away, and the edgy boredom that results can be quite blatantly indicative of an inner deadness and emptiness. On a less pathological level, I am struck by how often the complaint of "I'm bored" from a preschool or latency-aged child has little to do with a lack of activity choices and far more to do with a lack of connection to a parenting figure. This is why merely giving a child in that state a list of possibilities often has little effect but offering to engage in an activity with the child produces positive results. The child is missing the person and feeling his or her absence, so that the joint activity re-creates in the child the feeling of being "held," and the boredom usually vanishes.

TRANSITIONAL OBJECTS AND TRANSITIONAL PHENOMENA

Up until this point, Winnicott has presented us with a series of dualities: True vs. False Selves; "good enough" mothering vs. not good-enough mothering; psyche-soma or mind-psyche; communicating or not communicating; illusion or reality. We are now ready to stretch his paradigm to a third, intermediate area to present what most in our field consider Winnicott's most original and valued contributions—the concepts of transitional objects and transitional phenomena. He begins:

> It is well known that infants as soon as they are born tend to use fist, fingers, thumbs in stimulation of the oral erotogenic zone, in satisfaction of the instincts at that zone, and also in quiet union. It is also well known that after a few months infants of either sex become fond of playing with dolls, and that most mothers allow their infants some special object and expect them to become, as it were, addicted to such objects. There is a relationship between these two sets of phenomena that are separated by a time interval, and a study of the development from the earlier into the later

can be profitable, and make use of important clinical material that has been somewhat neglected. (p. 1)

In describing the "relationship between these two sets of phenomena," Winncott is perhaps at his most poetic. He writes:

I have introduced the terms 'transitional objects' and 'transitional phenomena' for designation of the intermediate area of experience, between the thumb and the teddy bear, between oral erotism and the true object-relationshp, between primary creative activity and projection of what has already been introjected, between primary unawareness of indebtedness and the acknowledgement of indebtedness. (p. 2)

Having defined these phenomena as inhabiting an intermediate arena, he goes on to establish their necessity in a theory of development, first vis-à-vis drive theory.

It is generally acknowledged that a statement of human nature in terms of interpersonal relationships is not good enough even when the imaginative elaboration of function and the whole of fantasy both conscious and unconscious, including the repressed unconscious are allowed for. (p. 2)

He then questions whether object relations (notably Kleinian) theory can stand alone without this intermediate arena.

There is another way of describing persons that comes out of the researches of the last two decades. Of every individual who has reached to the stage of being a unit with a limiting membrane and an outside and an inside, it can be said that there is an inner reality to that individual, an inner world that can be rich or poor and can be at peace or in a state of war. This helps, but is it enough? (p. 2)

If we are more than a tripartite model of consciousness, and more than a self in relation to the world, what else is needed to fully depict the human experience? Winnicott answers this confidently.

My claim is that if there is a need for this double statement, there is also a need for a triple one: the third part of the life of a human being, a part that we cannot ignore, is an intermediate area of **experiencing**, to which inner reality and external life both contribute. (p. 2)

I boldface the word experiencing because I want to stress its distinctness from experience. Winnicott uses a verb form because he is stressing the need for a phenomenological approach and emphasizing the dynamism inherent in living. The intermediate arena is always "on," engaged "in the perpetual human task of keeping inner and outer reality separate but interrelated" (p. 2). If we think back to high-school mathematics, Winnicott's model is akin to a Venn diagram, in which the overlap of the two spheres of inner and outer reality is the arena for transitional phenomena. The overlap is simultaneously part of and yet distinct from the two worlds it is made up of.

It is important here to stress the distinction between a transitional object and transitional phenomena. While I will trace Winnicott's history of how the first possession of the infant, its transitional object, occurs in a moment, it is useful to speak to how omnipresent the transitional phenomena are in adult life. Are some forms of obsessive-compulsive disorder a form of transitional phenomena gone amok? Does the adult find a "soother" in a given ritualistic behavior and then become stuck endlessly repeating it? When I teach, I'm often struck by how students typically take the same seats for each lecture, as if these seats have become part of their creating a comfort zone in which to take the class. Here's yet another example. There's a basketball program I'm involved in that has a large number of children from the third and fourth grade, so the players are eight or nine years old. At any tense moment during a game, when they're feeling the least mature and most vulnerable, you can see a good number of these children resort to transitional phenomena. At the finish of a very close game, for example, I noticed one of the leading players had placed the top of his T-shirt in his mouth while he was guarding his opponent! Now, much as with a much younger child, if you had stopped the game and said, "Stop chewing on your shirt," the child would have been mortified. I don't think in a million years he was aware that he was sucking his shirt. A little later in the game, you can see that he's calmer, his shirt is all the way down, and he's just playing.

I am struck, on a related plane, by the ubiquitous phenomenon in the United States of the sports fan who constantly wears memorabilia to connect to his favorite team or who screams in anguished passion at the television set, berating a coach or player. That fan is convinced on some level that the coach or player can hear him in his impassioned pleas or exhortations, much like a preschooler can believe that his play characters are real or that the boy with his "Velveteen Rabbit" in chapter 4 can "know" that his favorite rabbit is real. As Winnicott puts it:

> It is usual to refer to 'reality testing' and to make a clear distinction between apperception and perception. I am here staking a claim for an intermediate state between a baby's inability and his growing ability to recognize and accept reality. I am therefore studying the substance of illusion, that which is allowed to the infant, and which in adult life is inherent in art and religion, and yet becomes the hallmark of madness when an adult puts too powerful a claim on the credulity of others, forcing them to acknowledge a sharing of illusion that is not their own. (p. 3)

To take his point about the "hallmark of madness" to an absurd level, while the sports fan screaming at the coach through his television set may provoke our amusement or even compassion, should the fan state that he in fact believes that the coach both heard him and responded, we would quickly change our tune and think our fan quite mad!

What he is also saying is far more central to the creation and meaning of transitional phenomena. A transitional phenomenon predates established reality testing because if the child were already fully established in her reality testing, then she would know the object could not fully replace her mother and she wouldn't create it in the first place. Once reality testing is solidified, however, one cannot give an object these special transitional powers without deep confusion in the child. If a five-year-old who didn't yet have a transitional object was really upset and someone said to him, *Here, would you like this blanket? This blanket will help you feel better,* the child would look at that person as if he were crazy! It simply would not work. The child's reality testing is too solidly developed (and he had not previously "created" that blanket at a time before his reality testing was firmly established) so that he would know that the blanket is not the same thing as a comforting person. But if you took a five-year-old in the same situation who had had a transitional object but had not been playing with it for a period of time, I think the five-year-old would suddenly remember and say to itself, *Oh I'm going to go find my blanket,* and hold on to it in a way that he might not have done for a year or two or three because one can go back to this feeling of created safety with impunity.

Once again, these ideas create a vibrant dialectic; transitional phenomena arise when things are for the most part illusion and magical, and yet simultaneously they come from the reality that the baby needs something that is concrete and visceral that she can create. Importantly, the transitional object is a multisensory experience and the more sensory modalities it employs, the more real it is, the more useful it is. The fact that it feels a certain way that is soft and nice, that it smells a certain way, the way it feels when held against the baby's body, all of these multisensory components excite more memory centers in the' brain, making it more useful as a replacement for mother.

How does the first form of transitional phenomenon, the transitional object, develop? Winnicott describes a pattern where the nursing or thumb-sucking baby begins by "accidentally" taking a bit of sheet or blanket that gets held and/or sucked as part of its self-comforting behavior. This early behavior, including vocalizations, are all things he puts under the rubric of transitional phenomena. He then defines the birth of a transitional object as follows:

> Also, out of all this there may emerge some thing or some phenomenon—perhaps a bundle of wool or the corner of a blanket or eiderdown, or a word or tune, or a mannerism—that becomes vitally important to the infant to use at the time of going to sleep, and is a defense against anxiety, especially anxiety of the depressive type. Perhaps some soft object or other type of object

has been found and used by the infant and this then becomes
what I am calling a transitional object. The object goes on being
important. The parents get to know its value and carry it around
when traveling. (p. 4)

His linking the use of the object to a defense against depressive-
type anxiety is not unimportant. Depressive-type anxiety refers to
the fact that the child has reached the place in development where
she is a "unit" and thus must deal with the specific loss created by
the unavailability of the "not me" unit, i.e., her mother. The creation
of the transitional object is thus first and foremost a reparation, an
ego-related attempt to maintain continuity of being through the
substitution of the special object for the mothering person. It is
therefore given a wide range of time in which it begins to show up
(four to twelve months), but this wide range assumes the capacity
to become a unit. Without that capacity, the infant could not be
purposeful in creating an object from outside himself (he would
have no experience of an outside distinct from an inside in the "pre-
unit" stage) to use to cope with an inner distress.

Winnicott lists seven essential qualities of the relationship between the baby and her transitional object. I will list these qualities
and speak to underlying themes implicit in each statement.

1. The infant assumes rights over the object, and we agree to this
   assumption. Nevertheless, some abrogation of omnipotence is
   a feature from the start. (p. 5)

Winnicott notes quite ardently that it is clear that no one
should challenge the infant (or older child) as to the "realness" of
the object. Indeed, it would be an act of sadism to try and press the
child to give up the illusory aspects of this precious creation.
Nonetheless, the fact that the child has created it implies that he is
separate from his caretaker, knows on some level that he is separate, and that the taking of the object is "proof" of his loss of magical control and omnipotence.

2. The object is affectionately cuddled as well as excitedly loved
   and mutilated. (p. 5)

This brief sentence speaks volumes about Winnicott's inclusion of drive theory (excitedly loved), Kleinian theory (mutilated), and his own theory (cuddled) into a hybrid integration of the actual experience of the baby. In keeping with his poetic expressiveness, he is the master of the understatement as well.

> 3. It must never change, unless changed by the infant. (p. 5)

Because the primary function of the object is to maintain continuity of being, it follows that it should only be changed, if at all, by the baby herself. This is partly why its tactile, olfactory, or visual aspects should not be suddenly shifted. Often the baby uses the object in a particular way or with a particular posture, and the repetition of this pattern should also never be challenged as it is part of the transitional phenomena that can exist alongside the transitional object itself.

> 4. It must survive instinctual loving, and also hating and, if it be a feature, pure aggression. (p. 5)

This is really the result of the behavior stated in point two. The object must be durable enough to survive, at least in part. Nearly everyone who has had any experience of a transitional object, whether her own or someone else's, knows that the object often slowly erodes away from constant use. As long as even a fragment of cloth or worn toy remains, however, it maintains its salience and vitality to the child.

> 5. Yet it must seem to the infant to give warmth, or to move, or to have texture, or to do something that seems to show it has vitality or reality of its own. (p. 5)

The object, because it is a substitute for the aliveness of the mother, must begin with a sense of aliveness imbued to it by the child. A "dead" or inert transitional object cannot exist because it would be an atrocious substitute from the very start.

On another plane, it is striking to look at the words Winnicott employs to define the aliveness of the object: warmth, texture, and movement. It is not a coincidence to me that these three aspects of the object are the three hallmarks used to assess the quality and nature of Rorschach Ink Blot responses. Indeed, I believe the Rorschach is useful in the assessment of underlying personality organization precisely because the blots pull for these three determinants and because a psychodynamic approach to Rorschach assessment holds these three aspects of living up as vital components of the developmental process, just as Winnicott does.

> 6. It comes from without from our point of view, but not so from the point of view of the baby. Neither does it come from within; it is not a hallucination. (p. 5)

Winnicott describes the young infant as omnipotently creating the breast from his point of view because the attuned mother makes it "magically" appear just when he hallucinates it. If the mother can be a "good enough" blend of magical provider/subtle reality provider, the baby can gracefully make the transition to reality testing without undue hardship. In parallel fashion, although we perceive that the baby takes an already existing object as his own, the fact that the baby gives the object its comforting qualities makes it from the baby and not from the parent. At the same time, because of the aforementioned "unit" status that the baby has attained, he "knows" that it is not simply an imagined object hallucinated to fit the moment. It is striking in this context how early the transitional object is named by the baby, whether by a sound at six months or by a word at twelve months. Indeed, outside of a sound for mother or perhaps father, the baby's sound for his transitional object is often one of the first reliable words he creates. Parents then willingly label the object by this sound, attesting to its reality by this indirect symbol for a symbol.

> 7. Its fate is to be gradually allowed to be decathected, so that in the course of years it becomes not so much forgotten as relegated to limbo. By this I mean that in health the transitional object does not 'go inside' nor does the feeling about it necessarily undergo repression. It is not forgotten and it is not mourned. It loses meaning, and this is because the transitional

phenomena have become diffused, have become spread out over the whole intermediate territory between 'inner psychic reality' and the 'external world as perceived by two persons in common,' that is to say, over the whole cultural field. (p. 5)

This is an especially fascinating point. What I believe Winnicott is saying here is that as the baby attains "unit" status, the transitional object at first contains all the depth, creativity, intensity, and aliveness of the baby-mother dyad itself in a condensed form that allows the infant to play with what he means to feel alive. Over time, this condensed intensity becomes diffused out onto a variety of objects and experiences that grow in subtlety and variety as the baby does. The myriad forms it can take over a lifetime (art, religion, sports devotion, a favorite seat or color, etc.) allow the purpose of the object to remain viable without the need to necessarily keep the object itself at the center of the process. It thus can be placed in "limbo" without sadness or loss.

In a later paper entitled "The Location of Cultural Experience" (1967), Winnicott extends the idea of transitional phenomena to the term cultural experience in a more explicit manner. He claims:

The place where cultural experience is located is in the potential space between the individual and the environment (originally the object). The same can be said of playing. Cultural experience begins with creative living first manifested in play. . . . From the beginning the baby has maximally intense experiences in the potential space between the subjective object and the object objectively perceived, between me-extensions and the not-me. This potential space is at the interplay between there being nothing but me and there being objects and phenomena outside omnipotent control. Every baby has his or her own favorable or unfavorable experience here. . . . The potential space happens only in relation to a feeling of confidence on the part of the baby . . . confidence being the evidence of dependability that is becoming introjected. (p. 100)

Linking this "Location" paper to the transitional objects paper adds to our understanding of the concept of transitional objects and phenomena. First, he creates an arena for this intermediate experience and calls it potential space, a wonderfully named term in its dynamic, about-to-be-yet-not-quite-being quality. He then not only links the creation of this space to playing, but he also makes playing the precursor to the creative living that is manifested in cultural life. This puts play at its most exalted status in Winnicott's hierarchy of necessary ingredients for a vital life. Then he links the potential space to the now well-discussed arena of "me" and "not me" and the gradual relinquishing of magical control. Last, he links all of these capacities of the infant to his developing a sense of confidence, a confidence that is engendered by the root of all that is good, the "good enough" mother.

For Winnicott, transitional phenomena are at the crux of an enormously varied number of life experiences. The list he provides of such phenomena is remarkable.

> At this point my subject widens out into that of play, and of artistic creativity and appreciation, and of religious feeling, and of dreaming, and also of fetishism, lying and stealing, the origin and loss of affectionate feeling, drug addiction, the talisman of obsessional rituals etc. (Transitional Objects, p. 5)

We alluded to the links between transitional phenomena and play, art, religion, and to obsessional rituals earlier. It is especially intriguing to place drug addiction here, as the use of drugs to either numb the mind (the "without mind" state he describes in his "Mind" paper) or excite the mind to a False Self omnipotence would both easily fit into his paradigm of the nature and etiology of the transitional object. The linking of lying and stealing to transitional phenomena will be discussed more fully in chapter 11 when we discuss the meaning and origin of the antisocial tendency. The use of fetishistic objects can readily be seen as an erotization and displacement of the original use of the transitional object, while the simultaneously real but not-real feeling of the dream state can also be readily linked to the intermediate, potential space of transitional phenomena.

I will close with a brief review of the relationship between the transitional object and symbolism. Winnicott writes:

> It is true that the piece of blanket is symbolical of some part-object, such as the breast. Nevertheless, the point of it is not so much its symbolic value so much as its actuality. . . . When

symbolism is employed the infant is already clearly distinguishing between fantasy and fact, between inner objects and
external objects, between primary creativity and perception.
But the term transitional object, according to my suggestion,
gives room for the process of becoming able to accept difference and similarity. I think there is use for a term for the root
of symbolism in time, a term that describes the infant's journey
from the purely subjective to objectivity; and it seems to me
that the transitional object is what we make of this journey of
progress toward experiencing. (p. 6)

Thus while we as adults see the transitional object as a symbol of mother, from the baby's perspective, it is the *creation* of a
symbol for mother that matters. As the baby progresses and can
understand or even later put into words the use of a symbol, she
has had the transitional object to help tolerate the loss of mother
long enough to take on the world and to begin to use it and other
symbols to navigate it. The transitional object is the drawing board
for symbolization but is not a symbol in the traditional sense,
namely, the abstract cognitive capacity to make X stand for Y. It is
the first "prop" that allows the child to eventually give it full symbolic value because at first it is literally a replacement for a missing object. It is not a metaphor. It is a comforting object. Mother
at this stage is not a whole person either; mother is simply the
comforting being. So this transitional object is "Comforting Being
II." In that sense it's a replacement for, but doesn't symbolize, the
mother. As the child grows, from six months to a year to eighteen
months to two years, and progresses from the sensory-motor period to the full use of language, then the transitional object can be
used symbolically to stand for mother. When the child is eighteen
months old, for example, and gets upset, the mother says, *"Would
you like me to get . . . "Binky"?"* because the child knows "Binky"
means comfort is coming and it's going to be OK. By that point it's
a symbol.

I end this chapter with a reference to the remarkable Harry Potter series by J. K. Rowling. Both of Harry's parents died when he
was about a year old. But in many ways they gave him an abun-
dance of good-enough parenting. In book three of her series, Rowl-

ing creates the concept of the *Patronus*, as in patron. The Patronus is a magical, not quite internal and not quite external entity that can be conjured up only after a great deal of training. Harry, however, is able to conjure up his Patronus much more quickly, presumably because he had a great deal of devoted early parenting. Every person develops his or her own form of Patronus, which takes the form of an animal. A Patronus has magical properties that serve as the ultimate protection. Harry's father had a certain kind of Patronus, a stag, and appropriately enough, when Harry needs to conjure up this protective being, his Patronus is the same as his dad's! The gravest danger Harry faces in this book are creatures called Dementors. When a Dementor "kisses" you, it actually takes your soul from you and you remain alive but have a life without a soul ("without mind"?). The Dementor is thus a remarkably dreadful Kleinian-like character—the bad breast personified! If Harry can muster the necessary concentration to get his Patronus to materialize, it literally comes out of his body and kills the Dementors.

The point of these developments in the novel is that despite his father's early demise, Harry internalized him deeply enough that at the crucial moment he can conjure up his Patronus (symbolic father) and stop the soul killer from stealing away his soul. What a beautiful way to depict the notion of a transitional object! It is, in literary form, a structure from potential space that can be conjured up in the face of a soul-wrenching danger. It protects him in the ultimate way. It's really very Winnicottian!

Given the present context of evil "dementors," it is only appropriate to shift to the last major aspect of Winnicott's theorizing—the role that hate and aggression play in the developmental process.

Chapter Ten

<hr/>

Hate in the Countertransference

Dilemma: The need for hate, whether of mother for baby or therapist for patient, is an essential part of the capacity to relate fully.

Article reviewed: "Hate in the Countertransference" (1949).

> *There must be thirty ways*
> *To hate your baby*
> *Thirty ways to hate your baby . . .*
> *Treats me like a slave, Dave,*
> *Tries to hurt, Gert*
> *Don't need to be ruth, Ruth*
> *Just listen to me.*

> With apologies to Paul Simon and his great song, "50
> Ways to Leave Your Lover"

IN "PLAYING" WITH WINNICOTT, WE MAY well have reached his ultimate "sandbox" with this paper: that of the remarkably devoted pediatrician/child psychoanalyst who comes up with a list of some thirty-odd reasons why a mother hates her baby! Only someone with his level of love and faith in the "ordinary" mother could feel so comfortable with such hate. Here more than anywhere else, the process and content of his writing reveals a man who embodies his own theories. This is also why, if we were going to make a

161

"Greatest Hits of D.W. Winnicott" collection, then his "Hate in the Countertransference" paper would get as many votes as any of his other great works, if not more. Nearly sixty years after its publication, it still generates more relief, gratitude, acknowledgment, and dismay among clinical psychology graduate students than any other paper I know of. I often wonder about the level of uproar it must have caused at the time of its first presentation. In 1949 to come out and say that it is fully real and appropriate and necessary for analysts to hate their patients, and still more so that mothers hate their babies, often before their patients/infants hate them, was almost as revolutionary in its own limited way as Freud declaring that children have sexual fantasies and feelings was at a larger, more societal level. It was a revolutionary act and took an inordinate amount of bravery and self-confidence for Winnicott to be able to say it. Again I think it also speaks specifically to how much of his professional life as an analyst was spent analyzing very disturbed people. When one works deeply and in a prolonged way with severely troubled patients, one can begin to feel safe with the idea that the hate one experiences internally is not just a function of one's own inner conflicts. Winnicott was durable and fortunate enough to survive working with very disturbed patients. He experienced firsthand their deep regressions to primitive, "coincident" experiences of love and hate over a long time. He survived until more-developed conceptions of affective life could mature in their core experience. This permitted him to say, *This isn't me, it's this patient*, and to be able to distinguish between countertransference hate in the "bad sense," meaning the analyst hasn't been analyzed well enough, and hate in the very realistic and appropriate sense related to the patient doing hateful things. He then thought this distinction through to what it implies diagnostically, etiologically, and methodologically. In so doing he created a truly extraordinary paper.

It has become commonplace in certain large segments of the field of psychodynamically informed psychotherapy to see transferential and countertransferential paradigms as key in treatments of any length and intensity. I would suggest that it was this "Hate" paper that strongly helped galvanize this more "modern" view. Once countertransferential hate based on the therapist's own insufficient analysis and hate based on the patient's intrinsic properties could be distinguished from one another, it became far easier to use this distinction as the foundation for the notion that countertransferential feelings could be useful and productive. This "Hate" paper was thus a seminal catalyst in many ways in the field of interpersonal psychiatry, interpersonal therapy, and object relations therapy. I do wonder to what extent Winnicott had read the earlier work of Sullivan on transference. A dialogue between the two around these crucial issues would have been fascinating.

Let us now go back to the text of the paper itself. He begins by distinguishing types of countertransference.

> One could classify countertransference phenomena thus: (1) Abnormality in countertransference feelings, and set relationships and identifications that are under repression in the analyst. The comment on this is that the analyst needs more analysis, and we believe this is less of an issue among psycho-analysts than among psychotherapists in general (2) The identifications and tendencies belonging to an analyst's personal experiences and personal development which provide the positive setting for his analytic work and make his work different in quality from that of any other analyst. (p. 195)

Here is the crux of his argument as to the nature of the therapist's experience: that every therapy is intrinsically individual and what the analyst brings to the table is her stamp of individuality. This is a positive and valuable entity. He continues:

> From these two I distinguish the truly objective countertransference, or if this is difficult, the analyst's love and hate in reaction to the actual personality and behavior of the patient, based on objective observation. (p. 195)

While this is the crux of his paper, it is the next paragraph that brilliantly elaborates on the nature of countertransference through the lens of psychodynamic diagnosis and warrants being printed in its entirety.

> I wish to suggest that the patient can only appreciate in the analyst what he himself is capable of feeling. In the matter of motive: the obsessional will tend to be thinking of the analyst as doing his work

in a futile obsessional way. A hypo-manic patient who is incapable
of being depressed, except in a severe mood swing, and in whose
emotional development the depressive position has not been se-
curely won, who cannot feel guilt in a deep way, or a sense of concern or responsibility, is unable to see the analyst's work as an attempt on the part of the analyst to make reparation in respect of his
own (the analyst's) guilt feelings. A neurotic patient tends to see the
analyst as ambivalent towards the patient, and to expect the analyst
to show a splitting of love and hate; this patient, when in luck, gets
the love, because someone else is getting the analyst's hate. Would
it not follow that if a psychotic is in a 'coincident love-hate' state of
feeling he experiences a deep conviction that the analyst is also
only capable of the same crude and dangerous state of coincident
love-hate relationship? Should the analyst show love, he will surely
at the same moment kill the patient. (p. 195)

The usefulness of this passage perhaps lies in its implications for
the therapist's experience of each of these types of patients. Knowing
what the obsessional patient brings to treatment allows the therapist
with that type of patient to think more deeply about inner feelings of
futility or to struggle with the tendency to overthink with such a patient. Knowledge of the lack of guilt or depressive experience in the
hypomanic patient permits the therapist to better understand experiences of ruthlessness or depression stirred up by such a patient.
Treating a neurotic patient with this foresight should keep the therapist from "enjoying" the loving behavior of this patient without
searching for and helping to understand the hate that is displaced
elsewhere. Last, working with a psychotic patient under this rubric
should significantly warn the therapist that love feelings that are
evoked or expressed could produce every bit as dangerous an inner
experience in the patient as the most malignant of hateful feelings.

Students seem to react most strongly to the clinical vignette
Winnicott provides of a nine-year-old boy he worked with during
the Second World War. The boy's primary symptom was a constant
truancy, including running away from the hostel where he had been
placed. Winnicott first notes about the boy that

I had established contact with him in one interview in which I
could see and interpret through a drawing of his that in running

away he was unconsciously saving the inside of his home and pre-
serving his mother from assault, as well as trying to get away from
his own inner world, which was full of persecutors. . . . I was not
very surprised when he turned up in the police station very near
my home. . . . My wife very generously took him in and kept him
for three months, three months of hell. (p. 199)

Winnicott then describes for us this rather amazing three
months of "inpatient treatment." He describes an "all giving" phase
of establishing themselves (him and his wife) as "good enough" objects to the boy, who was given

complete freedom and a shilling whenever he went out. He had
only to ring up and we fetched him from whatever police station
had taken charge of him. (p. 199)

The boy was quite lovable during this phase but, just as Winnicott would have predicted, this loving phase, if felt as true by the
boy, would inevitably lead to his giving up truancy as a symptom and
expressing hateful feelings, both self-directed and aimed at Winnicott and his wife. Winnicott describes what transpired next:

It was really a whole-time job for the two of us together, and when
I was out the worst episodes took place. Interpretation had to be
made at any minute day or night, and often the only solution in a
crisis was to make the correct interpretation, as if the boy were in
analysis. It was the correct interpretation that he valued above
everything. The important thing for the purpose of this paper is
the way in which the evolution of the boy's personality engendered hate in me, and what I did about it.

Did I hit him? The answer is no, I never hit. But I should have
had to have done so if I had not known all about my hate and I
had not let him know about it too. At crises I would take him by
bodily strength, without anger or blame, and put him outside the
front door, whatever the weather or the time of day or night.
There was a special bell he could ring, and he knew that if he
rang it he would be readmitted and no word would be said about
the past. . . . The important thing is that each time, just as I put
him outside the door, I told him something: I said that what had
happened had made me hate him. This was easy because it was

so true. I think these words were important from the point of view of his progress, but they were mainly important in enabling me to tolerate the situation without letting out, without losing my temper and without every now and again murdering him. (p. 200)

This remarkable "treatment" is perhaps his best example of using a clinical vignette to embody his theory. It is interesting to compare Winnicott's stance with this boy with that of parents talking to their child about how he or she misbehaved. The parent guidance "model" suggests that we seek to help the parent assist the child in distinguishing between "bad" behavior and being a "bad" child. Here Winnicott is using this approach but with a most salient difference. He's saying, What you are doing is so awful, that I need to let you know that I hate it, in some very full way. Winnicott believes that what the child needs to hear at that moment is the reality of how full of hate the situation is. For Winnicott to say: "I hate you when you do that" is first and foremost a concrete strengthening of reality testing in the child. Second, it is saying that what you do is hateful, but it's not so hateful that it is beyond words. In fact it can be limited, it can be corralled by this notion of "I hate you." The child is not a wild horse running amok. But when a child is full of that level of chaos, what is most needed is a container. Words are Winnicott's first container, and the repetitive, almost ritualistic placing him outside the door is paradoxically the second container. It is the combination of the heartfelt words and the clear behavioral message that encompassed the first level of the containment process for this child. It is certainly pure paradoxical "Winnicott" to have the placing of the child *outside* of the most obvious container, his home, be, in fact, the container, not the abandonment of the boy. In that sense, the pairing of repeated phrases with containing behaviors is directly akin to the analytic experience with seriously regressed patients. What is so helpful about Winnicott's comments to the boy is that they serve as a membrane, a boundary for the boy's hate to bounce off of in a holding, secure manner. But it is important to stress how Winnicott's expression of his hatred for the boy's actions is not simply a container in the behavioral sense. To return to the "wild mustang" metaphor: putting the corral around the boy is essential, but it's not sufficient because a corral alone would not tame a mustang. The corral-making must be concomitant with going into the corral with the horse and having the horse eventually deal with the rider. Both aspects of the "treatment" have to be made available to the patient: the corral and entering into the corral. What Winnicott is describing in this paper is how his containment and articulation of hate enabled the boy to eventually become deeply connected to Winnicott and his wife.

It is absolutely crucial to add the role played by the bell at Winnicott's front door to the therapeutic aspects of this vignette. Winnicott stresses the idea that there is a special bell that the boy could ring and that if he rang it, he would be readmitted without a word said about the past. Given the availability of this special bell, it would have been a serious mistake if Winnicott had *not* said he hated the boy. Indeed, it is in the counterbalance of his expression of hate—with his statement to the child that he can always come back in and will not be made to then falsely comply—that allows Winnicott's voiced hatred to take on therapeutic value. In a sense, it is a return to the magically good mothering Winnicott assumed was missing for this boy. From the child's perspective, whatever mischief he had made was now erased by the press of a button, and once this button was pressed, *he would get back a good object.* In this way, Winnicott creates the setting for a magical moment, but he balances it by saying, *I hate you.* He is providing the good-enough magical illusion, but he's also saying *I hate you* when you behave like that. If the child is able to own both the hatred and the inevitable reunion, then this allows the child to become more integrated. If the child had only one and not the other, then he would have been prone to create False Self experiences and/or overly seductive illusion-making.

Another way to think about Winnicott's intervention with this boy has to do with the matching of affective intensity. Diagnostically, what Winnicott is saying is that there was nothing neurotic about this child. He was completely immersed in a hypomanic way of being. Given that this child had so little capacity for a more nuanced way of being, he experienced affect in an all-or-none manner. The most effective way to intervene with this all-or-none world,

Winnicott understood, was to be equally all or none in his response to the child. Thus his words and his actions combined to match the child's intensity, allowing him to match his amplitude, so to speak, with the child's impaired "hearing." In a child who is so chaotic and so confused, to find that there is an adult who can move with him in the same rhythm and intensity is revelatory. It aids the child in feeling that he is not so caught up in the moment and can thus start to take a bird's-eye view. That is the beginning of insight, of self-awareness. So the pendulum becomes less extreme. Over time, it may mean that he can become less psychotic and less hypomanic. At that point, Winnicott's "pendulum," his pace with the child, would also quiet down. His interpretations would become subtler, and he would not be putting the child outside of his house.

This vignette also makes me think of the distinction between hate and indifference. When you hate someone, you feel very strongly. There's nothing indifferent about it. That person is very much a part of you at that moment, and you are a part of that person. Hate and love are in this sense the parts of the circle that come around to be touching one another rather than polar opposites. Indifference is really the opposite of hate and love. When Winnicott is putting the child outside and telling him, *When you are ready you can ring the doorbell and come back and then we won't talk about it* is very different from *I'm putting you outside of my house, disappear forever!* When he picks this child up and he puts him outside the house, rain or shine, night or day, that is an action that is full of emotion, that is full of connection! When the doorbell can be rung and he is immediately let back in, that too remains full of connection. On another level, it is Winnicott saying that he can hate as much as the boy can and therefore, even in the experience of hatred, the boy can feel that he is not alone.

The second place in the paper where my students are shaken by Winnicott's actions is when he remarks:

> It was indeed a wonderful day for me (much later on) when I could actually tell the patient that I and his friends had felt repelled by him, but that he had been too ill for us to let him know.

This was also an important day for him, a tremendous advance-
ment in his adjustment to reality. (p. 196)

Students cannot bear the thought that Winnicott could be so
"cruel"! I tell them that they have to keep in mind that he probably
saw this patient for ten or twelve years. That he saw him four or five
times a week over that extended time frame and had journeyed with
this patient from a place of profound regression to dry, solid land.
But I think what he's also saying is that if you are fortunate enough
to have a patient change so profoundly, toward the end of treatment
she looks back on herself as if she were now a different person. She
knows how far she has gone and therefore to be able to talk about
how bad things were back then does not seem like an attack. It is
experienced more as a joint reflection of what patient and therapist
have come through and a look together in awe at how far they've
come.

What is the obligation of the therapist once he is aware of the
hate engendered by his or her patient? Winnicott notes:

The analyst must be prepared to bear strain without expecting the
patient to know anything about what he is doing, perhaps over a
long period of time. To do this, he must be easily aware of his own
fear and hate. (p. 198)

If you are going to take on the work of seeing a very troubled
patient, then so much of what you take on must be held quietly.
You may never, ever get to the point where the patient is or can be
aware of what the burden is. This paper raises the question, what
do you do as a therapist to soothe yourself with those patients who
require that you carry this burden, and how necessary is it that you
have people you can talk to about your cases, and/or have a life that
provides you with satisfaction outside of your consulting room?
Without at least one of these two "escape valves," there is a tremendous risk of doing your patients harm because there is insufficient
space in your life to carry on creatively without bearing that kind
of burden. It is also difficult when you have young children of your
own and you're trying to be a therapist at the same time, because
now you are serving as a container in two realms and that is quite

difficult. Winnicott's contribution to this dilemma is to accentuate how the acknowledgment of hate by the therapist attenuates the burdens of this difficult profession.

A more explicit point can be made about "bearing the strain" of working with a severely troubled child. When a therapist is working with a child who is more troubled than neurotic, and thus there is not a lot of "ego-relatedness" available, the therapist has to spend much of the treatment creating a forty-five-minute arena in which life *is* responsive yet nonretaliatory. This requires a tremendous amount of intactness yet openness in the therapist, an often exhausting combination. If the work is moving along well over a long enough period of time, the child develops, at first isolated pockets, but increasingly broader areas of intactness. The work of the therapist becomes less exhausting because there is less hate to hold. What then often happens is that the therapist has more access to all the things that he or she would have wanted to express to the child earlier but could not. Often this access is due to a combination of development in both the patient and the therapist. The therapist's changing experience of the patient frees up awareness of hatred in a manner roughly parallel to that of the child (but hopefully with far greater containment possible in the therapist!). This is what Winnicott is referring to when he speaks of "bearing the strain." The earlier on the therapist is aware of his or her own hate, the quicker he or she can find the potential space to hold that hate so that it doesn't destroy the treatment. As the patient gets stronger and better, both patient and therapist have more access to expressing this hatred in different, more useful ways because the patient can hold it and tolerate it.

Students then often ask the extremely useful follow-up question: What if there has been no satisfactory relationship in early infancy for the analyst to exploit in the transference?

This question may well have been addressed in another paper of Winnicott's, "The Deprived Child and How He Can Be Compensated for Loss of Family Life." He would say that with a person at such a profound level of disturbance, it is necessary to use residential care, where there would be the management of day-to-day life in a secure, reliable way. Only starting from that kind of management can there eventually be a place where psychotherapy can begin to be utilized. Winnicott discusses in the "Deprived Child" paper how the work of milieu workers in that context is every bit as "deep" as psychoanalysis. In the case of a true antisocial person, for example, there is nothing to hold on to internally so that a new type of experience must be created to anchor the individual. It is only after a long period of such management that one might have enough psychological traction to begin to turn the work into treatment of a more formal kind.

Winnicott always see parallels between the tasks of mothering the infant before he has become a unit and psychotherapeutic efforts with psychotic patients. These parallels are particularly salient for both dyads in the context of hate: this becomes the final theme of his paper. He begins to address this parallel in the following passage:

> Out of all the complexity of the problem of hate and its roots I want to rescue one thing, because I believe it has an importance for the analyst of psychotic patients. I suggest that the mother hates the baby before the baby hates the mother, and before the baby can know his mother hates him. (p. 200)

Why is it so important for Winnicott to make the timing of hatred so clear? Partly this has to do with his definition of hatred and when it can arise developmentally. Keeping true to his central notion of the difference in the baby as a "pre-unit" being vs. a "unit" being, he writes:

> Does this not mean that the personality must be integrated before an infant can be said to hate? However early integration may be achieved—perhaps integration occurs earliest at the height of excitement or rage—there is a theoretical earlier stage in which whatever the infant does that hurts is not done in hate. I have used the term 'ruthless' love in describing this stage. Is this acceptable? As the infant becomes able to feel to be a whole person, so does the word hate develop meaning as a description of a certain group of feelings. (pp. 200–201)

Here Winnicott stitches his concept of hate seamlessly to the rest of his theorizing. Before there is a "me" and "not me," the boundary between self and other is far too fluid to attribute the volition and directedness inherent in the concept of hate to the baby. As Winnicott puts it, the baby at this stage is "pre-ruth," it is before the capacity for caring for an "other" is possible. The baby is therefore truly ruthless in its quest to maintain illusory omnipotence.

But what of the mother? Winnicott is so clear on this point that he directly refutes Freud in his remarks about the concept. He states:

> The mother, however, hates her infant from the word go. I believe Freud thought it possible that a mother may in certain circumstances have only love for her boy baby; but we may doubt this. We know about a mother's love and we appreciate its reality and power. Let me give some of the reasons why a mother hates her baby, even a boy. (p. 201)

Putting aside the chauvinism of this aspect of Freud's theory ("even a boy"), it is compelling that the theorist who seems most comfortable with the fundamental tenet that the "ordinary" mother is "good enough" for her baby would be one and the same theorist to posit at least thirty explicit ways that a mother hates her baby a priori! This apparent contradiction takes us back to Winnicott's heartfelt, primary supposition that mental health is to be equated with creativity, spontaneity, and authenticity and not with rigidity, compliance, or clever niceties. Winnicott is creating a parallel between the "well-enough" analyzed analyst who can contain his or her hate for patients and the "good enough" mother who can do the same for her newborn. Winnicott is also saying that true maternal (or therapist) devotion is not derived through the use of neurotic reaction formation but through the amalgamation and integration of hateful feelings with loving feelings. It is precisely because the "good enough" mother can acknowledge her thirty ways of hating her baby that she can love him even more profoundly.

Partly because of their delightful explicitness, and partly because a number of these reasons for maternal hatred are important to understand, I present them all here:

The baby is not her own (mental) conception.

The baby is not the one of childhood play, father's child, brother's child, etc.

The baby is not magically produced.

The baby is a danger to her body in pregnancy and at birth.

The baby is an interference with her private life, a challenge to preoccupation.

To a greater or lesser extent a mother feels that her own mother demands a baby, so that the baby is produced to placate her mother.

The baby hurts her nipples even by sucking, which is at first chewing activity.

He is ruthless, treats her as scum, an unpaid servant, a slave.

She has to love him, excretions and all, at any rate at the beginning, till he has doubts about himself.

He tries to hurt her, periodically bites her, all in love.

He shows disillusionment about her.

His excited love is cupboard love, so that having got what he wants he throws her away like an orange peel.

The baby at first must dominate, he must be protected from co-incidences, life

must unfold at the baby's rate and this needs his mother's continuous and

detailed study. For instance, she must not be anxious when holding him, etc.

At first he does not know at all what she does or what she sacrifices for him.

Especially he cannot allow for her hate.

He is suspicious, refuses her good food, and makes her doubt herself, but eats well with his aunt.

After an awful morning with him she goes out, and he smiles at a stranger, who says: 'Isn't he sweet?'

If she fails him at the start he will pay her out forever.

He excites her but frustrates—she mustn't eat him or trade in sex with him. (p. 201)

What a remarkable list! Outside of a mother, perhaps only a pediatrician could have this sort of close, phenomenologically exact depiction of a baby! And perhaps only a child-psychoanalyst (and not a mother!) could make such a list and state it aloud!

A number of Winnicott's reasons for hate must be expanded upon before we link the list to work with psychotic patients.

"She has to love him. . . ." is noteworthy not only for the burden it places on the mother to once again be a "holding environment," but also for the notion that she may begin not to love him at times once he gets to the stage of integration where he may begin to doubt himself. This permission not to love is akin to Winnicott being able to tell his patient of many years that he used to be repelled by him.

"The baby at first must dominate, he must be protected from coincidences. . . . " Think of a baby in a high chair, practicing the dropping of his spoon ad nauseam, as he awaits his meal. If at the moment the spoon drops, the high chair should break and the baby start to fall, this coincidence will curtail, at least for a while, the baby's attempts to master what it means to be dropped or to drop something himself.

"At first he does not know at all what she does . . . " This is perhaps a summary of all the other reasons to hate the baby, because he has no gratitude in these early months, despite the enormous, sleep-deprived ministrations the mother provides.

"If she fails him at the start she knows he will pay her out forever." What a statement! Not only must the mother be "good enough" at enormous cost and deprivation, but, should she fail at her task, the resulting pathology in her child will haunt her in all aspects of her life for its entirety.

Why does Winnicott go to such lengths to demonstrate that a mother is filled with hate for her baby? It was the only way he knew of, I think, to state the parallel reasons for the hate he (and others working with similar patients) experienced working with psychotic patients. In Winnicott's view, acknowledging and even cataloguing these hatreds is the prime resource the therapist has available to work productively and understand meaningfully the inner lives of these troubled persons. He writes:

I think that in the analysis of psychotics, and in the ultimate stages of the analysis, even of a normal person, the analyst must find himself in a position comparable to that of the mother of a newborn baby. When deeply regressed, the patient cannot identify with the analyst or appreciate his point of view any more than the fetus or newly born infant can sympathize with the mother.

A mother has to be able to tolerate hating her baby without doing anything about it. She cannot express it to him. . . . The most remarkable thing about a mother is her ability to be hurt so much by her baby and to hate so much without paying the child out, and her ability to wait for rewards that may or may not come at a later date. (p. 202)

Thus, despite the myriad reasons for hating her baby, the mother rises above them all if she is "good enough." It is indeed the highest compliment Winnicott bestows when he says that the ordinary mother is "good enough." It becomes easy to see how his model for working with deeply troubled patients is to be able to hold them until they reach a profound regression and then hold them until they can hold themselves: it is a model inherent in the capable mother and that is hopefully replicable by the capable therapist if he or she can hold this hate the way a mother can hold it from her baby.

A last parallel between analysis with psychotics and the mother-baby dyad is expressed vis-à-vis the role of sentimentality in parenthood. He notes:

Sentimentality is useless for parents, as it contains a denial of hate, and sentimentality in a mother is no good at all from the infant's point of view. (p. 202)

What follows logically from this point is that the baby is incapable

of tolerating the full extent of his own hate in a sentimental environment. He needs hate to hate. (p. 202)

Which leads to his final point,

> If this is true, a psychotic patient in analysis cannot be expected
> to tolerate his hate of the analyst unless the analyst can hate him.
> (p. 202)

Thus, once again, it is the capacity to hate that breeds the capacity to live fully, in the nursery and in the consulting room.

We can now turn to the other extreme form of hatred in personality and review how it develops: the antisocial tendency. Winnicott's depiction of the nature and etiology of this tendency is, in my view, the equal of any of his theoretical constructs.

Chapter Eleven

―――――――――○―――――――――

The Antisocial
Tendency

Dilemma: "The child who steals an object is not looking for the object stolen but seeks the mother over whom he or she has rights."

Articles reviewed: "The AntiSocial Tendency" (1956) and "Aggression in Relation to Emotional Development" (1950–1955).

WITH SARDONIC TONGUE FIRMLY IN CHEEK, the great lyricist Sondheim provides remarkably sophisticated, if snide, commentary on the etiology of delinquency in his diatribe to Officer Krupke from *West Side Story*. The "Jets mock most aspects of the mental health/legal system, at one point noting how their "depraved behavior" stems from chronic depriviation. While not a paper on delinquency per se, the "Antisocial Tendency" speaks to notions of both delinquency and "untapped good," as well as to the phenomena in early childhood that spawn ubiquitous antisocial tendencies. The antisocial tendency provides a better lens for Winnicott to further his theorizing on personality development as he succinctly notes at the beginning of this paper.

> I have chosen to discuss the antisocial tendency, not delinquency. The reason is that the organized antisocial defense is overloaded with secondary gain and social reactions which makes it difficult for the investigator to get to its core. By contrast the antisocial tendency

can be studied as it appears in the normal or near-normal child, where it is related to the difficulties that are inherent in emotional development. (p. 306)

In this book I have presented Winnicott's theorizing conceptually chronologically. Nor I have focused on dilemmas inherent in the dynamism of the mother-baby dyad beginning with what makes the baby come alive; moving to what makes him experience life as a "unit"; going on to what allows him the capacity to be alone; extending the baby to the experience of a third, intermediate arena through the capacity to play; and, last, creating the milieu for creativity and authenticity through the integration of the capacity to hate. At every stage of this process, the parallels Winnicott presents between the developmental process and the analytic/clinical situation have been acknowledged and discussed. In this context, the "Antisocial" paper is a vital addition, for it now expands the vibrancy of his early baby phenomenology to the realm of how the slightly older baby (one to two years of age) loses or never gains the capacity for concern.

Winnicott begins by telling us what the antisocial tendency is not. It is not a diagnosis, comparable to neurosis or psychosis (although later he places its etiology in a developmental timetable between these two diagnostic entities). Indeed it can exist at any age and with any diagnosis. He then defines it as follows:

> The antisocial tendency is characterized by an element in it which compels the environment to be important. The patient through unconscious drives compels someone to attend to management. It is the task of the therapist to become involved in this, the patient's unconscious drive, and the work is done by the therapist in terms of management, tolerance and understanding. (p. 309)

Thus the antisocial tendency is a phenomenon of action. It is a psychological process that forces the person with the tendency to act on the environment and thus force the environment to engage, either reactively or proactively, this active protagonist. It is not something that remains for very long in the child's inner experience, although it is of course generated by the inner experience of his environment.

Winnicott then most poignantly places this active tendency to antisocial process in an interactive context from the perspective of the child. He writes:

> The antisocial tendency implies hope. Lack of hope is the basic feature of the deprived child who, of course, is not all the time being antisocial. In the period of hope the child manifests an antisocial tendency. This may be awkward for society, and for you if it is your bicycle that is stolen, but those who are not personally involved can see the hope that underlies the compulsion to steal. Perhaps one of the reasons why we tend to leave the therapy of the delinquent to others is that we dislike being stolen from. (p. 309)

Winnicott quickly acknowledges that linking deprivation to stealing is not an original conception and cites Bowlby, Klein, and Freud as evoking similar, earlier conceptualizations in that regard. What Winnicott contributes is his discussion of both what specific types of deprivation transpired between mother and baby to produce this "compulsion" and, crucially, when in the developmental process it typically is engendered. He begins by noting:

> Where there is an antisocial tendency there has been a true deprivation (not a simple privation); that is to say, there has been a loss of something good that has been positive in the child's experience up to a certain date and that has been withdrawn; the withdrawal has extended over a period of time longer than that over which the child can keep the memory of the experience alive. (p. 309)

There are several key implications of this passage. The child had to have been experiencing "good enough" mothering for a long-enough period of time to have achieved a "me" vs. "not me" unitary experience, otherwise there would be no means for understanding the concept of a memory to be kept alive in the child. Second, there has to have been an explicit taking away (stealing?) from the child (from its subjective perspective) of this positive experience, and this is a "stealing" regardless of whether the mother benignly or intentionally deprived the child. Last, the deprivation continues over time, so that presumably mother and baby have made numerous attempts to regain the positive experience to no avail. This experience over time is what engenders despair over the deprivation and yet hope that the deprivation can be deleted through action on the baby's part. This is why Winnicott states so early on in this paper that the antisocial tendency implies hope. He is constantly seeking to place the mother and baby in a dynamic context and, further, to describe each partner's active experience in that context from his or her unique perspective.

Winnicott then goes on to establish the dual trends inherent in the antisocial tendency—stealing and destructiveness. He has already described stealing by noting that:

> the child is looking for something, somewhere, and failing to find it seeks it elsewhere, when hopeful. (p. 310)

He then stretches this concept to include the need such a child has to "bump" up against the unavailable environment in some significant way.

> The child is seeking that amount of environmental stability which will stand the strain resulting from impulsive behavior. This is a search for an environmental provision that has been lost, a human attitude, which, because it can be relied on, gives freedom to the individual to move and act and to get excited. (p. 310)

This passage ties the etiology of the antisocial tendency to the prime ingredient in the development of a life of creativity: the reliability of the environment, whose holding function has been put into question by its overly long withdrawal from the child. Time is the crucial variable here, on two different levels. First, in the usual course of events, the baby "recovers" from episodic unreliability in the mother and vice versa. But if the poor attunement persists and the child's evocative memory for previous positive attunements is no longer viable, the baby is left either despairing (withdrawing) or frantic (object seeking and hence potentially destructive). Interestingly, Winnicott rarely speaks in any of his papers to the depressed baby; he more often, as he of course does here, focuses on the frantic but hopeful baby with the tendency to violate the social boundaries because of its desperation. Time is also relevant in this formulation on another level. If this prolonged unreliable attunement occurs earlier, before the child has achieved "unit" status, the result is psychotic-level fears and feelings of annihilation. This is why Winnicott places the antisocial tendency as a development in the second year of life.

Winnicott then takes us more deeply into the etiology of this tendency through his assessment of the nature of stealing. He writes:

> The child who steals an object is not looking for the object but seeks the mother over whom he or she has rights. These rights derive from the fact that (from the child's point of view) the mother was created by the child. The mother met the child's primary creativity, and so became the object that the child was ready to find. (p. 311)

This is an important synthesis of the act of stealing with the optimal role of the mother in the processing of the baby from illusion to disillusion. It is precisely because the mother was "good enough" (i.e., available, waiting to be found) in the earliest months of life that the baby has developed a healthy belief in his creation of the mother. Once again we have a paradox, namely, that if the mother had not been so "good" early on, the older baby would not feel "entitled" (that he has the right) to have the mother "on call." The presence of the antisocial tendency thus indicates that a significant step in the humanizing process has been achieved.

In the preceding chapter we reviewed the vital role that the integration of hate with love has in the capacity to become authentic and creative, whether through "good enough" parenting or "good enough" analysis. In this paper, Winnicott refers to such integration as "fusion." With reliable-enough parenting, particularly the ability of the mother to tolerate a variety of the baby's spontaneous gestures and affects, he becomes able to fuse his inherent motility (later, his aggression) with his libidinal wishes to connect with the mother. The resulting fusion lends greater depth and genuineness to the baby's experience or, in the language of earlier chapters, adds instinctual experience to the service of ego-relatedness, strengthening the baby. On a more basic level, if the child is supported in her capacity to achieve fusion, she is able to integrate the wish to destroy with the wish to connect. This allows passion, in the sexual, sublimated, and aggressive senses, to be "bathed" in "the milk of human kindness," so to speak, bringing creativity and aliveness to the forefront of the human experience.

In the present paper, Winnicott takes the concept of fusion and places it at the core of what happens in the creation of the antisocial tendency. Because the mother has become unreliable before the child has fully fused these object-seeking (libidinal) and destructive (motility turning to aggression) trends, they remain potentially toxic to the child's experience. In other words, neither the trend toward object seeking nor the trend toward object destructiveness produces a viable response from the mothering figure. Winnicott sees only one way out for the child in this predicament:

> I suggest that the union of the two trends is in the child and that it represents a tendency toward self-cure, cure of a de-fusion of instincts.
>
> When there is at the time of the original deprivation some fusion of aggression (or motility) roots with the libidinal, the child claims the mother by a mixture of stealing and hurting and messing, according to the specific details of that child's developmental state. (p. 311)

This is the condition that persists in the "near-normal" child, one with the better prognosis, which Winnicott will address shortly. In more disturbed children,

> When there is less fusion the child's object-seeking and aggression are more separated off from each other, and there is a greater degree of dissociation in the child. This leads to the proposition that the nuisance value of the antisocial child is an essential feature, and is also, at its best, a favorable feature indicating a potentiality for recovery of lost fusion of the libidinal and motility drives. (p. 310)

At the risk of being facetious, the "potentiality for recovery of lost fusion" is roughly equivalent to Sondheim's sarcastic lyrics that for the delinquent, "deep down inside us there is good." The fact that the antisocial tendency leads the baby to be a "nuisance" puts in Winnicott's terms the now clichéd notion of a "cry for help." What makes Winnicott's thinking more than clichéd, however, is what he views as constituting "help." The baby is not simply crying out for "spoiling"; rather (as discussed in the previous chapter), his demands must be met by the reliable provision of love and hate. Winnicott's comments on sentimentality are again relevant here: the baby cannot feel fully real if her nuisance behavior is met by reaction formations and false sentiment. It is only if the mother is capable of fused relating that the baby can recover from her previous failures in reliability and get back "on track" toward creative living.

There is perhaps no other paper where Winnicott better integrates his skills as a pediatrician with his acumen as a psychoanalyst than this one. This integration is marvelously implied when he discusses the antisocial tendency in the context of its mild beginnings in early infantile behavior. In a seamless manner, he threads the everyday signs of normal infant entitlement, behaviors he must have seen in the pediatric clinic thousands of times, with the first seeds of pathological deprivation tendencies in infant-mother interaction. He notes, for example:

> I suggest that the first signs of deprivation are so common that they pass for normal; take for example the imperious behavior which most parents meet with a mixture of submission and reaction. This is not infantile omnipotence, which is a matter of psychic reality, not of behavior. (p. 311)

Winnicott emphasizes the distinction between infant imperiousness, which is willful and conscious and comes from the baby who is already a "unit," and omnipotence, which appears in the first six months of life, before the baby has a firm awareness of "me" and "not me." The distinction is always in the forefront of his thinking in this arena because it is vital to his depiction of the antisocial tendency as a later developmental hurdle, a reaction to something that was lost as opposed to never having been found in the first place.

Winnicott struggles with the notion of whether deprivations of the infant during this later period can be fully repaired. He presents this struggle in the context of his work on greed and greediness. About greediness, he writes:

> If we study greediness we shall find the deprived complex. In other words, if an infant is greedy there is some degree of deprivation and some compulsion toward seeking for a therapy in respect of this deprivation through the environment. The fact that the mother is herself willing to cater for the infant's greediness makes for therapeutic success in the vast majority of cases in which this compulsion can be observed. (p. 312)

Here Winnicott is describing the baby who, typically in the second year of his life, has had significant-enough experiences of poor attunement to feel deprived as part of the beginning of a chronic pattern. The deprivation forces the baby to experience a near-constant neediness, yet the baby feels connected enough and hopeful enough to voice discontent in the form of a relentless greediness, of a demand for more of the mother. If the mother recognizes this need early enough on, she can cater to the infant and make reparation. But are these reparations equivalent, *from the baby's perspective,* to a mother-infant dyad that has not had these deprivations and thus not experienced this greediness?

Winnicott takes on this question by first distinguishing greediness from greed. Unlike greediness, which is focused and intent on a given object, greed is a more global, earlier phenomenon, linked in time to the baby's first steps in separating "me" from "not me" and hence less related to a specific person outside of herself. Greed must be distinguished from greediness by Winnicott for two reasons: one, because it allows him to maintain the distinctions between the experiences of the baby before and after she has a separate sense of self and "other"; and two, because the distinction allows him to link aspects of drive theory that he finds quite useful and accurate with aspects of his own theorizing about the developmental process. Greed in this context becomes synonymous with instinct and drive,

while greediness becomes a part of the older infant's attempts to balance neediness with its awareness of the needs of her mother.

As a parenthesis, it may be useful to look at anorexia as an experience of inverted greediness. Unable to integrate libidinal and
destructive aspects of the self, the child inflicted with greediness
also splits the experience of aggression from potential abandonment. Now that the child is unable to acknowledge aggression, the
child's greediness can then, if other salient variables prevail, be
turned on herself, making the child hungry to eat at herself and
needing to starve herself as a result.

Winnicott then makes what I believe to be the central point of
his "Antisocial" paper. He writes:

> In parenthesis, it is sometimes said that a mother must fail in her
> adaptation to her infant's needs. Is this not a mistaken idea based
> on a consideration of id needs and a neglect of the needs of the
> ego? A mother must fail in satisfying instinctual demands, but she
> may completely succeed in 'not letting the infant down' *in cater-
> ing for ego needs*, until such a time as the infant may have an in-
> trojected ego-supportive mother, and may be old enough to main-
> tain this introjection in spite of failures of ego support in the
> actual environment. (p. 312)

Instinctual needs of the infant *must* occasionally not be met by
the mother so that the baby can create the bridge from magical omnipotence to shared reality. Although minimally in the first days and
weeks of life, when the baby's needs are near absolute, Winnicott
makes clear throughout his work that the occasional lack of adaptation to instinct is exactly what the baby needs to develop its ego-relatedness, its awareness that there is a reliable "not me," and hence
a sturdy-enough "me." But here he adds a crucial point; in the realm
of noninstinctual need, in the realm of emotional availability, the
mother can be absolute in her responsive care and ideally *is* that absolute. The mother allows the baby as many opportunities for meaning-making as possible in these next months (through at least to the
point where constant language-producing is possible). This provides
the baby with a vital, creative-enough shield to take on the rest of
the world and its potential failures in ego support.

Winnicott adds further refinement and dimensionality to his discriminations between greed and greediness and id and ego adaptations by parsing "love impulses" by the baby from greediness. He notes:

> The primitive love impulse is not the same as ruthless greediness. In the process of the development of an infant the primitive love impulse and greediness are separated by the mother's adaptation. The mother necessarily fails to maintain a high degree of adaptation to id needs and to some extent therefore every infant may be deprived, but is able to get the mother to cure this sub-deprived state by her meeting the greediness and messiness, etc., these being symptoms of deprivation. (p. 312)

Here Winnicott establishes a third level of mother-infant functioning vis-à-vis deprivation at this later phase of infancy. As described earlier, there is the most profound deprivation that eventually causes ruthlessness; here there is no memory of the reliable mother to draw upon, leaving the infant a ruthless exploiter. There is then the beginning of a deprivation "complex" in which the baby experiences the mother as erratic in her ego support and becomes compulsively greedy in his quest to get reparation for what he has "missed out on." In the passage above, Winnicott describes a third, "normal" level, in which some deprivation is universal and ruptures are easily repaired by the mother's reliable and benign response to the brief symptoms of the child's transient deprivations.

Having created this three-level hierarchy of deprivation, Winnicott quickly moves back to the mid-level experience of greediness, of which the antisocial tendency is the result. He adds:

> This greediness is antisocial; it is the precursor of stealing, and it can be met and cured by the mother's therapeutic adaptation, so easily mistaken for spoiling. It should be said, however, that whatever the mother does, this does not annul the fact that the mother first failed in her adaptation to her infant's ego needs. (p. 312)

This is new territory that Winnicott is venturing into. He is now addressing the age-old question of the degree of permanence of early disruptions; is there such a thing as a fixation or arrest at an early developmental phase, and what is the baby's and the environment's capacity for full reparation? Winnicott never completely tells us in this paper, nor in any other, whether the mother's successful "therapy" with her baby can actually annul her earlier failures. But he does tell us clearly that there are pitfalls in the way a mother attempts to make reparation that will surely curtail the baby's capacity to feel fully repaired. If the mother has initially been successful in providing the ego support necessary to handle the very young baby's love and motility impulses, the baby feels no obligation to the mother for her "kindness." This is simply another way of saying what Winnicott said in earlier chapters, that the baby in this situation has no need to be "reactive," he can "go on being," develop the capacity to be alone, etc. If the mother has failed often enough in this task so that the baby feels deprived at this middle level, then, to use his words,

> There is some feeling of obligation as the result of the mother's therapy, that is to say, her willingness to meet the claims arising out of frustration, claims that begin to have a nuisance value. Therapy by the mother may cure, but this is not mother-love. (p. 312)

This last sentence is an astounding one. It is astounding because it exalts "mother-love" to a stratospheric level, even while it remains within the achievements of the "ordinary," "good enough" mother. Mother-love is thus the kind of love that masters the earliest phases of the mother-infant dyad, creating the authentic, alive baby. Its "indulgence" of the baby is not indulgent at all, in that it provides optimal ego support while optimally nonsatisfying but not depriving the infant when appropriate. In fact, Winnicott adds:

> Mother-love is often thought of in terms of indulgence, which in fact is a therapy in respect of a failure of mother-love. It is a therapy, a second chance given to mothers who cannot always

be expected to succeed in their initial most delicate task of primary love. (pp. 312–313)

Winnicott is now left to address the question of the nature of this therapy and its consequences.

> If a mother does this therapy as a reaction formation arising out of her own complexes, then what she does is called spoiling. In so far as she is able to do it because she sees the necessity for the child's claims to be met, and for the child's compulsive greediness to be indulged, then it is a therapy that is usually successful. Not only the mother, but the father, and indeed the family, may be involved. (p. 313)

On one level, Winnicott is positing a viable second chance for the mother and family to successfully cure the baby whose first months were not optimal. The burden is once again placed on the facilitating environment to be able to be empathic enough to readjust its behavior and to then tolerate the nuisance of a greedy baby long enough for the baby to regain reliability. On a second level, he is providing a vivid diagnostic context for clinicians who work with infants of this age and their families. Helping the mother (and family) to distinguish between their reaction formations (their false compliance, to use another aspect of Winnicott's terminology) and their empathic awareness of their baby's needs becomes the core treatment goal for any clinical intervention at this juncture.

On a third level, the parallels Winnicott creates between the mother's attempt to "cure" her baby's deprivations and the therapy process with highly disturbed adults or older children should be clear. Therapy with patients whose pathology stems from disruptions during this period must have reliability as its bulwark. It must include in this reliability the capacity of the therapist to tolerate the patient's "messy, greedy" hate and yet to not simply indulge the patient's instinctual demands.

Winnicott has up to this point in the paper both established the root causes and captured the phenomenology of different levels of deprivation and the resulting complications they present for adequate parental response. He then takes us down one final path and outlines the necessary measures that must be taken to work through these chronic deprivations and live fully. He tells us:

> Surely it is an essential feature [of the antisocial tendency] that the infant has reached to a capacity to perceive that the cause of the disaster lies in an environmental failure. Correct knowledge that the cause of the depression or disintegration is an external one, and not an internal one, is responsible for the personality distortion and for the urge to seek a cure by new environmental provision. (p. 313)

Not only does the antisocial tendency arise late enough in infancy for the infant to already have attained "unit" status, but the baby, by virtue of this status, knows that the "problem" has been caused by the "outside," which is why she becomes so greedy in the pursuit of external supplies to counter this problem. On the positive side, this makes the child at this stage far better off than her potentially psychotic cohorts who did not have such a firm inside and outside at the time of their deprivation. It also is what makes the child hopeful, as her insides have not been experienced as toxic in some way, causing the deprivation.

If, however, these deprivations persist indefinitely, the antisocial tendency becomes calcified into an antisocial child and these children

> are constantly pressing for this cure by environmental provision (unconsciously, or by unconscious motivation) but are unable to make use of it. (p. 314)

Three conditions, each quite difficult in its own right, have to be satisfied to enable the now antisocial child to be repaired. The child must be placed in a new setting in which reliability is plentiful so that her nuisance behavior becomes manifest (the child feels hopeful again). The child must then become a nuisance and the environment must

> be tested and retested in its capacity to stand the aggression, to prevent or repair the destruction, to tolerate the nuisance, to

recognize the positive element in the antisocial tendency, to provide and preserve the object that is to be sought and found. (p. 314)

This Herculean task is simply the first condition to be met. Out of this condition comes the possibility that the child may come to

find and love a person, instead of continuing the search through laying claims on substitute objects (stealing) that had lost their symbolic value. (p. 314)

This is the fulfillment of the second condition. The next stage is not only crucial to full life but also provides us with his complete answer to the question of whether a child can be fully repaired even if he or she "only" has the antisocial tendency and is not fully anti-social. Winnicott adds:

In the next stage the child needs to be able to experience despair in a relationship, instead of hope alone. Beyond this is the real possibility of a life for the child. (p. 314)

These two sentences integrate not only the constructs he plays with in this paper but also many of his most important the-oretical propositions. Hope alone, Winnicott implies, simply leaves the child back at the point in infancy where his newly established "me-ness" is still woefully inadequate to meet the psychological demands of the environment. The hope-only child has heretofore felt that the world is reliable enough although he is not yet capa-ble of handling that environment without ongoing ego support. More importantly perhaps, the hope-only child has had insuffi-cient experience with the integration of hate into his conceptions of self and other. It is here that the "Antisocial" paper draws upon, by implication, many of the facets of his "Hate in the Countertransference" paper. When the antisocial child (or pre-sumably adult) reaches the hope-alone stage through reliable in-tervention and experiences love toward a therapeutic object, he is much like the healthy child who is about to take on the task of acknowledging hate toward the love-object. The therapist's ca-pacity to handle the patient's hate then allows the patient to struggle with his own hate for those aspects of his environment that were not reliably available. This parallels the healthy child's expression of hate toward the parent. This, in turn, allows the patient to experience the despair associated with this unreliability. The working through of the despair and hate is what raises the possibility of a full life for the patient, much as the acknowledgment of everyday disappointment allows the healthy child to experience life as a True Self.

It is also important and useful to extend these points from the present paper to Winnicott's "Transitional Objects" paper. The baby at the point of hope is also able to create a transitional object to maintain hope. Transitional phenomena allow the child to maintain hopefulness because she can use the object(s) to symbolically recreate the absent internal experience of the parent and thus avoid despair and loss. The transitional arena in which the baby can engage the created object is also the arena for play. The capacity for play, as we have seen, allows the baby to safely replicate and even risk new experiences with herself, her inner world, and with the environment of people and things. As the antisocial child is brought firmly to the stage of nuisance/hope and then to love and eventually despair, she presumably gains a greater capacity to evoke transitional phenomena to augment her inner world. The availability of a potential play space simultaneously promotes the capacity to be alone in the presence of (now) reliable others. Most concretely, it allows for greater access to True Self configurations as opposed to the False Self compliant behaviors so commonly seen in antisocial persons, who falsely comply in an attempt to "get away" with something they've "stolen" as part of their ultimately fruitless attempt to feel real.

In Winnicott's paper "Aggression in Relation to Emotional Development," he adds several points on the etiology of aggression that are useful here. Winnicott notes:

> At origin aggressiveness is almost synonymous with activity. . . .
> In so far as behavior is purposive, aggression is meant. Here immediately comes the main source of aggression, instinctual experience. Aggression is part of the primitive experience of love. (pp. 204–205)

These lines fill in several small gaps in Winnicott's description of the etiology and implications of aggression. He notes that aggression can only be deemed aggressive if there is purpose and intention behind it. Since there is not yet a fully discrete "me" and "not me" in the first few months of life, there can be no real intent. Thus aggression is at first motility. When "me" and "not me" are established, the baby's simultaneous seeking to make contact and expanding his behavioral repertoire spontaneously in ways that "destroy" the mother are part and parcel of one another. Each and every foray into making connection comes with a foray soon after toward making disconnection. If mother can "hold" the baby during these dialectical processes, that is, respond to the baby with reliability, the infant's unit status gets strengthened.

This paper then expands on notions laid out in prior papers.

> Now comes the stage described by Melanie Klein as the 'depressive position' in emotional development. For my purpose I will call this the Stage of Concern. The individual's ego integration is sufficient for him to appreciate the personality of the mother figure, and this has the tremendously important result that he is concerned as to the results of his instinctual experience, physical and ideational. (p. 206)

Here we have a description of that which does not occur consistently enough for the child exhibiting the antisocial tendency. That child has lost the mother (from the point of view of her reliable attunement and availability) at precisely the time when he could have fully established a capacity for concern for her. His expressions of hope (i.e., his "nuisance" behaviors) are generated without this concern. Unfortunately for the baby, this lack of concern puts additional pressure on the parent to retaliate instead of hold at precisely the moment when holding would be essential. It is therefore all too likely that the mother will experience the baby's "hopeful" acts as further indication that he does not show any concern for her; the mother is all too correct in this assessment. She is then likely to reply as if being exploited at the very moment that the baby's actual exploitation must be seen as hope if mother and baby are to thrive. It is here that Winnicott's comments on the necessary role of fathers and others to aid in disrupting this potential vicious cycle become germane. The parents' need for outside help to avoid reaction formations in their approach to their "entitled" baby is also quite relevant to clinical work and should inform our interventions.

Why is the Stage of Concern so vital? Winnicott notes:

> The stage of concern brings with it the capacity to feel guilty. . . . The guilt refers to the damage which is felt to be done to the loved person in the excited relationship. In health the infant can hold the guilt, and so with the help of a personal and live mother is able to discover his own personal urge to give and to construct and to mend. In this way much of the aggression is transformed into the social functions, and appears as such. In times of helplessness (as when no person can be found to accept a gift or to acknowledge effort to repair) this transformation breaks down, and aggression appears. Social activity cannot be satisfactory except it be based on a feeling of personal guilt in respect of aggression. (pp. 206–207)

Winnicott suggests that guilt marks a vital achievement in the humanization process. It is also an enormously useful aspect, both on the individual and the societal level, of the creative yet connected process of being fully alive with fully alive others. Aggression is thus viewed as a result of the infant's inability to make reparation and/or connection (a gift or a repair as Winnicott puts it) with the person she is interacting with. This view of aggression thus sets the platform upon which "The Antisocial Tendency" paper rests and allows us to understand the paradigm whereby the fortunate baby gets to use aggression constructively to further develop her sense of vitality, while the unfortunate baby is left without a consistent way of expressing the desire to connect. In the latter case, the now frustrated baby acts more like a nuisance than the mother can bear, further spiraling them down a path where the antisocial tendency can flourish.

Having linked these constructs in the abstract to the formation of an antisocial tendency, we can now turn to linking many of these same constructs to clinical work with patients who are struggling mightily with aggression and its vicissitudes. Hence the final two chapters will directly address clinical work with these types of patients.

Chapter Twelve

───────────○───────────

The Aims of
Psychoanalytic
Treatment

"In doing psychoanalysis I aim at:
        Keeping alive
        Keeping well
        Keeping awake"

Articles reviewed: "The Aims of Psychoanalytical Treatment" (1962) and "The Case of Ada" from *Therapeutic Consultations in Child Psychiatry* (1971).

> *Albus Dumbledore had gotten to his feet. He was beaming at the students, his arms opened wide, as if nothing could have pleased him more than to see all of them there. "Welcome," he said., "Welcome to a new year at Hogwarts! Before we begin our banquet, I would like to say a few words. And here they are: Nitwit! Blubber! Oddment! Tweak!"*
>
> J. K. Rowling, *Harry Potter and the Sorcerer's Stone*, p. 123

UP TO THIS POINT, THE GREAT BULK of our "play" has been the exposition of Winnicott's theorizing on the developmental process. Clearly he has time and again linked multiple aspects of the interplay between mother and baby with the interactions of therapist

195

and patient in the clinical setting. He has connected interactive and internalizing processes in the first months of life with similar processes with deeply regressed, psychotic patients. He has tied interactions with older babies to clinical work with depressed and antisocial children and adults and, less often, with anorexic patients. Because his theorizing is so deeply environmental in its etiology, the tasks of the "good enough" mother are explicated in precise, comprehensive detail, and the consequences of her "failures" are the source of his thinking on psychopathology. In parallel fashion, he places a similarly heavy burden on the therapist to provide the milieu for therapeutic change. In these last two chapters, our attention will be focused more specifically on his writing about what therapists must do and not do in order for their patients to thrive. In chapter 12 we will first focus on what he calls the aims of treatment and use the case of Ada to shed light on the therapeutic endeavor. In our final chapter, we will look at his writings on transference and countertransference with an eye toward synthesizing his clinical and theoretical work.

Winnicott's work "The Aims of Psychoanalytical Treatment" is deceptively dense for such a short (four pages) paper. He begins and ends the paper with a kind of "puckish" oversimplification of the analytic process, but it quickly becomes clear that despite his brevity, his expectations for the behavior of the therapist are simultaneously simple yet profound. He begins:

> In doing psycho-analysis I aim at:
> > Keeping alive
> > Keeping well
> > Keeping awake
> I aim at being myself and behaving myself. Having begun an analysis I expect to continue with it, to survive it and to end it. (p. 166)

Hopefully the parallels between this remarkable introduction to psychoanalysis, presented at a meeting of the British Psychoanalytic Society, and Professor Dumbledore's introduction on the first night at the Hogwarts School of Magic are obvious. Both men are obviously British, both at this point in their lives are wise, honored, respected sages, and both are known for their eloquent ability to tweak and revere their roles and themselves simultaneously. You can even argue that they both are leaders of magical institutions, but I may be pushing the comparison a bit far!

In any case, the aims Winnicott presents at the start of this paper are not only far from simple, they are directly derived from the fundamental principles of his theorizing. "Keeping alive," for example, cannot be more basic and simplistic, yet as we have come to learn, a sense of aliveness is the highest form of being for Winnicott and is derived from an infancy that is "good enough" to breed authenticity and minimize compliance. "Keeping well" is similarly deceptive in its brevity, as it privileges the intactness of his internal life despite the potentially seductive, malevolent, or chaotic inner lives of his patients. It also implies that he can avoid the dominance of internal "moods" so that he can be available for empathic response to his patients as an antidote to the presumed lack of such empathy from the patient's familial circumstances. "Keeping awake," as any therapist discovers, is an extension of his first two aims, as it connotes an inner vitality that affords the luxury of attentiveness, often despite the internal struggles of the therapist. "Being myself" is a simple, direct reference to his notion of the True Self and the minimization of false compliance, yet the attainment of this True Self, as we have reviewed, is always fraught with potential impingement. "Behaving myself," as he will show us quite soon when he describes the role of interpretation in analysis, is also elemental yet multifaceted.

The integrity of Winnicott's attitude toward work is not something I have directly commented upon up until now, but it reveals itself in his next passage:

> I enjoy myself doing analysis and I always look forward to the end of each analysis. Analysis for analysis' sake has no meaning for me. I do analysis because that is what the patient needs to have done and to have done with. If the patient does not need analysis then I do something else. (p. 166)

There is such elegant balance in this passage, both in the balance of his prose and in the balance he creates between the profound necessity and pleasure of the work on the one hand and its equally profound need to end and to be useful on the other. Utility is the key word here. As discussed in chapter 6, the capacity to use objects (relationships) is a significant developmental achievement, an integration of love and hate that produces an abiding faith in others and in the self. Winnicott expects this capacity of himself and seeks to establish or augment it in his patients via the therapeutic process. This, in turn, implies that Winnicott knows that he is to be "used" for the treatment to flourish, which means he must also be discarded when no longer needed. Indeed, usage implies the capacity to not use, to "have done with." The fact that he can enjoy the process as well as enjoy its conclusion speaks mightily to his capacity to "use" in the best sense.

What qualities should a therapist have to be able to conduct analysis (or any form of psychoanalytically informed treatment)? Winnicott tells us explicitly in his introduction to *Therapeutic Consultations*.

> For instance, one can say at once that there must be evident a capacity to identify with the patient without loss of personal identity; there must be a capacity in the therapist to contain the conflicts of the patient, that is to say, to contain them and to wait for their resolution in the patient instead of anxiously looking around for a cure; there must be an absence of the tendency to retaliate under provocation. Also, any system of thought which provides an easy solution is of itself a contra-indication since the patient does not want anything but the resolution of internal conflicts. . . . Needless to say the therapist must have professional reliability as something that happens easily; it is possible for a serious person to maintain a professional standard even when undergoing very severe personal strains in the private life and in the personal growth process which, we hope, never stops. (p. 2)

Turning back to his "Aims" paper, Winnicott then presents a definition of "standard analysis," which, in a typically Winnicottian way, he defines on his own terms, with his own terminology.

> For me this means communicating with the patient from the position in which the transference neurosis (or psychosis) puts me.

In this position I have some of the characteristics of a transitional phenomenon, since although I represent the reality principle and it is I who must keep an eye on the clock, I am nevertheless a subjective object for the patient. (p. 166)

Winnicott thus adheres to a typical definition of analysis as a function of transference, but he subsumes transference into his concept of transitional phenomena, as his being simultaneously "inside" and "outside" for the patient creates a third, intermediate arena for the therapy to proceed.

Winnicott next discusses his reasons for making interpretations. Here we get a better feel for the actual experience of what he is like with his patients. He describes two reasons to interpret to a patient.

If I make none the patient gets the impression that I understand everything. In other words, I retain some outside quality by not being quite on the mark—even by being wrong. (p. 167)

This is a direct analog to mother-infant interaction, wherein it is the misattunements that the mother makes that help lead the baby out of complete omnipotence and into the world of "me" and "not me." It is also markedly consistent with infant research revealing the enormous number of such "mistakes" in any useful mother-baby interaction.

His second reason for interpretation is also a direct outgrowth of his theoretical work. He writes:

Verbalization at exactly the right moment mobilizes intellectual forces. It is only a bad thing to mobilize the intellectual processes when these have become seriously dissociated from psychosomatic being. (p. 167)

As discussed in chapter 9, many things have to go well in the first years of life in order to continue to feel an integration of psyche and soma. Too much impingement on the baby makes him reactive, a "mood forecaster" rather than someone who can "go on being," and causes an overly precocious use of mind to defend against a loss of bodily integrity. Winnicott thus implies that patients with this type of pathology must be worked with in a more visceral, less intellectual manner.

We have also not discussed Winnicott's wonderful use of humor, often self-deprecatory humor, often presented in the midst of a most serious discussion. The following is as good an example of this use of humor as I could find in his writing:

> My interpretations are economical, I hope. One interpretation per session satisfies me if it has referred to the material produced by the patient's unconscious co-operation. I say one thing, or say one thing in two or three parts. I never use long sentences unless I am very tired. If I am near exhaustion point I begin teaching. Moreover, in my view an interpretation containing the word 'moreover' is a teaching session. (p. 167)

Winnicott is thus teaching us here! Moreover (ha, ha), is not his use of simple, short sentences again a link to mothers talking with their babies? And is not his admission and comfort with the fact that he does get tired and does occasionally "teach" his patients another modeling of his enormous personal integrity and humility?

There are two other points he makes in this paper that warrant discussion. The first concerns his fundamental sense of the nature of transference, which is in stark contrast to a drive theory model of transference. He notes:

> Although psychoanalysis may be infinitely complex, a few simple things may be said about the work I do, and one is that I expect to find a tendency towards ambivalence in the transference and away from more primitive mechanisms of splitting, introjection and projection, object retaliation, disintegration, etc. I know that these primitive mechanisms are universal and that they have positive value, but they are defenses in so far as they weaken the tie to the object through instinct, and through love and hate. At the end of endless ramifications in terms of hypochondrical fantasy and persecutory delusion a patient has a dream which says: I eat you. Here is stark simplicity like that of the Oedipus complex. (p. 167)

Here he begins with the idea that the patient brings the inclination toward more ambivalent and less pre-Oedipal defenses to the transference, which would suggest a theoretical stance more akin to Freud than to Klein. But Winnicott then adds that this tendency toward ambivalence manifests itself because of the primary need the patient has to more fully experience the therapist and to not hide from loving and hating feelings. This will lead the patient to a fundamentally oral fantasy, to a place once again where mother and baby reside in "stark simplicity" and not to a later, Oedipal configuration.

The last aspect I wish to stress from this paper is his discussion of when he modifies his treatment approach from standard analysis to "working as a psychoanalyst," meaning using his knowledge of psychoanalytic theory but not conducting an analysis. This line of thinking is useful both in terms of what conditions preclude analysis in his theorizing and in his statement about the role of diagnosis. Psychoanalysis is precluded, he writes:

(a) Where fear of madness dominates the scene.
(b) Where a False Self has become successful, and a façade of success and even brilliance will be destroyed at some phase if analysis is to succeed.
(c) Where in a patient an antisocial tendency, either in the form of aggression or stealing or of both, is the legacy of deprivation.
(d) Where there is no cultural life—only an inner psychic reality and a relationship to external reality—the two being relatively un-linked.
(e) Where an ill parental figure dominates the scene. (pp. 168–169)

Each of these conditions speaks to diagnostic entities that Winnicott has repeatedly described in his writings. Condition A refers to the primitive fear of disintegration akin to infants who have not attained "unit" status and fear "falling forever." Condition B refers to those persons where the True Self has become so hidden and fragmentary that a fundamental challenge to their False Self could shatter their identity. Condition C refers to those persons whose feelings of deprivation are so profound that they cannot contain their need to act on the environment, thus requiring management more than psychoanalysis. Condition D refers to those persons who have never developed the capacity for transitional phenomena or an intermediate space between inner and outer reality. These people do not have the psychic space within which treatment can occur. Condition E refers to those child treatments where the pathology of a parent or parents is so severe that they could not tolerate the likely, if transient, regressions their child might evoke in treatment and/or could not tolerate the child's deepening tie to the therapist.

These considerations, taken as a whole, lead Winnicott to his most definitive depiction of the role of diagnosis. He notes:

> These and many other illness-patterns make me sit up. The essential thing is that I do base my work on diagnosis. I continue to make a diagnosis of the individual and a social diagnosis as I go along, and I do definitely work according to diagnosis. In this sense, I do psychoanalysis when the diagnosis is that this individual, in his or her environment, wants psycho analysis. . . . By and large, analysis is for those who want it, need it and can take it. (p. 169)

This fundamental point is worth stressing. By emphasizing the active role diagnosis plays at all points in his treatment work, Winnicott is doing two important things. One, he is stating that the therapeutic process must constantly be monitored for shifts in the patient's organization and for the implications of such shifts in terms of the strengths and pathologies of the patient. Two, by constantly attending to diagnosis, he is simultaneously telling us that his clinical work is always integrated with his theorizing, so that each informs the other in a dialectical fashion.

THE CASE OF ADA

It is easy to see this dialectic of theory and practice in action when we turn to the case of Ada. Ada, an eight-year-old girl, is diagnosed by Winnicott as struggling with an antisocial tendency. Although this case could therefore easily have been discussed in the previous chapter, his integration of technique with his theorizing on this type of developmental disturbance makes it more pertinent to discuss it here.

Ada is referred by her school for persistent stealing. Winnicott lets us know that she lives too far away for ongoing treatment to be practical and her diagnosis (see condition C above), would have not made her a suitable candidate for "standard analysis" in any case. He notes in two ways his urgency to take on her symptoms in as full a way as possible. First he tells us:

> It was therefore necessary for me to act on the basis that I must do everything possible in the first psychotherapeutic consultation. (p. 220)

He then adds that he wanted to see the child first, before seeing the mother, because

> I was concerned with getting the patient to give herself away to me, slowly as she gained confidence in me, and deeply as she might find that she could take the risk. (p. 220)

It is important to stress here that because Winnicott views the antisocial tendency as a developmental phenomenon where good mothering was once present but lost, this pathology seems particularly well suited to his consultation style, which seeks to unearth an early obstacle and bring it into the light of day. Because Ada loved to draw, moreover, Winnicott conducted the session through watching and commenting on her own drawings, the squiggle game not being needed.

Ada's first three drawings—flowers in a vase; a lamp hanging from the ceiling, and swings in a playground under two clouds (more about them later)—were viewed as conventional, even "poor" drawings by Winnicott, without much meaning attributed to them. I was struck by the notable absence of people in the drawings, the flowers in the first drawing as a potential fertility symbol that she comes back to in later pictures, as well as by the focus on "light" in the last two drawings. Was she trying to conjure up warmth in some way? And, if so, was this warmth a hungering for closeness?

Her fourth drawing begins a revelation process that Winnicott uses to full advantage. She draws a pencil, sticking straight up, but she is dismayed that there is something wrong with the drawing and asks for an eraser. Winnicott doesn't have one (!) and though she alters the drawing, it remains "too fat." Winnicott tells us that he is aware of the fat pencil as potentially symbolic of:

(1) erect penis; (2) pregnant belly and (3) pudgy self. (p. 223)

She at first moves away from any underlying feeling stirred up by her "fat" pencil and her fifth drawing is a pleasant, if well defended, scene of house, flower, sun, and clouds. Although he has made no interpretations or even comments yet, it is clear that he is encouraged by her capacity to provide so symbolic a drawing early on. He is "rewarded" for his patience by drawing number six, where she draws a very large girl, her cousin, with her hands behind her back. Ada adds, "I can't draw hands." (p. 224)

This, for Winnicott is the turning point of the session. He notes:

I was now growing confident that the theme of stealing would appear, and so I was able to lean back on the child's own 'process.' *From now on it did not matter what I said or did not say, except that I must be adapted to the child's needs and not requiring the child to adapt to my own.* (p. 224)

The fact that Winnicott wrote the last sentence in italics is worthy of discussion. Here again we see his integration of theory and technique in thoroughly seamless fashion. As we know from his theoretical writings, he believes that the compulsion to steal stems from the need to take something from the person from whom one is "entitled" to steal (mother). This entitlement speaks to an earlier capacity by the mother to be available "for the taking" but to a later lack of reliability in that regard. That it was available once allows Winnicott the faith to follow Ada's "process" rather than having to "feed" her the way he might be drawn to do with a child with a developmentally earlier pathology. It is also crucial, in keeping with his diagnostic assessment, that what a child is in need of, as reparation, is the mother's (therapist's) renewed empathy, so that the child feels like her demands on the environment can be heard and met. Thus it is of paramount necessity that he not impose his own needs, even more so than if the child were more "neurotic." His approach is also in keeping with his notion that additional false compliance on Ada's part would further estrange her from her True Self, as well as his belief that through play she might create an intermediate arena where her concerns could be voiced.

This last point emboldens Winnicott to help Ada speak to what these hidden hands might be up to. He tells us that theoretically he has linked their being hidden to both stealing and masturbation but of course hopes that Ada can take him to her own meanings. When she rationalizes that the cousin is hiding a present, he pushes her to draw the present. When she does so, he asks if she can draw where she bought the present from and she curiously draws a large curtain down the center of the drawing that has no apparent reason for being there. Winnicott doesn't comment but asks about the lady buying the present. Remarkably, Ada again hides the person's hands, this time behind the counter where she is buying the present. Winnicott notes:

> The theme of buying and giving presents had entered into the child's presentation of herself, but neither she nor I knew that these themes would eventually become significant. I did know, however, that the idea of buying is regularly employed to cover the compulsion to steal, and the giving of presents is often a rationalization to cover the same compulsion. (p. 226)

Winnicott is clear that the hidden hands signify a conflict blatantly stated if not understood. He thus craftily tells Ada:

> I would very much like to see what the lady looks like from behind. (p. 226)

Surprising herself, Ada draws the person and immediately iden-
tifies with her, noting that they have the same long arms, and the
girl is wearing the dress she (Ada) is wearing to the consultation,
which used to be her mother's! The hands are finally drawn, with
very fat fingers that remind Winnicott of the fat pencil Ada drew.

Winnicott feels strongly that Ada is indeed revealing herself and
that the revelation will make sense of her need to steal. He of
course does not know if Ada is capable of pursuing this theme more
deeply so again he uses his theorizing to move the session forward.
Not sure if drawing remains a principal means of communication,
he asks about another aspect of experience that fits into the intermediate zone between inner and outer reality: he asks about getting
to sleep. She then draws her beloved transitional object, a big teddy
bear, and links this directly to her next drawing, her younger
brother's hand, drawn with very large, fat fingers. Ada has now
drawn three examples of fat objects, all linked in some symbolic
fashion to pregnancy, to early nurturance, and to the potential loss
of nurturance due to the arrival of something (someone) phallic.
Winnicott further notes that the drawing of Ada's brother's hand is
accompanied by large, breast-like shapes just above it, markedly
similar to the cloud shapes on two other drawings so far. Importantly, Winnicott sees no need to interpret any of this material. The
aliveness with which she is producing these symbolic representations on her own, coupled with his stated acknowledgment that
he must follow her lead, allows him the comfort to let her set the
pace, without interference. Going back to the two conditions he
describes in his "Aims" paper for making interpretations, we are
reminded that neither is met here. He has no need to let her know
the limitations of what he understands because she is actively
producing meaning for the two of them. He also has no need to
mobilize her intellectual forces at the moment because he sees
her as "hanging fire" (p. 228) and thus fully and viscerally in the
moment, making intellectualization a potential defense and not a
mobilization.

She then shifts gears and draws a "proud climber" on the top of
a large mountain. Although Winnicott doesn't go in this direction, I
am struck by how the climber is right at a huge breast (sun), mak-

ing me think that she has now identified with the male figure who gets the breast (her younger brother) rather than seeing herself as deprived. In any event, Winnicott sees this drawing as indicative of

> Ada's capacity to experience an achievement, and in the sexual field to reach a climax. I was able to use this as an indication that Ada would be able to bring me her main problem and give me the chance to help her with it. (p. 228)

Heartened by her signaling him that she was willing to further explore her inner life, he turns to another way to speak to her transitional, intermediate arena of playfulness; he asks her about her dreams, specifically relating the question to mountaineering so that he is following her content and her pace. She immediately responds by describing a disjointed, chaotic nightmare that led to her spending the rest of the night in her mother's bed. Winnicott notes:

> She was evidently reporting an acute confusional state. This was perhaps the center point of the interview, or *the essential reaching to the bottom of her experience of mental illness.* If this be true, then the rest of the session could be looked upon as a picture of the recovery from the confusional state. (p. 229)

Once again we see how Winnicott's theorizing makes sense of the case material, directs his understanding of the session, and informs his technique. If the basis of Ada's stealing results from an antisocial tendency, then it also is a defense against the deep chaos experienced by the baby who is insufficiently "held" before there is sufficient internal ego strength to shield herself from the environment's impingements. He would then *expect* that if the session were indeed meaningful to Ada, she would eventually get to this deeper, unformed place. The remaining question would be how to help her make sense of this deep regression.

Ada then draws four drawings. The first, a paintbrush and box, can be easily seen as an attempt to move away from the chaos of her nightmare through a concrete, pleasant rendition of her "favorite hobby." Her next three drawings tell us that she is unsuccessful in maintaining this well-defended stance. Her drawing of a spider plant is an outgrowth of other scary dreams of stinging scorpions; she draws a confused picture of a part-mobile, part-stationary home and then a poisonous spider. Winnicott links this last drawing to the fat fingers in her drawing of her younger brother and hence to her masturbatory wishes as a compensation for conflicts over stealing. I am struck by the continued persecutory and separation themes that were part and parcel of her nightmares. He asks her, interestingly in this context, about sad dreams and she immediately speaks of her parents dying, then coming back to life. This harkens back to his description of the tasks involved in providing an antisocial child the chance for a productive life as described in chapter 11. After the child has had his expressions of hate contained by a reliable environment, he must experience (reexperience?) the despair that flows from the original loss in relation to the mother. Winnicott bringing up sad dream content is his way, in the incredibly abridged context on a one-time consultation, of allowing Ada to experience the process of regression and then progression in a shorthand form. This is further reinforced by her comment that she has a box with thirty-six colored pencils at home, indirectly belittling him for his insufficient supplies. The fact that he does not retaliate after her "attack" allows her to "use" Winnicott, so that she can then reveal the source of her need to steal. She reports that she had a "burglar dream," a direct reference to stealing. Winnicott writes:

> Now the final stage of the interview started. It will be observed that Ada's drawings became much more bold at this point, and to anyone watching her it would have been clear that she was actuated from deep impulse and need. One felt almost in touch with Ada's unconscious drives and source of fantasy. (p. 230)

She then draws two remarkable drawings. The first is of a black man killing a woman with a large hatchet-like object, again with large, fat fingers, this time coming up behind the man. She then immediately draws a burglar, "funny like a clown," again with fat fingers. Most importantly and intriguingly to Winnicott, there is a large, breast-like shape opposite from the burglar with a tied bow attached to it. She describes the burglar as stealing jewels from a rich lady so that he can give a present to his wife because he could not wait to save up. Winnicott notes:

> Here, at a deeper level, appears the theme represented earlier by
> the woman or girl buying handkerchiefs from a store to give as a
> present to someone. It will be seen that there are shapes like the
> clouds of the earlier drawings, and these are now like a curtain,
> and there is a bow.
>   I made no interpretation, but found myself interested in the
> bow, which, if untied, would reveal something. This could be a
> pictorial representation of nascent consciousness, or release from
> repression. (p. 232)

It is striking to me how the drawing of a smiling burglar could
also represent her brother, who not only has a penis but is also
markedly near the bow (nipple) of the curtain (breast). She later
notes that this burglar is really very kind. I think this last depiction
of the burglar struck Winnicott as too much of a reaction formation,
an attempt to defend against her rage at her brother for stealing away
her mother's comfort and nurturing. He then, for the first time in the
session, describes what he does next as an intervention: he asks her
about the bow. Here he no longer simply adapts to her process but
prepares himself to make an interpretation. I think he feared her re-
treating from a full reaching to her early disruptions and thus had to
"mobilize her intellectual forces" before it was too late. In response
to his asking about the bow, she drew drawing twenty-one,

> which shows a juggler. This could be thought of as an attempt to
> make a career out of the unresolved problem. Here again were
> the curtain and the bow. The dissociation is represented by the
> fact that the picture is in two halves in that the curtain is down,
> but also it is up, and the juggler's act is on. (p. 232)

Here the juggler is a step "up" from reaction formation as a defense, in that it could represent a sublimation of her conflicts with
stealing and/or masturbation. However, Winnicott is not content to
let her "merely" sublimate the conflict without some attempt to put
the source of the conflict into words. He is strengthened in his re-
solve to not "settle" for her sublimation by the curtain she places
between the juggler and the bow (nipple). This curtain can be seen
as her resignation to not getting to enjoy the breast, being forced instead to perform for others, rather than to live life fully. Given all
we have reviewed about his definition of health as opposed to mere

living, he could hardly be expected to settle for Ada's False Self rendition of a split-off juggler without some attempt to have her directly address her stealing and its meaning.

So Winnicott now feels ready to "pop the question" to Ada, and he asks her directly if she steals things herself. Her response is a telling example of a typical child's conscious response to a question that taps unconscious material. Her immediate response is a vehement "No!" but at the same time she takes another piece of paper and makes an incredible drawing. The drawing is simplicity itself: a large tree with bountiful leaves, grass, flowers, and a little animal near the base of the tree. Toward the top of the drawing are two large apples, with stems pointing upward. Winnicott tells us knowingly:

> This showed what was behind the curtain. It represented the discovery of the mother's breast which had been hidden, as it were, by the mother's clothes. In this way a deprivation had been symbolized. The symbolism is to be compared and contrasted with the direct view depicted in Drawing 12 which contains a memory of the baby brother in contact with the mother's body. (p. 234)

This drawing was so explicitly in response to Winnicott's question about whether Ada herself steals that it seemed a direct, if still preconscious to Ada, presentation of her wish to have access to her mother's breasts. It was these breasts, as it were, that Ada was once entitled to and then was deprived of without understanding or reliability. Winnicott then himself feels entitled to make his only interpretation of the session. He says to her:

> Oh, I see, the curtains were mother's blouse, and you have reached through to her breasts. Ada did not answer, but instead she drew with obvious pleasure. . . . '[T]his is mother's dress [she said], that I love best. She still has it.' (p. 235)

Winnicott is true to his word from his "Aims" paper about the nature of his interpretation. His sentence is short and simple, with no "teaching" or using of the word "moreover"! The interpretation is heard fully by Ada in that she can move immediately to an important drawing that reveals the lost object now rediscovered. It is crucial and not at all coincidental that Ada reveals that her mother still has the very special dress that she draws. She thus can recover something that had not been annihilated but had been lost, a dramatic rendition of what Winnicott sees as the crux of the antisocial tendency. Winnicott writes of this last drawing:

> The dress dates from the time when Ada was a little girl and indeed it is so drawn that the child's eyes are about at the level of the mother's mid-thigh region. The theme of breast is continued in the puff sleeves. The fertility symbols are the same as in the early drawing of a house, and are also changing into numbers. (p. 235)

The idea that Ada draws the dress from the perspective of what a little girl would see when looking up at her mother is striking. It speaks to the crystal-clear regression to this earlier period evoked by the session, and specifically by Winnicott's getting to the heart of her need to steal. It is then not surprising that

> the work of the interview was now over, and Ada wasted a little time 'coming to the surface,' playing a game which continued the theme of numbers as fertility symbols. Ada was now ready to go, and as she was in a happy and comfortable state I was able to have ten minutes with the mother who had been waiting an hour and a quarter. (p. 236)

Seventy-five minutes to get to an unlocking of a four-year-long conflict! Is it any wonder why graduate students reading his "Consultations" are utterly intimidated and awestruck by his work! Not only does she hear his interpretation and respond by a "working through" of a repressed memory of her fertile, alive mother, she can then end the session with a sublimation of her eventual capacity for fertility: an adding of numbers in ever-increasing quantities. We're even told that Ada stopped stealing immediately after the interview and did not steal again over a six-year follow-up period. Mother also reported an immediate change in Ada's relationship with her, "as if a block had been removed," and Winnicott notes that

> this recovery of an old intimacy has persisted, and it seems to show that the work done in the interview was a genuine

re-establishment of infant-mother contact which had been
lost. (p. 238)

Despite the remarkable success of this interview, I hope it does
not come across to the reader as "magical." Winnicott would not
have wanted his work (at least consciously!) to be experienced as
the young infant experiences the magical omnipotence of "creating"
the mother when he needs her. Rather, I hope that the presentation
of this clinical consultation alongside the description of his theorizing will place each and every one of his interventions in theoretical
context, flowing creatively from his theory and not from magic

Two last points need to be made regarding the brief interview
he had with Ada's mother. Importantly, we find that the deprivation
he discussed in theory was not actually solely of her mother. When
Ada was four years and nine months old, her younger brother fell
seriously ill and remained ill for a long time. Her older sister, who
had taken on a strong mothering role with Ada, now switched her
attention "absolutely" to her younger brother, leaving Ada deprived
of her two mothering figures. Mother noted that she and her hus-
band did not realize the extent of this deprivation for a long time,
so that it was almost two years before Ada started to recover from
this loss. Strikingly, it was at the time of her recovery that her stealing first began. This fits with Winnicott's timetable for the antisocial child needing to first get satisfactory caretaking of a long-
enough duration before hate can be expressed. The "hate" in this
case took the form of stealing as a displacement from what she was
entitled to get from her mother/sister. There is little question that
her satisfactory development for almost five years and the two years
spent by the family trying to repair her deprivation were also central
ingredients in her capacity to get to this material in one session and
in the effectiveness of the session itself to remove her "block."

Let us now turn, in the final chapter, to a review of Winnicott's
theorizing and clinical work through the lens of transferential and
countertransferential experience.

Chapter Thirteen

───────○───────

Winnicott as Therapist More Than Theorist

"Being reliable in all respects is the chief quality we need."

Articles reviewed: "Advising Parents" (1957); "Countertransference" (1960); and "The Case of Robert" from *Therapeutic Consultations in Child Psychiatry* (1971).

IN THIS, THE FINAL CHAPTER, I will focus primarily on Winnicott's thinking about being a clinician, with his theorizing taking a backseat. We will focus on how he conceptualizes what it takes and what it means to be a professional therapist. We will then conclude with "The Case of Robert," where, of all his "consultations," he does the most "therapy." This case beautifully illustrates the integration of Winnicott the clinician with Winnicott the theoretician/scholar.

In his essay entitled "Advising Parents," Winnicott closes with a stunningly clear description of how he envisions the proper practice of psychology. He writes:

> Psychology if practiced at all must be done within a framework. An interview must be arranged in a proper setting, and a time limit must be set. Within this framework we can be reliable, much more reliable than we are in our daily lives. Being reliable in all respects is the chief quality we need. This means not only

213

that we respect the client's person and his or her right to time and concern. We have our own sense of values, and so we are able to leave the client's sense of right and wrong as we find it. Moral judgement, if expressed, destroys the professional relationship absolutely and irrevocably. The time limit of the professional interview is for our own use; the prospect of the end of the session deals in advance with our resentment, which would otherwise creep in and spoil the operation of our genuine concern. (p. 120)

In this passage, Winnicott focuses on two aspects of the practice of psychology: the setting of a time limit and the importance of avoiding moral judgments. Winnicott's focus on both of these aspects underscores the central role reliability plays in all of his thinking. If Winnicott as therapist has as a model certain key aspects of the role of the mother in early life, chief among these aspects is her "good enough" reliability, her ability to "be in the moment" with her baby. Because the therapist lacks the mother's primary maternal preoccupation, the therapist can only show "genuine concern" if there is a time limit to this concern. Similarly, the "good enough" mother is also reliable in her limiting the impingements on the baby's spontaneity and creativity. This is analogous to the therapist's effort not to impinge on the patient by imposing moral values or judgments on his or her actions or thoughts. Just as the over-impinging mother destroys the child's True Self capabilities and creates a false compliance, so too will the impinging therapist crush the patient's authentic relationship to them.

"Advising Parents" was directed primarily at medical professionals who crossed the line into advising parents on psychological issues. It thus does not speak more subtly to the nature of the therapist's role and training in the process of psychotherapy. His paper entitled "Countertransference," however, is quite helpful in extending his theoretical conceptions to the clinical domain.

He begins the paper by first defining transference.

Transference is not just a matter of rapport, or of relationships. It concerns the way in which a highly subjective phenomenon repeatedly turns up in an analysis. Psycho-analysis very much consists in the arranging of conditions for the development of these phenomena, and in the interpretation of these phenomena at the right moment. (p. 159)

This is a clear statement that not all behavior by the patient toward the analyst is transference, only those repeatedly drawn, "highly subjective" states of mind. This definition is the counterpart to his equally narrow definition of countertransference offered in his "Hate in the Countertransference" paper. The present paper significantly expands his thinking by focusing on what the professional role brings to the patient's experience and how this role embodies unique aspects of being that form the basis of being a professional. He begins his argument in this way:

> Professional work is quite different from ordinary life, is it not?
> All this started up with Hippocrates. He perhaps founded the professional attitude. The medical oath gives a picture of a man or woman who is an idealized version of the ordinary man or woman on the street. Yet *that is how we are when professionally engaged.* Included in the oath is the promise that we do not commit adultery with a patient. Here is a full recognition of one aspect of the transference, the patient's need to idealize the doctor, and to fall in love with him, to dream. (p. 160)

In the italicized section of the passage, Winnicott makes a simple yet profound point. Because we have adopted a professional attitude in our work, we are no longer simply an "ordinary" man or woman during the treatment hour. Thus a great deal of a patient's idealizing transference is induced by the therapeutic stance, if indeed he or she can maintain the requirements of the professional attitude. So far this is basically a restatement of Freud's description of the importance and necessity of the positive transference. Winnicott takes this basic principle in a new direction when he speaks to what constitutes this "professional attitude" and what the impediments are to maintaining it. He writes:

> Freud allowed for the development of a full range of subjective phenomena in the professional relationship; the analyst's own analysis was in effect a recognition that the analyst is under strain

in maintaining a professional attitude. It is on purpose that I use this wording. I am not saying that the analyst's analysis is to free him from neurosis; it is to increase the stability of character and the maturity of the personality of the worker, this being the basis of his or her professional work and our ability to maintain a professional relationship. (p. 160)

There are many points to be made here. One is that a professional attitude is not a given, but a developmental achievement that can be easily straining. The second point is that what is strained is the stability of character of the therapist. This extends his definition of reliability in a new direction: the therapist must be reliable enough not to fall in love with the patient's idealization of him or her. I'm reminded of the classic Woody Allen movie *Annie Hall*. There is a scene in the movie in which the Diane Keaton character is about to make love with Woody but wants to smoke marijuana first, as it relaxes her. Woody protests vehemently, his argument being that if she smokes, he won't know whether her pleasure in lovemaking is derived from him or from the marijuana. In an analogous way, Winnicott is telling us that the intrinsic idealization of the therapist by the patient stems at least initially from our professional attitude (the marijuana) and that the therapist needs to be on guard to distinguish the effects of this "marijuana" from his or her actual character. Thus, only the stability of the therapist's character can shield the patient and the therapist from this inflated self-assessment by the therapist.

Winnicott then speaks to an inherent danger in the creation of the professional attitude. He notes:

A professional attitude may, of course, be built up on a basis of defenses and inhibition and obsessional orderliness, and I suggest that it is here that the psychotherapist is particularly under strain, because any structuring of his ego-defenses lessens his ability to meet the new situation. The psychotherapist must remain vulnerable, and yet retain his professional role in his actual working hours. I guess that the well-behaving professional analyst is easier to come by than the analyst who (while behaving well) retains the vulnerability that belongs to a flexible defense organization. (p. 160)

This is an extension of the True Self/compliant False Self dichotomy to the realm of the therapist's defense organization. The more rigidly, falsely organized therapist may be able to maintain the professional attitude under most circumstances but is clearly at risk for both greater strain and/or a loss of professionalism should the particular fit between therapist and patient organization be a maladaptive one.

What exactly is the "professional attitude"? In its most basic aspect, this refers to a stance that cannot be maintained in ordinary life.

> What the patient meets is surely the professional attitude of the analyst, not the unreliable men and women we happen to be in private life. (p. 161)

If we remind ourselves of Winnicott's "gold standard" for health, the capacity to be creative and authentic, then surely it is only when the therapist maintains his or her professional attitude that the spontaneous gestures of the patient can be "held." The therapist's capacity to be surprised without undue strain is thus every bit as crucial to an effective treatment as is the therapist's reliability when caught in repeated, transference-laced interactions with the patient. At either extreme, or indeed at any place along this continuum of "new" and "old" patient experience, the ability of the therapist to remain available is of the highest value in creating new understandings and new behavioral paradigms for the patient.

A professional attitude is therefore a function of the therapist's own degree of authenticity and creativity resting on a foundation of character stability and hence maximum flexibility to the inner life of the patient and the therapist. But it is not simply all that. Winnicott adds an interesting phrase here:

> I want to state that the working analyst is in a special state, that is, his attitude is professional. The work is done in a professional setting. In this setting we assume a freedom of the analyst from personality and character disorder of such a kind or degree that the professional relationship cannot be maintained, or can only be maintained at great cost involving excessive defenses. (p. 161)

The phrase of interest to me is that of the "special state" of maintaining a professional attitude. Winnicott is not saying that the therapist has to be of such enormously healthy stature that the professional attitude is a way of being. He is saying instead that this attitude is protected by the special state of the work setting and further protected, as we discussed earlier, by the time limits inherent in such a setting. Once again, he creates a parallel between therapist and mothering figure. Just as the mother is not expected to maintain absolute attunement beyond the very first days of life, if at all, the therapist cannot be perfectly attuned beyond the rigid time frame of the patient "hour." As a further parallel, it is the ending of the hour that demonstrates quite clearly to the patient that the therapist is not a perfectly attuned mother. The space created between therapist and patient at the close of the session mirrors the mother's weaning of her child from illusory omnipotence to "good enough" adherence to the reality principle.

Winnicott describes this space between patient and therapist in an intriguing way. He writes:

> The professional attitude is rather like symbolism, in that it assumes a distance between analyst and patient. The symbol is in a gap between the subjective object and the object that is objectively perceived. (p. 161)

The ability of the therapist to adopt a professional attitude is what makes the therapist different from a friend, stranger, colleague, or relative of the patient. Thus to the patient, the professional attitude ensures (except perhaps at psychotic moments for the patient) that the therapist is not solely a subjective object (i.e., not a hallucination or figment of the patient's imagination) nor a purely objective perception. That is, the therapist's genuine concern makes it impossible for the patient to always see the therapist with utter objectivity, as this concern fulfills profoundly gratifying needs in the patient. Importantly, the idea that the professional attitude creates an intermediate area between inner and outer reality is obviously not a coincidence in Winnicott's theorizing. As we have learned, psychotherapy occurs in the overlap of the play space, the potential space of this intermediate area for both patient and therapist. Thus, the professional attitude creates the very arena where therapy can be most profitable.

Winnicott repeatedly highlights this notion of professional attitude because it frees him from looking at transference and hence countertransference phenomena as omnipresent in the therapist-patient relationship. He contrasts this with Jung's writing on transference.

> [Jung] compares the analytic relation to a chemical interaction, and continues that treatment can "by no device . . . be anything but the product of mutual influence, in which the whole being of the doctor as well as the patient plays a part." Later he is very emphatic that it is futile for the analyst to erect defenses of a professional kind against the influence of the patient. (p. 161)

Winnicott is not denying the mutuality of the patient-therapist interaction by any means. He is positing, however, that it is not the "whole being" of the doctor that is involved. He notes:

> I would rather be remembered as maintaining that in between the patient and the analyst is the analyst's professional attitude, his technique, the work he does with his mind. (p. 161)

This is a most intriguing statement by Winnicott, as it suggests that the professional attitude is no longer a state of mind protected by a specific setting with rigid time frames but is rather a function of technique, or, worse yet, a function of the cognitive work of the therapist's mind. This would be a blatant contradiction of all we have reviewed in which Winnicott repeatedly states his abhorrence for the "clever" therapist or stresses the falsity inherent in the mind-psyche, as opposed to the integrated psyche-soma, capable of "going on being."

Winnicott therefore immediately clarifies what he means by the use of the therapist's mind as a factor in the professional attitude. He adds:

> Now I say this without fear because I am not an intellectual and in fact I personally do my work very much from the body-ego, so

to speak. But I think of myself in my analytic work working with easy but conscious mental effort. Ideas and feelings come to mind, but these are well-examined and sifted before an interpretation is made. This is not to say that feelings are not involved. On the one hand I may have stomach ache but this does not usually affect my interpretations; and on the other hand I may have been somewhat stimulated erotically or aggressively by an idea given by the patient, but again this fact does not usually affect my interpretative work, what I say, how I say it or when I say it. (pp. 161–162)

This may be the most explicit statement Winnicott makes about his view of himself as a therapist. For him, his mind is by definition an integration of psyche and soma, so that the use of his mind precludes mere intellectualization. Feelings, ideas, and bodily states are equally valid and usually available to him in trying to make sense of an idea from a patient. These abilities are reliably available to him when within his role as an analyst, and thus the professional attitude he can evoke separates his "self" from his role and allows this separation to make him different and hence symbolic to his patients. This permits him to disagree wholeheartedly with Jung and defy his idea that the whole of the therapist's being is involved. On another level, this disagreement may also harken back to Winnicott's notion that we are, at our core, unknowable by another and thus an isolate. If this core, this True Self, is unknowable, then it follows that the True Self cannot be readily influenced by a patient, thus challenging Jung's notion of utterly mutual, whole human beings influencing one another. It is intriguing to contrast Winnicott's theorizing in this arena with the views of the "interpersonal" school of psychoanalysis, a topic for another paper.

Winnicott takes his argument about the lack of ubiquity of transference and countertransference to its logical conclusion by first defining what an analyst is and is not, leaving him with a succinct definition of what countertransference is and is not. He defines an analyst as

objective and consistent, for the hour, and he is not a rescuer, a teacher, an ally or a moralist. The important effect of the analyst's own analysis in this connection is that it has strengthened his own ego so that he can remain professionally involved, and this without too much strain. (p. 162)

Having defined and constrained the professional attitude, and having shown to his satisfaction that its existence implies that not all behavior by the patient is transference or even wholly interpersonal, he is left with a quite specific and constrained definition of countertransference. He notes:

In so far as all this is true the meaning of the word countertransference can only be the neurotic features *which spoil the professional attitude* and disturb the course of the analytic process as determined by the patient. (p. 162)

Countertransference is thus defined quite functionally: it is not simply the existence of neurotic constructions in the therapist, nor is it all feelings or behaviors of the therapist toward the patient. It is only those neurotic features in the analyst that limit the professional attitude, that prevent the therapist from fully attending to where the patient is at the moment. It is also crucial to note his phrase "as determined by the patient," for here again he is speaking to his gold standard of non-impinging therapeutic interventions that best allow the patient's True Self to flourish.

I will close this chapter by focusing on his clinical consultation with Robert, a nine-year-old boy. I choose to end with this case for a number of reasons. Most important is the fact that Winnicott makes use of interpretations in this consultation to a far greater extent than in any of the other cases presented. This allows us to see this side of his working for the first time. The interpretations he makes, moreover, are more strongly linked to "Freudian" notions of phallic and Oedipal concerns than to the infantile issues that predominate in Winnicott's ideas about etiology. His ability to integrate drive theory with earlier, infantile material is one of the unique aspects of his theorizing. This integration is beautifully detailed in this case. As we have not "played" with Winnicott in this way before, it makes for a fitting ending to this examination of his work.

The Case of Robert

Robert is nine and has two younger sisters. His family is described by Winnicott as a "going concern" with a great deal of responsibility and tolerance on the part of the parents. Although he has an IQ of 130, he does very poorly in school, hates reading, and always feels rushed and pressured by teachers. His history is dominated by a great deal of war-related stress on the family while he was in his infancy and by a jealous rage at his younger sister, born when he was two. There are symptoms of mild depression and lethargy, torturing of "mother" and "father" newts in his garden, and being a bad sport in play with peers. Winnicott also stresses the boy's great fondness for his mother and some potential gender concerns. Regarding this area, Winnicott notes:

> There is a maleness about the boy which is satisfactory, but there is also a very obvious envy of the mother's productive capacity, and his latent woman-identification is closely bound up with his affection for his father. In regard to sexual matters, he seems to be unable or unwilling to ask for information, and the parents have never found the right position from which to tell him about sex except in regard to the growth of the baby inside the mother. (p. 91)

Winnicott meets the boy with his mother for a few minutes, and Robert admits to his school difficulties, then speaks of his fondness for gardening. He makes an "odd spontaneous" remark that the gardening "brightens up a dull patch" (p. 92). Winnicott links this almost immediately with the rather depressed, constricted presentation of his mother.

Robert and Winnicott begin with the squiggle game. The first two drawings become railway loops, while the fifth is an octopus that loops back on itself to become yet another form of railway. Winnicott uses the suckers drawn by Robert on the octopus to ask about thumb sucking. This leads Robert to talk about his "horrible, filthy Tissie," a transitional object he retrieved from its prior role as a floor cloth. He noted that his mother could eventually no longer stand this dirty rag and burned it, to which Robert reacted by "crying a lot till he forgot it" (p. 95). His describing it as horrible and filthy suggests his all-too-pervasive compliance with the mother's view of his treasured creation, while his crying at its loss at least implies some mourning but no rage at the mother's unempathic behavior. Strikingly, he draws Tissie in drawing six, but then, in his seventh drawing, draws himself taking the rag out of the bucket. To his own great surprise, he draws himself at this time wearing a skirt. Winnicott notes:

> He was very surprised indeed to find that he had a dress on, and it seemed that he had reached to a deep memory.
> He was now ready to talk about nightmares. (p. 97)

Much as with the other three cases, Winnicott uses the squiggle game to stir the patient to a deep place and then asks about dreams now that the "gate" to the unconscious is "open." It is here that Winnicott begins interpreting Robert's material. Robert draws a picture of a house on fire in a dream. Winnicott responds:

> I interpreted this as sexual excitement and he understood because he gets an erection associated with the dream. At this point I gave him some sex information for which he was longing. I told him to go and ask his father if he wanted to know more. (p. 98)

Obviously we can only wish that we knew precisely how and what Winnicott said to the boy about "sexual excitement" and what information he told the boy. The fact that the boy divulged that he had an erection associated with the dream clearly speaks to his finding the interpretation accurate both in content and timing.

Robert tells about another nightmare, this one of burglars who steal jewels, but as he says he cannot draw it, Winnicott was going to "leave this aside." Robert strikingly then asks Winnicott to draw a burglar going into a house. This tells Winnicott that the boy wished to go further in pursuit of the meaning of these dreams. Robert's drawing shows a man with a pistol right where his penis would be, he has smashed a window with this pistol in order to enter into the house. Winnicott interprets the drawing directly.

> I was able to point out that the pistol that broke the glass was a picture of his erect penis. I said that as he was not yet able to

have the emission that belongs to grown-up men he has to use the magic of the pistol shot. (p. 98)

This interpretation led to Robert and Winnicott reviewing their three drawings of houses broken into or set on fire. Winnicott now makes this rather remarkable developmental interpretation:

Here was a hole in the window from the pistol shot. I joined this up with the first thing he said to me, which was that his garden brightens a dark patch. I then said: 'You see at first you were a baby and you loved mother and you bit the holes in the Tissie. One day you will be a grown-up man like Daddy and you will marry and have children. Now you are half-way between. You love someone and you dream of the house burning up because it feels so exciting. And you shoot your way in because there is no emission, and instead of giving babies you steal jewels.' I went on: 'There is someone you love when you are dreaming these dreams' and he said: 'I think it's Mummy.' So I said: 'Well if you were a burglar and you got into the house you would have to knock down Father.' He said: 'Well, I would not like to do that.' I said: 'No, because you are fond of him too and sometimes because you are fond of him you wish you were a girl.' He said: 'Only a little tiny bit.' (p. 98)

Well, so much for the therapist who rarely makes interpretations! This is truly Winnicott at both his most magical and most grounded in theory. I have yet to come across in any of his writings a better clinical example of his capacity to integrate drive theory with his own theorizing. While obviously an interpretation of Oedipal desires and Oedipal fears, presented with a clarity that would make any Freudian proud, he links these fantasies with the boy's transitional object. He does not take the path of Robert's mother needing her "dark patch brightened" by the boy's false compliance, which would have been a more usual stance theoretically by Winnicott. But by bringing Tissie into his interpretation he implicitly reminds the boy of his wish to wear a dress (to be a girl) and hence identify with mother. This leads him to speak with Robert about his "very difficult relationship" with his sister. Winnicott interprets their fighting by saying to Robert:

Well, it looks to mother and father as if you and your sister are jealous of each other, and I would say you are jealous of her for being a girl, and she is jealous of you for being a boy. At the same time you are in love with each other, and as you are not grown-up the nearest thing you can get to making love is to pester each other and fight. (p. 98)

He seemed very relieved about all of this, and decided that he had finished all that we wanted to do and that it was time to go, with which I fully agreed. (p. 100)

Robert was thus able to not only hear and make use of an Oedipal interpretation, he was able to make similar use of his incestuous feelings and fantasies toward his sister! The fact that it took ten drawings to reach this remarkable conclusion is perhaps yet another dramatic example of why Winnicott can be so intimidating to the rest of us mortals. Winnicott tries to temper the magical power of both his understanding and his technique by repeatedly stressing the health of the child, despite the power of his symptomatology. He notes:

I felt that the interview might well be a healing one for him because of what he was ready for and because I was not dealing with illness. (p. 100)

He seemed very relieved about all this, and decided that he had finished all that we wanted to do and that it was time to go, with which I fully agreed. (p. 100)

Later in the paper, he adds in the same vein:

I have described a very simple case. I think a point is that this child might have been your child or mine. (p. 102)

Yet he later adds:

In regard to the psychoanalysis of this child, I want to make it quite clear that if these parents could afford and could easily manage a five times a week treatment over a long period, I would advise psychoanalysis, not because the child is very ill but because there are enough troubles to make a treatment worthwhile, and the more normal a child is the more rich and quick is the result. (p. 103)

He concludes by noting:

> The boy has passed through all the early emotional developmental stages well enough and is not liable to psychotic breakdown. His problems are in the rich field of interpersonal relationships and of the bringing together of the two types of relationship, the affectionate and that which rides on waves of instinct. In my remarks to this boy I brought in sexual matters, and in dealing with children who are developing well we fail if we cannot follow the children wherever they lead. (p. 103)

Thus Winnicott insists that his work with Robert was far from magical but rather was based firmly on developmental theory. Despite the presence of transitional object themes and maternal depression, Winnicott felt clear in his diagnosis of neurotic-level pathology. The ability of his parents, especially his mother, to be abundantly available to her other children, led him to see Robert's earlier difficulties as more situational than indicative of true mother-child disruptions. This allowed him to focus more productively on the Oedipal nature of the material. Robert's developmental sturdiness, coupled with the fact that the situation warranted a one-time consultation, paved the way both for the content and the rushed process of his interpretations. The obvious fact that Robert did not hesitate to positively respond from the very start to Winnicott's comments made it that much easier for Winnicott to proceed as he did.

CONCLUSION

In attempting to "play with" Winnicott, I chose a particular heuristic. I began with a baby with predatory ideas and a mother wishing to be attacked by that hungry baby. The mother has to be created by the baby, yet be there ready to be found. The consequences for authenticity and falseness are profound if the baby is forced to primarily react to the mother's needs. A baby with a "good enough" mother in this regard develops the capacity to be alone in the presence of another without distress and without falseness. This leads to the ability to hate the now separate mother and for her to optimally survive this "hatred" in order for the baby to become fully fused or integrated. I use the case of Bob to illustrate this capacity. This case amply demonstrates how the capacity to play is the gold standard for eventual health. Play is made still more meaningful in the context of the creation of transitional phenomena, the arena for the growth of cultural life. Culture and society on a macro level, and personal experience on an intrapsychic plane, cannot be fully described without a fuller discussion of the role of hate, which further clarifies the parallels between mother-infant and therapist-patient dyads. Fully acknowledging hate allows us to discuss the antisocial tendency, a way of looking at hate as an expression of hope for something lost and a battle against deprivation. The case of Ada provides a clinical milieu for understanding the antisocial tendency. By linking Winnicott's theoretical constructs in this manner, the final two chapters allow for a focus on the aims of treatment and a discussion of the characteristics involved in being a therapist. The case of Robert was included to demonstrate that Winnicott could be as facile with Oedipal material as he could with pre-Oedipal configurations, and that his capacity to integrate drive theory with his theorizing is among his most important contributions to the field.

This was simply one heuristic. These constructs could have been presented in many other permutations and certainly have been by many other authors. There were also many other constructs that I did not include (i.e., his work on the manic defense; his discussion of sadism and masochism; and a more complete analysis of his long-term work with child and adult patients, among others). I am also aware that many others have written on the contributions of Winnicott in a more comprehensive manner that what was attempted here. I resort to one last quote from Winnicott in this regard:

> I am only too happy, when after making my own statement, I find that what I have said has been said previously by others. Often it has been said better, but not better for me. ("Birth Memories, Birth Trauma, and Anxiety," p. 177)

I have wrestled with how best to end this book. It should be abundantly clear to even its most casual reader that this has not been a critical or even a neutral examination of Winnicott's work. It is also probably clear that Winnicott is a treasured internalized object to me. Teaching him to graduate students for many years and now writing this book has felt like passing down the best aspects of one's parents to one's children. Playing with Winnicott has therefore been a matter of continuity-making for me and for those I have taught.

I hope I have done him justice.

Bibliography

Escalona, S. (1967). *The roots of individuality.* Chicago: Aldine Books.

Freud, A. (1936). *The ego and the mechanisms of defense.* New York: International Universities Press.

Gergely, G. (2001). The development of understanding of self and agency. In U. Goshwami (Ed.), *Handbook of childhood cognitive development.* Oxford: Blackwell.

Hoffer, W. (1949). Mouth, hand and ego-integration. *Psychoanalytic study of the child, 3,* 49–56.

Klein, M. (1975). Envy and gratitude. In *Envy and gratitude and other works 1946–1963,* (pp. 176–235). New York: Delacorte Press/Seymour Lawrence.

LeBoyer, F. (1975). *Birth without violence.* New York: Knopf.

Menninger, K. (1963). *The vital balance.* New York: Viking.

Ogden, T. (2001). Reading Winnicott. *Psychoanalytic Quarterly, 70,* 299–323.

Piaget, J. (1936). *The origins of intelligence in children.* New York: International Universities Press, 1952.

Stern, D. (1985). *The interpersonal world of the infant: A view from psychoanalysis and developmental psychology.* New York: Basic Books.

Sullivan, H. (1962). *Schizophrenia as a human process.* New York: Norton.

Tronick, E. (1989). Emotions and emotional communication in infants. *American Psychologist, 44,* 112–119.

White, R. (1981). *The abnormal personality.* New York: Wiley.

WORKS BY WINNICOTT

From: *The Maturational Processes and the Facilitating Environment*. New York: International Universities Press, 1965.

The Capacity to Be Alone (1958)
The Theory of the Parent-Infant Relationship (1960)
Ego Distortion in Terms of True and False Self (1960)
Countertransference (1960)
The Aims of Psychoanalytic Treatment (1962)
Communicating and Not Communicating Leading to a Study of Certain Opposites (1963)

From: *Therapeutic Consultations in Child Psychiatry*. New York: Basic Books, 1971.

Case IV: The Case of Bob
Case V: The Case of Robert
Case XI: The Case of Hesta
Case XIII: The Case of Ada

From: *Playing and Reality*. London: Tavistock Publications, 1971.

Transitional Objects and Transitional Phenomena (1951)
Playing: A Theoretical Statement (1971)
The Use of an Object and Relating through Identification (1971)
The Location of Cultural Experience (1967)
Mirror-Role of Mother and Family in Child Development (1967)

From: *The Family and Individual Development*. London: Routledge, 1965.

Advising Parents (1957)
The Deprived Child and How He Can Be Compensated for Loss of Family Life (1950)
Group Influences and the Maladjusted Child (1955)

From: *Through Pediatrics to Psychoanalysis*. London: Routledge, 1965.

Clinical Varieties of Transference (1955–1956)
The Antisocial Tendency (1956)

Aggression in Relation to Emotional Development (1950–1955)
Hate in the Countertransference (1947)
Mind and Its Relation to the Psyche-Soma (1949)
Birth Memories, Birth Trauma and Anxiety (1949)
Reparation in Respect of a Mother's Organized Defence against Depression (1948)
Primitive Emotional Development (1945)

Index

About the Author

Steve Tuber is Professor of Psychology and Past Director, Doctoral Program in Clinical Psychology of the City University of New York at City College. He has published and presented over 80 papers on the interplay between assessment and treatment in children and adolescents and teaches courses on psychological testing, child psychotherapy and the work of Donald Winnicott. He also has a private practice in New York City.